Seventeenth-Century Imagery

PUBLISHED UNDER THE AUSPICES OF

THE 17TH AND 18TH CENTURIES STUDIES GROUP

UNIVERSITY OF CALIFORNIA, LOS ANGELES

Publications of
THE 17TH AND 18TH CENTURIES STUDIES GROUP, UCLA

I.

Seventeenth-Century Imagery: Essays on Uses of
Figurative Language from Donne to Farquhar
Edited by Earl Miner

2.

England in the Restoration and Early Eighteenth Century
Essays on Culture and Society
Edited by H. T. Swedenberg, Jr.
William Andrews Clark Library Professor, 1969–1971

VISIO SIMILITVDINIS GLORIÆ DOMINI. *Ezech.*

From the title page of Antonius Fernandius, *Commentarii In Visiones Veteris Testamenti* (Loudun, 1617) (see essay by Maren-Sofie Røstvig). This drawing illustrates the traditional interpretation in biblical exegesis of Ezekiel's vision (Ezek. 1, 10), showing Christ seated at rest in the middle and imposing harmony (or unity) through the quaternions of the created universe and the four gospels. Other tetractys devices and typological symbols are also set forth in the illustration.

Seventeenth-Century Imagery

Essays on Uses of
Figurative Language from
Donne to Farquhar
Edited by
EARL MINER

1971
UNIVERSITY OF CALIFORNIA PRESS
BERKELEY · LOS ANGELES · LONDON

University of California Press
Berkeley and Los Angeles, California
University of California Press, Ltd.
London, England
Copyright © 1971 by The Regents of the University of California
ISBN: 0-520-01825-7
Library of Congress Catalog Card Number: 76-132417
Edited by Grace H. Stimson
Designed by W. H. Snyder
Printed in the United States of America

VIRO BONO DOCENDIQUE PERITO

H. T. SWEDENBERG

IAM LXV ANNOS NATO

IN HONOREM

Hesperii Laris Antistes, cui copia torrens
Dicendi, validi semper comes argumenti.
His super exemplis iampridem accensa Juventus
Instituit primos [Divo] Musisque Labores.

—ABSALON ET ACHITOPHEL

FOREWORD

The 17th and 18th Centuries Studies Group has been founded at the University of California, Los Angeles, with the aim of bringing together students of various disciplines to advance understanding of the lives and the culture of peoples during a crucial period of human experience. To this end the group has undertaken a variety of enterprises (with the support of the Chancellor and the deans at UCLA), including teaching programs, conferences, and symposia designed to cross departmental lines. The aim is to foster studies involving numerous disciplines and to encourage participation by other universities in the United States and abroad. One such enterprise is the publication of a series of books covering a wide spectrum of interests and attracting contributors in various fields.

The group hopes to draw upon the libraries, talents, and resources of one university in a way that will engage the efforts and be worthy of the attention of a more than local fraternity of scholars. Individual volumes are planned to pursue a variety of topics. We welcome comments and suggestions from scholars interested in these two centuries and hope that our endeavors will stimulate comparable study and activity at other universities.

EARL MINER
*Chairman, The 17th and 18th
Centuries Studies Group, UCLA*

PREFACE

English literature of the seventeenth century holds its admirers by virtue of its variety and its scale. The variety finds some recognition in this volume in its topics, interests, and approaches and, indeed, in the nationalities of its contributors. The scale, or quality, is implicit throughout. What the authors of these essays share with one another is an interest common to seventeenth-century writers as well as to generations of critics. If diction, figurative language, and rhetoric cannot be claimed as the unique possession of literature from Donne to Farquhar, certainly concern with these matters is central to our understanding of that literature. And such concern finds repeated justification in what seventeenth-century writers wrote or wrote about.

Many of those writers, including some not represented in this book, were revolutionary in seeking out what may well be termed natural languages: Donne, Jonson, Bacon, Burton, Hobbes, and Dryden are but a few. At the same time, seventeenth-century writers often were counterrevolutionary in their adherence to older decorums, and writers such as Browne, Milton, Bunyan, and Congreve heightened art languages, even while seeking their own version of what was most natural. What was common to all was a concern with language, a concern deepened by worry over the unstable condition of their mother tongue and heightened by knowledge of the alternatives offered by classical and by other modern languages. Each of the writers named, and perhaps all but one of those treated in this volume, were prodigious linguists by our restricted modern standards. They would have understood entirely Pope's remark about a Grub Street poet who was, Pope said, totally illiterate, not even knowing French. If it sometimes seems that most of them went up to Cambridge or were christened John, or both, that was no doubt accidental. They shared a remarkable degree of learning, profane and divine. Their classically based rhetorical training taught them that metaphor was, technically, an "abuse" of language. They were concerned with the uncertain state of their language, taking strenuous measures to order and enrich it. They were bred on parabolic readings of Scriptures, and they were more given to searching for truth in analogies between varieties of reality or experience than to establishing facts. We would say that to them language was crucial to ontology, epistemology, and metaphysics. To them it clearly implied the governance of states, the understanding of God's works, and the salvation of one's soul.

It was of course a commonplace that language distinguished man from other creatures beneath the angels. Equally obviously, language required discipline; to qualify its user for literacy, it needed intensifying by rhetoric or by artistic "abuse." And yet writers who valued nature exhibited a nervousness over the validity of rhetoric and questioned the adequacy of their native tongue. Carew's praise of Donne emphasized the conquest of the English language which was the triumph of Donne:

> Thou shalt yield no precedence, but of time,
> And the blinde fate of language, whose tun'd chime
> More charmes the outward sense; Yet thou maist claime
> From so great disadvantage greater fame,
> Since to the awe of thy imperious wit
> Our stubborne language bends.

Burton, characteristically denying in practice what he affirmed as principle, insisted that he was the plain man,

and writ with as small deliberation as I do ordinarily speak, without all affection of big words, fustian phrases, jingling terms, tropes, strong lines, that like *Acestes'* arrows caught fire as they flew, strains of wit, brave heats, elogies, hyperbolical exornations, elegancies, &c. which many so much affect. I am *aquae potor*, drink no wine at all, which so much improves our modern wits, a loose, plain, rude writer, *ficum voco ficum, & ligonem ligonem*, and as free as loose, *idem calamo quod in mente*, I call a spade a spade, *animis haec scribo, non auribus*, I respect matter, not words.

These are certainly valuable assurances, since we are not likely to have known as much otherwise. Edmund Waller, for his part, went so far as to doubt that lasting achievement was possible in his language:

> Poets that lasting marble seek,
> Must carve in LATIN or in GREEK:

We write in sand, our language grows,
And, like the tide, our work o'er flows.

Bacon, Herbert, and Hobbes—each masterly in creating images
that neither their age nor others since could forget—similarly
sought for linguistic order, for an identity of words with things
which their own writings belied.

For some time it has been fashionable to regard Bacon, Hobbes,
and the Royal Society as un-English forces, subversive of poetic
language like the French Academy, or at least as purgers of En-
glish who sought to reform the necessary abuses of literary lan-
guage into a plain, naked way of writing. Then as now, however,
example meant more than precept. What one discovers in Bacon's
Wisdom of the Ancients or in the sententiae of his *Essays* is some-
thing approaching perennial philosophy. "Tully well saith" was
enough to commend moral wisdom. And, toward the other end of
the century, we discover the Hon. Sir Robert Boyle writing on the
style of Holy Scriptures (I invite anyone to inspect the remarkable
mixture of titles of his works in Wing's *Short-Title Catalogue*), or
Thomas Burnet enunciating a theory of the earth in majestic prose,
or Sir Isaac Newton intermitting his studies in astrology, gravita-
tion, and alchemy to write a commentary on so mystical a prophet
as Daniel. Donne's language is at once immediate and conceited.
Jonson knew the jargon of mountebanks and the slang of London-
ers as well as the Latin of Horace and Vives. The pressures exerted
by Milton and Dryden on English to yield a new kind of order and
a new kind of revelation share much with the altogether artful
homeliness of Walton, Aubrey, Pepys, and Bunyan.

None of us has the rhetorical training that was flogged into these
writers in their boyhood, and few of us possess their familiarity
with more than one or two languages besides our own. But all of us
know that language and imagery (if not, because of our almost
total ignorance, rhetoric) are central to the study of seventeenth-
century writers. They are central because they are not merely
ornamental (although imbued as they were with ceremony, deco-
rum, and rhetoric, our writers certainly did seek out jewels for
bedizening naked truth). Above all, the one Book that was central
to the life of every seventeenth-century writer was constantly be-
ing subjected to figurative interpretations. Even those arguing for
literal interpretation of the Bible meant that at times, with the Can-
ticles, for example, the figurative interpretation was the literal one;
everyone believed that the Old Testament prefigured the New.

Painting, music, science, divinity, law, and even medicine depended upon systematic transference from one realm of language (that is, verbal representation of ideas and experience) to another.

Such evident truths do not imply that the seventeenth century was medieval. Nor do they imply that the writers of the century are interchangeable. Most of the writers altered their religious or their political allegiance, or both, at least once; all hesitated on such questions as whether the sun went around the earth or the earth around the sun; and all looked forward as earnestly as they looked backward. In 1678, for example, an all but unknown divine, Nathaniel Wanley, published (with a dedication to the Master of the Rolls of "immortal memory," Sir Harbottle Grimstone) *The Wonders of the Little World: Or, a General History of Man*—a very good title for the century. He confesses that he was inspired by Bacon to make his compendium of the "*Wonders of Humane Nature.*" Here, then, is the "New Philosophy." The first entry in the first chapter of the first book is "*Of such Infants as have been heard to cry while they were in the Womb of their Mothers.*" Our writers are temporal amphibians all.

There is something fetching in our attempts to chart unity in such blessed contradictions. Much has been made, for example, of a "Senecan" or "Stoic" revolution in prose styles and thought during the early reach of the century, and some critics feel passionately that for a few decades this Stoic revolution possessed intimate correspondence with poetic language. But in fact Stoic writers were printed more often after the Restoration than during the half century before the death of Donne. And that grand master, or bogeyman, of rhetoric, Cicero, had published as many editions and translations of one work, *De Officiis*, as did Seneca in his total canon. This fact, as also the additional one that "Tully's Offices" are themselves Stoic, seems as yet barely to have penetrated our assumptions. How many people teach Restoration poetry in accordance with the fact that during the period divine poets were more popular than secular (with the exception of Dryden, if he is an exception)? How many people are aware that between 1660 and 1690 the poetry of Chaucer, Donne, and Herbert was published, whereas that of Jonson was not, or that between 1667 and 1700 there were twenty-five editions of Milton's poems? How many people, one must ask again, really teach seventeenth-century literature with a recognition that, among poets first published before 1660, those published most frequently during the century were Quarles, Ovid, and Dryden, in that order? That all other poets followed way behind, and that Herrick's *Hesperides* was published only in 1648?

Questions and problems (whether we relate the phrase to Aquinas or Donne) such as these may be taken as an excuse for looking at the seventeenth century again and yet again.

It would be disingenuous of me to say that such problems were set for the contributors to this volume. (In fact, these random remarks were written after their essays were in hand.) Rather, in inviting them to contribute to this book I was seeking several kinds of balance. It seemed natural that a volume commissioned under the auspices of UCLA should contain a number of essays by people from the parent institution and by people at other branches of the University of California. Equally, I felt it desirable to approach leading students of seventeenth-century literature at other universities in the United States and abroad. Happily, there was no dearth of especially qualified men and women to approach, even on short notice. (It may be remarked parenthetically that, for what reason I do not know, the number of women preeminent in study of the literature of the century has been and continues to be altogether exceptional, and I take pleasure in including in this volume two of the most eminent, although I approached them of course for their eminence rather than for their sex.) But I conceived that success if not perfection was possible by striking a balance between two desiderata: a topic of importance and contributors of proven ability. That is not to say that other interesting topics and other able critics do not exist. With a variety of approaches to the general subject, one must be struck by the fact that the essays on the drama turn centrally upon language and action; that two essays center on critical abuses; that two essays (on Donne and Dryden) seek to define ill-understood genres; and that varieties of Neoplatonism are raised in essays touching figures as far removed as Spenser and Dryden. Such a balance may be precarious, but why else risk walking the critical wire? (The last essay assures the reader of a safety net.)

The search for another kind of balance naturally led to the attempt to include essays on major seventeenth-century writers. In the event, I have slighted drama and prose, not intentionally, but no doubt by a barely conscious prejudice in favor of poetry. I am by no means convinced of the propriety of a compiler-editor's including a piece of his own. (If invited by another person, I should have offered to write on topics that interest me nowadays in the writing of Milton or Butler.) I felt, however, that a volume of this kind could not afford to omit Dryden, and this conviction accounts for my appearance as essayist as well as editor. Given my concern for balance, I am particularly grateful to my friend, Stanley Stewart, for agreeing to provide an essay on Marvell, although his first preference was to write on Traherne. For any other omissions, I plead guilty—with a *caveat lector*. The reader will be hearing from the contributors on other occasions.

Two essays in this volume may seem somewhat severe in strictures leveled at individuals. I confess to considerable hesitation over this matter. The singling out of individual scholars for reprobation may smack of a degree of polemic not to everyone's taste. The matter was decided for me, however, when happily or unhappily Professor Legouis's very bracing essay arrived. Replying to my request for an essay on "definitions and caveats" in the study of seventeenth-century imagery, he found occasion to castigate me two or three times, with, of course, perfect scholarly manners. If, as compiler and editor, I sponsor criticism of myself, surely all readers will welcome the greater liveliness of the naming of names by contributors who believe that the cause of truth is served by pointing out the errors of the errant. As a matter of simple courtesy, I have sent an advance copy of the one essay taking flight from the work of a single critic who is, I firmly believe, eminent and dextrous enough to look out for himself. He and I are capable of responding, actively or silently, to such attention without loss of equanimity. Each of us has yet much to learn about seventeenth-century literature and about ourselves, not least because the relation between the two is manifestly of the highest importance.

In numerous respects, this volume does not exhaust the subject with which it is concerned, and I hope it is evident how much I should welcome further study. If this enterprise is successful, however, we shall have heightened awareness and advanced understanding of a central feature of seventeenth-century English literature. I am especially pleased with the variety of ways in which the essays raise fundamental questions about individual works, authors, styles, and ways of thought. I hope it is not just an editor's partiality to think that the essays do open numerous lines of study without turning idiosyncratic or novel for novelty's sake. At all events, I consider it impertinent to impose, whether on the reader or the contributors, my summary of what may so readily be found in the ensuing essays. Of the contributions to this volume (excepting my own, of course) it may be said with assurance that their quality and variety speak for themselves.

E. M.

Los Angeles
December 1969

ACKNOWLEDGMENTS

My principal debt is of course owed to the contributors themselves. I am particularly grateful to the Office of the Chancellor at UCLA for providing funds for subvention of publication and for research assistance, and to the University of California Press for undertaking to publish this volume. Mr. Ronald S. Baar, Mr. Steven Sharp, Mrs. Ruth Wolson, Miss Nancy Nakano, Mr. Dennis Martin, Mr. Saul Steier, and Mr. Robert Luzardo—all graduate students at UCLA —have given me material assistance. The first two assisted in checking references and in verifying quotations. The last four helped me to read proof, which arrived during term examinations and just before Christmas, 1970. My colleague, Philip Levine, has aided me with the Latin dedication, borrowed in part from a characterization of the elder Cato. The Central Stenographic Bureau at UCLA has assisted with prompt and accurate typing. Finally, I take great pleasure in acknowledging for a second time my debt to the superior editing of Mrs. Grace H. Stimson, whose canons of clarity and accuracy I envy.

This book is dedicated to my colleague, H. T. Swedenberg. Neither his modesty nor the occasion makes possible a *Festschrift*, but I fancy that as an active scholar he will take more pleasure in a dedication than in the rites, however sincere, of formal celebration. I cannot say more than that he is a man whom I have admired and loved these fifteen years, and that by dedicating this book to him I feel that I have indicated the standards I have intended to observe in it. I hope that neither he nor the contributors to this volume will take it amiss that I close this paragraph with the address by Dryden to Congreve in the last line of his poem: "You merit more; nor cou'd my Love do less."

CONTRIBUTORS

ROBERT M. ADAMS is Professor of English at the University of California, Los Angeles. He was graduated from Columbia University, where he also took his advanced degrees. He has taught previously at Rutgers University and Cornell University. In addition to *Ikon: John Milton and the Modern Critics* and numerous essays and reviews, he has published several books in modern, French, and comparative literature.

IAN DONALDSON is Professor of English at the Australian National University. He took First Class Honours degrees at the University of Melbourne and the University of Oxford. Before returning to Australia, he was Fellow of Wadham College and Lecturer in English; he has also taught as a visiting professor at the University of California, Santa Barbara. In addition to numerous essays, and to his work for *Essays in Criticism*, he has published *The World Upside-Down: Comedy from Jonson to Fielding* and is preparing an edition of Jonson's poems for the Clarendon Press.

STANLEY FISH is Professor of English at the University of California, Berkeley. He is a graduate of the University of Pennsylvania and received his Ph.D. from Yale University. He has published *John Skelton's Poetry* and *Surprised by Sin: The Reader in Paradise Lost*. He has edited a casebook for *Samson Agonistes* and a collection of essays on seventeenth-century prose for the Oxford Galaxy Modern Essays in Criticism series. He has in progress a book prospectively entitled *Distinguishing into Mercies: Literary and Life Styles in the 17th Century*.

CHRISTOPHER GROSE is Assistant Professor of English at the University of California, Los Angeles. He was graduated from Amherst College and took his advanced degrees at Washington University. He has written an essay on *Paradise Lost* and has edited John Evelyn's account, *The History of Sabatai Sevi*. He is preparing a study of rhetorical strategies in *Paradise Lost*.

TOSHIHIKO KAWASAKI is Professor of English at Nagoya University, Japan. He is a graduate of Kyoto University and received his graduate degrees from the University of Wisconsin. He has taught Japanese literature as a visiting professor at Stanford University, and his main lines of interest are implied by the titles of his books (published in Japanese): *The New Criticism; An Analytical Approach to Japanese Literature;* and *Donne's World.*

PIERRE LEGOUIS is *Professeur honoraire* at the University of Lyons. He was a student at the Ecole Normale Supérieure and took the *agregation d'anglais.* He has held professorships at the University of Besançon and the University of Lyons. He has written numerous articles and reviews and has written or edited the following books: *André Marvell: Poète. Puritain. Patriote; Donne the Craftsman; Poèmes Choisis de Dryden; Poèmes Choisis de Donne;* and *Andrew Marvell: Poet. Puritan. Patriot.* Most recently Professor Legouis has been revising and enlarging H. M. Margoliouth's edition of *The Poems and Letters of Andrew Marvell* in the Oxford English Texts Series.

BARBARA K. LEWALSKI is Professor of English at Brown University. Her graduate degrees were taken at the University of Chicago, and she taught at Wellesley College before going to Brown University. She has published numerous essays on Shakespeare, Milton, and various seventeenth-century topics. Her books include: *Milton's Brief Epic: The Genre, Meaning and Art of "Paradise Regained";* editions of certain of Milton's prose works in *Milton's Prose* (general editor J. Max Patrick), of *Much Ado About Nothing,* and (with Andrew Sabol) of *Seventeenth-Century Poets.* She has in progress *John Donne's Anniversaries: The Poetry of Praise as a Symbolic Mode.*

EARL MINER is Professor of English at the University of California, Los Angeles, where he is also chairman of the 17th and 18th Centuries Studies Group and Associate General Editor of the California Edition of *The Works of John Dryden.* He took his academic degrees from the University of Minnesota. He taught at Williams College before going to UCLA and has held Fulbright lectureships at Kyoto and Osaka universities and the University of Oxford. In addition to editing volumes in *The Works of John Dryden,* he has published *Dryden's Poetry* and *The Metaphysical Mode from Donne to Cowley.* Besides these and some other volumes on the seventeenth century, he has published books on Japanese and comparative literature and has in press a study of the Cavalier poets.

ALAN ROPER is Associate Professor of English at the University of California, Los Angeles. He took First Class Honours at Cambridge University (where he proceeded M.A.), an M.A. at Dalhousie University, and a Ph.D. at the Johns Hopkins University. He was an Instructor at Harvard University and a Research Fellow in English at Queens' College, Cambridge, before going to UCLA. Apart from articles on various subjects, he has published *Dryden's Poetic Kingdoms* and *Arnold's Poetic Landscapes*. He is editing Dryden's translation of *The History of the League* for *The Works of John Dryden*.

MAREN-SOFIE RØSTVIG is Professor of English Literature at the University of Oslo. She proceeded as Candidate of Philology at Oslo University and took her Ph.D. at the University of California, Los Angeles. She has published numerous studies, among them *The Happy Man: Studies in the Metamorphoses of a Classical Ideal* (Vol. I, 1600–1700; Vol. II, 1700–1760). The extensive revision of the first volume of *The Happy Man* makes it almost a new book. She has contributed to *The Hidden Sense and Other Essays* and has written "Marvell and the Caroline Poets" for *The Sphere History of Literature in the English Language* and "Structure as Prophecy: The Influence of Biblical Exegesis upon Theories of Literary Structure" for *Silent Poetry* (ed. Alastair Fowler).

STANLEY STEWART is Professor of English and Chairman of the Department at the University of California, Riverside. He was graduated from the University of California, Los Angeles, where he also took his advanced degrees. Besides essays on seventeenth-century literature and other subjects, he has written *The Enclosed Garden: The Tradition and the Image in Seventeenth-Century Poetry* and *The Expanded Voice: The Art of Thomas Traherne*. In addition, he has edited *The Unity of Prose: From Description to Allegory* and is contributing "Wilson's *Christian Dictionary* and the 'Idea' of Marvell's *Garden*" to a collection of essays edited by Howard Weinbrot.

CONTENTS

I

IMAGES OF PERFECTION

Maren-Sofie Røstvig

Edmund Spenser's *Fowre Hymnes* (1596) is rightly considered a splendid example of the Neoplatonic theme of the ascent from lower to higher levels of being; equally Neoplatonic are the definition of creation in terms of a preconceived "wondrous Paterne" and the insistence that this pattern of perfect beauty cannot be perceived by "mortall sence," but only by means of the "inward ey" of the mind.

Because of the vagueness of its outlines, Renaissance Neoplatonism is an uncommonly awkward tradition to assess. In the long run it may, perhaps, be wiser to abandon the term altogether in favor of a less specific word. In *Neoplatonism in the Poetry of Edmund Spenser* Robert Ellrodt rightly insists on the importance of observing the distinction between the Neoplatonic and the Christian view of the ascent from lower to higher levels of beauty. The Christian must necessarily abandon, and even condemn, the lower steps, just as he invests the idea of the return to God with a temporal dimension. Salvation (or regeneration) can be achieved only in time, through the course of human history. If these two attitudes are alien to Platonic and Neoplatonic thought, and if Ficino and Pico della Mirandola are justly described as "consistent and orthodox Platonists,"[1] then we must perforce conclude with Professor Ellrodt that Spenser must have been indebted to the Christianized Platonism of the Middle Ages rather than to the Florentine Neoplatonists. But is it possible to accept a characterization of Ficino

[1] Robert Ellrodt, *Neoplatonism in the Poetry of Edmund Spenser* (Geneva, 1960), p. 149.

1

and Pico as "orthodox" Platonists? It is, of course, perfectly true
that the Middle Ages failed to distinguish properly between Chris-
tian doctrines and the philosophy of Plato and the Neoplatonists,
and that they even went so far as to identify the Platonic account
of creation in the *Timaeus* with the Mosaic account. It is equally
true that Ficino and Pico mark a return to Platonism proper,
stripped of the Christian framework. While the Middle Ages were
familiar with Plato only as transmitted in Christianized commen-
taries on the *Timaeus* or as assimilated into Christian doctrines and
biblical exegesis, the Renaissance marks a restitution of the basic
texts and concepts. Ficino's work as translator and editor exempli-
fies this restitution, and so does Pico's *Commento* on Benivieni's
hymn on love. But the *opera omnia* of Ficino, as of Pico, modify
our impression of their historical role so strongly that it is impossi-
ble to accept a clear-cut differentiation between the Platonism of
the Middle Ages and that of the Renaissance. Plato's *Timaeus* may
have been a medieval classic, as Professor Ellrodt so often reminds
us, but it remained a classic—and a Christianized classic—through-
out the Renaissance. Ficino's own commentary on the *Timaeus*
represents a direct continuation of the medieval tradition, its pur-
pose being to demonstrate "the harmony between Moses and Plato,
whom Numenius called a second Moses." [2] Pico's *Heptaplus*
(1489) similarly reconciles Moses with Plato and Pythagoras and
displays a thoroughly syncretistic bias. Further evidence of the
continuity of the medieval tradition can be found in a letter written
by Ficino on 12 June 1489 in response to a request for a list of
books on Platonic thought. This letter recommends not only
Hermes and Plotinus, but the great medieval treatises such as Chal-
cidius' commentary on the *Timaeus* and Macrobius' *In Somnium
Scipionis*. In Dionysius the Areopagite *omnia sunt Platonica;* in
Augustine, *multa.* [3]

It is a fairly simple matter to prove that Augustine's Christianized
version of Platonic thought influenced not only the Middle Ages
but also the Renaissance, so that it may be wiser to refer to Renais-
sance syncretism rather than Renaissance Neoplatonism whenever
the reference is to works like Pico's *Heptaplus* or Ficino's *Theo-*

[2] Chap. XXIV of the *Commentarium in Timaeum;* see *Opera Omnia* (Paris,
1641), II, 406. See also chapters IX–X and XIX for similar statements. I wish to
express my indebtedness to Miss Valerie Smith of Oxford University for her
competent assistance in helping me to understand the Latin of Ficino's text.

[3] *Opera Omnia*, I, 926 f. Both Ficino and Pico believed that Plato prophesied
of Christian doctrines because he was a follower of Moses.

logia Platonica.[4] The fact that this syncretistic tradition has received such scant attention reflects a failure to grasp the nature of the syncretistic vision of the one truth and the various ways in which this vision influenced the poets. The many syncretistic accounts of creation published during the Renaissance illuminate themes and images of frequent occurrence in English poetry from Spenser to Milton, especially images of perfection. Our failure to do justice to the syncretistic tradition therefore has deprived us of important insights, so that many of these images have been poorly understood, or not at all. This is particularly true of what one may call mathematical images of perfection.

I hope Professor Ellrodt will forgive me for illustrating this failure by means of a quotation from his excellent study of Spenser, where he refers to Renaissance syncretism as "a seething mass of confused thinking":

The syncretic nature of Renaissance Platonism is well known and requires no further emphasis. Zoroaster, Pythagoras, "thrice-great Hermes," the Orphic hymns, the Cabbala and Arab philosophy entered into it, together with Plato and Plotinus. . . . All known systems of philosophy were tortured into harmony by the minds of men more alive to likenesses than sensitive to discrepancies; and the whole was loosely related to Christianity. That seething mass of confused thinking will be referred to as *Neoplatonism*.[5]

Spenser similarly is accused of a lack of proper discrimination. His mind "was not discriminating: he could blend several notions, associate several traditions with little regard for philosophic consis-

---

[4] The continuity of the tradition is seen quite clearly by comparing Augustine's *De ordine, De Musica*, VI, *De vera religione*, and *De libero arbitrio* with Bonaventura's works (particularly *Itinerarium mentis in Deum*) and with Ficino's *Theologia Platonica*. We know that Augustine transmitted Platonism to the Middle Ages (and to Dante), but he exerted an extraordinary influence also on the Florentine Neoplatonists. See, for example, Ficino's reference to Augustine's evaluation of Plato in the proem to *Theologia Platonica;* and it is worth noting that chapter XII, 5, is a verbatim rendering of Augustine, *De vera religione,* XXIX, 53–XXXII, 60, whereas Ficino's chapters XII, 6–7, summarize the argument of Augustine's *De Musica*, VI. For examples of Bonaventura's use of the same Augustinian sources, see in particular *Itinerarium mentis in Deum*, II, 5–10, and III, 3–4. Bonaventura's *Collationes in Hexaemeron* contains many good examples of a syncretistic juxtaposition of Plato and Plotinus with the Bible (see, for example, V, 15, 17; VI, 6, 7). Behind the Platonism of Ficino as of Bonaventura is the father figure of Augustine, a man whom they are not content merely to invoke; both summarize and include extensive quotations from his works.

[5] Ellrodt, *Neoplatonism*, p. 9.

tency." [6] The habit of referring to philosophers like Cusanus, Ficino, and Pico as exhibiting "a tolerant eclecticism" is fairly common,[7] but it is grossly unfair, as we realize the moment we turn to the primary sources. After having read Cusanus, Ficino, and Pico (preferably as supplemented by a liberal dose of patristic, medieval, and Renaissance theology) we must concede that not only is there a very real logical basis for their syncretism, but that this phenomenon was much more pervasive than has so far been realized. The belief that Plato was Moses Atticus and that Pythagoras borrowed from Moses is a logical consequence of the completely orthodox typological attitude to the Old Testament. Augustine is perhaps the most authoritative source for the view of history as a gradual unfolding of the divine scheme of redemption; this scheme was presented at first only through types and shadows, and then in full clarity in the life of Christ.[8] The prevalence of typology was increased, rather than diminished, by the Reformation, and it is possible that a man like Zwingli accepted Pico's syncretism without reservation simply because he attached so much importance to typology.

If one believes that the historical events narrated in the Old Testament are prefigurations of events in the life of Christ, then similar "prefigurations" may easily be attributed to other pre-Christian sources such as the Orphic hymns, Greek myth, and the Hermetic and Platonic dialogues. This assumption would be particularly plausible if one posited biographical links, for example, a secret oral transmission. The well-known, popular story of the death of Pan and of the cessation of oracles at the birth of Christ underlines the universal nature of this event.[9] The coming of Christ

[6] *Ibid.,* p. 81.

[7] The phrase is taken from Paul J. W. Miller's introduction to Pico della Mirandola, *On the Dignity of Man; On Being and the One; Heptaplus* (Indianapolis, 1965), p. x (hereafter cited as Pico, *Heptaplus*).

[8] See Jean Daniélou, *From Shadows to Reality: Studies in the Biblical Typology of the Fathers* (London, 1960). George Herbert, Marvell, and Milton illustrate the widespread use of typological imagery in the poetry of the first half of the seventeenth century. Exodus imagery was particularly frequent in the pamphlets of the Civil War, and many will remember Milton's comment, after the Restoration was a fact, that the English, in their "epidemic madness," had chosen "a captain back for Egypt" and renewed bondage. The close connection between typology and syncretism is illustrated by Dr. John Everard, the translator of the Hermetic dialogues (1650) and of Dionysius' *Mystical Theology* (1653), whose published sermons (1653 and 1659) are full of typological expositions. The popularity of typological exegesis may be illustrated by reference to William Guild's *Moses Unvailed* (1620), a handbook setting out the chief Old Testament types.

[9] A good exposition of the typological and syncretistic interpretation of history may be found in Ficino's *De Christiana religione* (*Opera Omnia,* I, 1–73), trans-

affected the whole world and not just the tribes of Israel, and by arguing that "Apollo from his shrine / Can no more divine" (Milton, *Nativity Ode*, ll. 176–177) one is in fact admitting that the so-called pagan world had its types or prophecies of Christ. It is in the very nature of types that they cease to function the moment that the antitype, Christ, appears. It is also part of their nature that types are grasped only after considerable mental effort resulting in what we today should consider oversubtle, strained interpretations. The same is true of the technique employed to reconcile, for example, the Mosaic and the Platonic accounts of creation; one must always consider the "inner meaning" of the text, as Pico explains in the first proem to his *Heptaplus*. If Moses seems "an unpolished popularizer rather than a philosopher or theologian or master of great wisdom," it is because he wrote about the truth in such a manner that only the few could understand it. This common practice was employed as well by Plato, who "concealed his doctrines beneath coverings of allegory, veils of myth, [and] mathematical images," just as Christ taught the crowd by means of parables, reserving an open explanation, without figures, for His disciples, and even these could not be told everything.[10] When, therefore, a Renaissance popularizer like Mario Equicola (*Di Natura d'Amore*, 1563) states that Plato and Plotinus presented the truth only through veils and shadows (*per velo & per ombra*), his phrasing could easily be a direct echo of Pico. But this possibility is not seen

lated into French by Guy Lefèvre de la Boderie in 1578. Chapter IX states that the advent of Christ was prophesied from the beginning of the world by the prophets and the sibyls through divine inspiration, and chapter XXII affirms that with the advent of Christ all errors were expelled, and all evil rites and sacrifices ceased. Not even Hercules could have achieved so complete a victory over demons, and Plutarch is cited as the great authority on the death of Pan and the cessation of oracles. The chapter concludes with a long list of those who prophesied about Christ before His coming, and Augustine is again cited as the great doctor of the Church who affirmed that the inspiration of the Platonists was of divine origin. Chapters XXIV–XXV comment on the prophetic role of the sibyls; chapter XXVI explains the germ of truth conveyed by pagan fables, such as the one concerning Deucalion's flood (one of the pagan parallels adduced by Milton in *Paradise Lost*). Numenius' characterization of Plato as Moses Atticus is quoted once again, while the doctrines of Hermes Trismegistus are said to become apparent in Moses and his life. Ficino is therefore one of those who posited that Hermes preceded Moses, and not the other way round. Chapter XXXIV connects the two Testaments in Pauline fashion by means of Platonic terminology: the Old Testament relates to the New as shadow to body, or as body to form. More easily accessible is Sir Walter Ralegh's *A History of the World* (1614), the first few chapters of which summarize the traditional theological interpretation of the early stages in the history of man. The bias is syncretistic.

[10] Pico, *Heptaplus*, p. 69. See also Augustine, *De doctrina Christiana*, II, vi, 7–8; II, xvi, 25; IV, viii, 22.

by Ellrodt, who instead interprets Equicola's view as evidence of a medieval bias alien to men like Pico and Ficino, but sympathetic to a poet like Spenser.[11] I cannot see that this conclusion has any validity; I would argue, instead, that we must accept that the Florentine Neoplatonists were syncretists in the tradition established by Augustine, and that this long-lived interesting tradition is the source for much of the imagery in Renaissance poetry.

I imagine that the ladder of ascent as portrayed by Spenser in *Fowre Hymnes* is the best known of the "Neoplatonic" themes of the Renaissance. There is a distinct tendency to think of this ladder almost exclusively in terms of degrees of beauty and to associate it with love, but it is important to give this image a less literal interpretation and to relate it to a number of other concepts or images of equal, or even greater, poetic significance.

According to William G. Madsen, Milton's description of the *scala creaturarum* (*Paradise Lost*, V, 469–512) conveys the familiar Neoplatonic theme of the "ladder of love." [12] This comment, although true enough, is inadequate; Milton's scale stresses the different faculties invested in the *res creatae*, and the higher steps represent higher faculties. Ficino's *Theologia Platonica* defines the ascent in terms typical of Renaissance syncretism:

thus far

Ascendimus hactenus a corpore in qualitatem, ab hac in animam, ab anima in Angelum, ab eo in Deum, unum, verum et bonum, auctorem omnium atque rectorem. Corpus appellant Pythagorici multa, qualitatem multa et unum. Animam unum et multa. Angelum unum multa. Deum denique unum.[13]

lastly

One and Many (or Multitude) are the basic terms, and the ascent is from *body* (Many) to *quality* (Many and One), from quality to *soul* (One and Many), from soul to *angelic being* (One Many), and from angelic being to *God*, who alone is One or Unity. The ascent is marked by an increasing degree of unity and a decreasing degree of multitudinousness. And Unity is that which all things desire, to quote from that most authoritative and supposedly orthodox of treatises, Dionysius' *On the Divine Names* (I, 5). In celebrating "the bountiful Providence of the Supreme Godhead we must draw upon the whole creation," because this Godhead is the central force of all things and their purpose. Through the existence

---

[11] Ellrodt, *Neoplatonism*, p. 174.

[12] William G. Madsen, *From Shadowy Types to Truth* (New Haven, 1968), p. 87.

[13] *Theologia Platonica*, III, 1 (*Opera Omnia*, I, 112).

of the Godhead the world is brought into being and maintained, "and It [i.e., the Godhead] is that which all things desire—those which have intuitive or discursive Reason seeking It through knowledge, the next rank of beings through perception, and the rest through vital movement or the property of mere existence belonging to their state." [14] The emphasis here is not on love and beauty, whether earthly or heavenly, but on the fact that all things seek God (defined as Unity) through their proper faculties: knowledge, sense perception, vital movement, or mere being. Milton also makes this point in his description of the prelapsarian world, and it is a constantly recurring theme in Henry Vaughan.

Although Unity (God) is at the top of the ladder and Multitude (body) at its foot, all things have a share in the divine Unity. Many of the key images of *Paradise Lost* result from this numerical definition, notably stated in VIII, 419–426:

> No need that thou
> Shouldst propagate, already infinite;
> And through all numbers absolute, though one;
> But man by number is to manifest
> His single imperfection, and beget
> Like of his like, his image multiplied,
> In unity defective, which requires
> Collateral love, and dearest amity.[15]

One could gloss this passage by quoting from Dionysius' *On the Divine Names* (II, 11), where God is said to be able to multiply without loss of unity: "from Its Oneness it becomes manifold while yet remaining within Itself." God "remains One in the act of Self-Multiplication"; He is "an Undifferenced Unity in Himself and without any commixture or multiplication through His contact with the Many." [16] As I have argued elsewhere, the fall both of angels and of man in *Paradise Lost* is a fall away from unity into a multiplicity utterly devoid of unity,[17] and for this reason Milton's strategy is to contrast images of discord with images of perfection, the former being defined by absence of union.

[14] Dionysius the Areopagite, *On the Divine Names and the Mystical Theology*, trans. C. E. Rolt (London, 1966), pp. 60–61.

[15] All quotations from Milton are from *The Poems of John Milton*, ed. John Carey and Alastair Fowler (London, 1968).

[16] Dionysius, *On the Divine Names*, pp. 79 f.

[17] "Milton and the Science of Numbers," *English Studies Today*, 4th ser. (Rome, 1966), pp. 267–288. The "images of imperfection" used to describe the fallen angels in *Paradise Lost*, I–II, stress the qualities usually attributed to the concept of multiplicity devoid of unity: size, weight, number, movement, mutability, and uncertain reasoning powers.

Although the idea of order as expressed in the *scala creaturarum* has its hierarchical aspect, we must not limit our attention to the codified systems of social levels in the kingdoms of this world or the next. We should rather think of order in terms of the harmony it creates at all levels of being. Unity is achieved through a harmonious arrangement of parts, and so important is this idea that it conditions the titles of many of the syncretistic treatises of the Renaissance, for example, Francesco Giorgio's *De harmonia mundi* (1525 and 1536; French trans., 1579).

Music is an obvious example of the kind of harmony that can be perceived by the senses, and as such it is only a pale reflection of the harmony that prevails in a well-ordered soul, or in the mind of God. Thus the *itinerarium mentis in Deum*—the title of Bonaventura's most popular treatise—is a progress from visible to invisible forms of harmony. This stress on the value of harmony was no recondite idea; Shakespeare found it suitable for presentation on the stage, letting one of his characters state that he whose soul is lacking in harmony cannot relish the harmony of music:

> The man that hath no music in himself,
> Nor is not moved with concord of sweet sounds,
> Is fit for treasons, stratagems, and spoils,
> The motions of his spirit are dull as night,
> And his affections dark as Erebus:
> Let no such man be trusted.
> (*The Merchant of Venice*, V, i, 83–88)

In a letter written on 8 September 1479 Ficino quotes Augustine on the same topic: "Our Aurelius Augustine writes in his book *De musica* that he is not harmoniously composed who does not delight in harmony." Ficino goes on to state that this argument is not without good reason, since it is necessary that he who fails to be moved by harmony should himself somehow be without it. If it were at all permissible, he would say that such a man could not have been created by God, as God loved harmony to such an extent that He created a world where each part possesses a harmonious relationship to the whole. Through the intellectual power and the goodness of its Author, therefore, the universe is truly in harmony with man. Ficino's final point is that God disposed the celestial spheres so that they create an incomparable harmony, as the Pythagoreans and Platonists maintain.[18]

---

[18] *Opera Omnia*, I, 794 f. The topic of the letter is given in the heading: Non est harmonice compositus, qui harmonia non delectatur.

The theological orthodoxy of this Augustinian adaptation of the classical concept of harmony was universally accepted. The truth of the Pythagorean and Platonic numerical formulas for the harmony of creation appeared from the Bible itself, where God was said to have created all things in number, weight, and measure.[19] The Wisdom who orders all things sweetly [20] was believed to have done so by means of the universally valid numerical formulas for harmony, and it is because they are arranged in this manner that the *res creatae* are capable of achieving a return to God, and it is for the same reason that the heavens declare the glory of God.

The syncretistic fusion between the schemes of creation and redemption on the one hand and, on the other, Plato's lambda formula for the harmony of the universe may be illustrated by reference to the portrayal of Christ in a Genesis initial in a Bible dating from about 1070. As Harry Bober explains in an article drawing attention to this portrayal,[21] such highly adorned initials often contained images of exegetical importance by presenting, for example, some of the better-known typological parallels between the Old Testament and the New. In this particular initial, however, Christ is shown seated and surrounded by four framing bands of medallions, each of which depicts personified elements and to each of which is given the number that assures harmony when the four are joined. The cubes of 2 and 3—8 and 27—are given to the extremes represented by fire and earth, and these extremes are harmonized by the mean numbers 12 and 18 representing air and water.[22]

---

[19] Wisd. of Sol. 11:20 (Vulg., 11 : 21). Ficino, *Commentarium in Timaeum*, XII, identifies the Mosaic account of the six days of creation with the six numbers in Plato's lambda formula: 2 and 3 plus these numbers squared and cubed. These six numbers issue out of the creative Monad, placed at the top:

$$1$$
$$2 \quad 3$$
$$4 \quad 9$$
$$8 \quad 27$$

The Pythagorean tetractys includes only the first four numbers, 1, 2, 3, and 4, whose sum is 10, which denotes a return to unity. The numbers in these formulas create the ratios productive of harmony; thus the ratio 2:1 creates the octave, or diapason.

[20] Wisd. of Sol. 8:1.

[21] Harry Bober, "In Principio: Creation before Time," in *Essays in Honor of Erwin Panofsky*, ed. Millard Meiss (New York, 1961), I, 13–28.

[22] A good medieval exposition of the harmony imposed on creation by Plato's lambda numbers is found in Bonaventura's *Collationes in Hexaemeron*, IV, 16, as based on Augustine, *De Genesi ad litteram*, IV, 7, 14. Bonaventura explains that 8 relates to 12 as 18 to 27, since 8 plus half of 8 (i.e., 4) is 12, and 18 plus half of 18 (i.e., 9) is 27. The ratio is therefore the same. The classical medieval exposition

This portrayal of Christ is in complete agreement with the interpretation usually given to Ezekiel's vision of the chariot with the four wheels and a man seated in the middle (Ezekiel 1, 10), a vision of Christ imposing harmony through the 4 of the elements and the 4 of the Gospels.[23] The harmony of the elements presented in the Genesis initial is therefore a type or a prophecy of the harmony restored to man through the 4 of the Cross and the 4 of the Gospels.

Christ the Creator thus has the same function as Christ the Redeemer, in that both acts consist in the imposition of harmony. The syncretists would describe this act as a reconciliation between multiplicity and unity through those numerical ratios that ensure a return to unity, and the popularity of a work like Pierre de la Primaudaye's *The French Academie* [24] reveals the extensiveness of the syncretistic trend toward the end of the sixteenth century. Other publications that testify to the prevalence of syncretistic arguments around the turn of the century are Jean Bodin's *Universae Naturae Theatrum* (1596) and *The Six Books of A Commonwealth* (1st French ed., 1576; 1st English ed., 1606). Bodin continues the medieval tradition of assigning to the four elements the numbers that create musical harmony and, like Pierre de la Primaudaye, argues that these ratios must be made to prevail in man and in society.[25] The continuity of patristic and medieval traditions may be observed also in the *Catalogus Gloriae Mundi* (1617) by Bartholomaeus Chassanaeus, an author whose indebtedness to Pico is very evident. The agreement between Milton's description of hell and that of Chassanaeus is no doubt owing to a commonly shared tradition derived from Augustine. Chassanaeus, like Augustine, places hell within the divinely established order; hell imitates the hierarchical structure of Heaven united under one head, but what is missing is the harmonious disposition of the elements. With respect to these there is no order or place, no active or

of the lambda numbers is, of course, Chalcidius' commentary on the *Timaeus*, a critical edition of which, edited by Raymond Klibansky, was published by the Warburg Institute in 1962.

23 See below, pp. 20 f. In an essay now in press I give a survey of the exegetical tendency to invest biblical structures with prophetic import ("Structure as Prophecy," in *Silent Poetry*, a volume of essays edited by Alastair Fowler and published by Routledge).

24 Numerous editions of La Primaudaye's work, in both French and English, came out toward the end of the sixteenth century and at the beginning of the seventeenth.

25 Jean Bodin, *The Six Books of A Commonwealth* (London, 1606), pp. 788 f.

passive.[26] When making the familiar comparison between the four elements and the four evangelists, the author refers to Ezekiel 1 and hence to that vision of the chariot which Milton was to exploit as his chief image of perfection.

Before I conclude this brief exposition of some aspects of Renaissance syncretism, a final important point must be made. To a greater or lesser extent, and more or less clearly, all the great syncretists proclaim that the literary artist must imitate the creative technique of the Deity. He, too, must create harmony by imposing number, weight, and measure (Wisd. of Sol. 11:20), by disposing everything *suaviter* (Wisd. of Sol. 8:1). As Pierre de la Primaudaye phrases it, a harmonious organization is proof that the origin is in the unity that is God.[27] This idea is explicitly applied to literary creation by the brothers Guy and Nicholas Lefèvre de la Boderie in the prefaces to their translations of Giorgio's *De harmonia mundi* and Pico's *Heptaplus*, published in one volume in 1579. Thus the structure of a literary work, whether in prose or verse, may constitute an image of perfection, like the created universe and the scheme of redemption, by embodying the same numerical formulas for harmony. Moses is the great example of the inspired poet-prophet, so that to imitate Moses is to imitate Nature herself, and to imitate Nature is to imitate God, the creator of Nature. And God, as Spenser well knew, created according to a preconceived "wondrous Paterne" of such beauty that it cannot be perceived by "mortall sence." We come closest to God's pattern by means of those mathematical ratios that reflect an eternal, immutable beauty above the world of the five senses. According to Guy Lefèvre de la Boderie (himself a poet) the artist must imitate God by conceiving, in his mind, a design or model of his work incorporating "la plus parfaicte Idée qu'il puisse imaginer & depeindre au tableau de son Entendement." And this most perfect idea may be grasped, in studying the structure of the universe, if, like Giorgio, one is capable of proceeding from the visible to the invisible.[28]

[26] Bartholomaeus Chassanaeus, *Catalogus Gloriae Mundi* (1617), pp. 130 f. That there is no order with respect to active or passive is a reference to odd and even numbers, the former being considered masculine and active, the latter, feminine and passive. The lambda numbers are ranged accordingly, odd numbers to one side and even numbers to the other.

[27] See *French Academie*, Bk. III, chap. xi.

[28] These prefaces are important documents in the history of Renaissance poetics, and they ought to be closely studied for the light they shed on Renaissance syncretism and its influence on theories of poetic creation.

Although in the following it may not be possible to pursue a strict sequence, since one image so often connects with a related one, I begin by focusing on the circle as an image of perfection and on the androgyne (a kind of circle), and conclude with examples of structural images of perfection based on the ratios productive of harmony.

There is Platonic and Hermetic as well as biblical authority for the view that God may be compared to a circle,[29] the biblical *locus classicus* being the statement that "I am Alpha and Omega, the beginning and the end" (Rev. 1:8, 11; 21:6; 22:13).[30] Circular patterns had been attributed to the Bible as a whole and to individual parts. Thomas Aquinas, on observing that a certain psalm begins and ends with the same verse, at once concluded that its form was circular, and it seemed equally obvious to exegetes that the Bible begins with the same vision with which it concludes: a tree placed in the middle, respectively, of the Garden of Eden and of the Heavenly Jerusalem. This tree is Christ, the center of both Testaments and the center for the temporal scheme of human existence from creation to Judgment Day. The image of the circle therefore connects with the concept of a center, and a circular arrangement with one that is symmetrical (i.e., a division into two or around a midpoint in the manner advocated by Augustine in *De Musica*, VI, and in *De vera religione*).

When Milton has Adam and Eve praise God, he makes them define His being as first, last, midst, and without end (*Paradise Lost*, V, 165), and he has them do so in a perfect universe whose love of God is manifested in a never-ceasing circular motion. This universe is so constituted that it is itself an image of perfection—a logical necessity, since earth (or the universe) is a shadow of Heaven. The circular movement of the universe is a reflection of the circular movement of the angels around the throne of God, and this throne is always in midheaven. It is sufficiently easy to spot all the direct references in Milton's text to circles, orbs, or circular

---

[29] See, for example, Bonaventura's discussion in the *Itinerarium mentis in Deum*, V, 8. God is, as it were, both the center and the circumference, because He is eternal and most present (*praesentissimum*) and hence circumscribes and penetrates all things (*omnes durationes ambit et intrat*). The Hermetic statement that God is a sphere whose circumference is everywhere and whose center is nowhere is quoted, but it is attributed to Alanus de Insulis (*Regulae Alani de sacra theologia*, 7).

[30] The standard exegetical comment on these verses is that they prove the circular nature of the Deity. Some exegetes adduced as additional proof the fact that the three letters in the name of God (Jehovah) are the three circular numbers 5, 6, and 10 (Hebrew letters are numbers as well).

movements in Heaven as in the universe at large, or in Eden. It is, perhaps, less obvious that groups of four form circles, but Adam and Eve say as much when they invoke the elements "that in quaternion run / Perpetual circle" (V, 181 f.). The hours, too, move in a perpetual circle, not merely because all temporal cycles are circular (like the four seasons), but because there is another quaternion in the four chief hours of the day and night—morning, noon, evening, and midnight—which are constantly referred to in the course of the epic action. There are, then, quaternions of elements, qualities, humours, passions, hours, seasons, winds, and quarters of the earth, which through their balanced arrangement achieve the kind of harmony that reflects the Deity whom they praise by moving in their appointed order. The four qualities of hot, cold, moist, and dry are so perfectly poised or balanced that no one quality prevails in Eden, and the same is true of the four passions and the four humours in the microcosmos of man. As long as man fulfills his natural function or purpose, to love and to praise God, he remains in a state of union and obedience and hence of harmony, and the same is true of the universe in which he has been placed.

An epic concerned with "man's first disobedience" may therefore be said to be concerned with the breaking of this circle. Adam stops his metaphorical circling around God the moment that he prefers Eve, and, ironically enough, this exercise of free will to ensure conjugal union entails the breaking of the circle formed by Adam and Eve. On man's commitment to God depends all union—union between man and woman and even the union between the four elements and all the other quaternions of existence. This is shown most clearly in the epic action of *Paradise Lost*, more subtly in the imagery. The frequent references to the joining of hands bring home to us the essential unity of Adam and Eve before the Fall: "Thus talking hand in hand alone they passed / On to their blissful bower" (IV, 689 f.) and "into their inmost bower / Handed they went" (IV, 738 f.). The first step toward the Fall is taken when Eve, "Thus saying, from her husband's hand her hand / Soft she withdrew" (IX, 385 f.), an act that occurs after Adam has vainly urged the importance of union or that perfect balance between opposites which is the definition of concord, in strong contrast with "the hateful siege / Of contraries" (IX, 121 f.) from which Satan necessarily suffers. In man before the Fall there can be no such siege; delight is joined to reason (IX, 243) as Eve to Adam, and it is in recognition of the importance of this union that Adam pleads in favor of "our joint hands" (IX, 244), warns against severing this union (IX, 252 ff.), and affirms that Satan cannot hope to "circumvent us joined" (IX, 259). When, in the last lines of the epic, Adam and Eve take their solitary way through Eden, the fact that they do so "hand in hand" is evidence of harmony restored, albeit only in part. What has happened cannot be undone: the perfection of the cosmic structure has been ruined so that inequality replaces equality or perfect balance. This is true in the most literal sense: the movements of the celestial bodies have become erratic so that the temporal scheme displays a similar absence of perfect regularity, the reason being that God, as "some say, "bid his angels turn askance / The poles of earth twice ten degrees and more / From the sun's axle" (X, 668–670). In this manner the poised symmetry of the universe is destroyed, and it is no longer a perfect reflection of the unity that is God. Days and nights no longer display equality (X, 680); change has replaced permanence and must do so the moment that Sin and Death effect their entrance. Discord, Milton states (X, 707–709), is the daughter of Sin, and she introduces Death "through fierce antipathy."

This definition of Sin in terms of discord exemplifies that fusion between Greek philosophy and Christian doctrines which gained the sanction of patristic and medieval theology. The Pythagorean origin is indicated when Milton uses the term "quaternion," another word for the Pythagorean *tetractys* or *progressio quaternaria;* but Milton has placed the reference to the quaternions of the created universe within a cluster of biblical echoes, thus indicating the absence of contradiction.[31]

The strength of the syncretistic tradition may be illustrated by reference to the imagery employed by Henry Vaughan [32] or Andrew Marvell, where we often pass from what is Hermetic or Platonic to what is Christian. Again it would be anachronistic to posit a transitional jolt; if Marvell shared the intellectual bias of his employer, Lord Fairfax, he would have believed in the impeccably Christian character of the Hermetic dialogues.[33] The androgyne is one of the half-Platonic, half-Hermetic concepts that caught Marvell's attention. This concept is closely related to that of the

[31] See Fowler's footnotes (*Poems of Milton*) on *Paradise Lost*, V, 153–208.

[32] Henry Vaughan's "The World" (the better known of his poems with that title) fuses Hermetic, Platonic, and biblical imagery. See my article on this subject in *Papers on Language and Literature*, V (Fall, 1969).

[33] The British Museum owns the MS volume in which Fairfax entered his incomplete translation of the commentary on the Hermetic dialogues published in French by François de Foix in 1579 (see my study, *The Happy Man* [rev. ed.; Oslo, 1962], I, 162–166). Fairfax translated the section where de Foix comments on the Hermetic account of the creation of an androgynous man.

circle, in that the bisexual or androgynous character of man as first created was conceived of as a kind of circle. Hermetic and Platonic dialogues state that man was created as a bisexual being, and syncretistically inclined theologians interpreted Genesis 1:27 ("male and female created he them") so as to agree with Plato and Hermes. Renaissance commentaries on the Hermetic account of creation identify this bisexual state with the prelapsarian state of perfection, the division into two being associated with the Fall. The state of perfection, moreover, was defined as one in which mind is in complete command of the world of matter, while conversely the divided state is marked by the supremacy of the body and the bodily passions, and hence of movement. The bisexual state reflects the state of God[34] insofar as it is capable of procreation without external aid, and insofar as it is marked by rest and union instead of movement and separation.

Marvell alludes to this syncretistic version of the prelapsarian state in several poems, most clearly in "The Garden" and "The Definition of Love." "The Garden" begins with praise of repose and a rejection of mere earthly passion, and its evocation of paradise before the Fall is stated in terms of "that happy Garden-state" before Adam had acquired a "mate":

> Such was that happy Garden-state,
> While man there walked without a mate:
> After a place so pure, and sweet,
> What other help could yet be meet!
> But 'twas beyond a mortal's share
> To wander solitary there:
> Two paradises 'twere in one
> To live in paradise alone. (ll. 57–64)

If "paradise" is taken as a metaphor for the sexual organs (a sufficiently common usage), then the concluding couplet would describe the androgynous state. This state is, however, "beyond a mortal's share," since mortality is a direct consequence of the division into two sexes. As in Milton's *Paradise Lost*, the Fall is connected with division and discord, perfection with complete union and harmony. Although some poets inevitably exploited the idea of bisexuality merely for fun,[35] the representation of Francis I in

[34] Fowler's comments (*Poems of Milton*) on *Paradise Lost*, I, 20 f., cite the various sources for this belief.

[35] Thomas Randolph uses bisexuality in this way in "Upon an Hermaphrodite" (1640), and so does John Cleveland in a poem of similar title, "The Author to his Hermaphrodite."

a portrait as half man and half woman is proof of the strength of the tradition associating prelapsarian perfection with an androgynous creation. The ruling monarch must be made to share one of the divine attributes.[36]

Marvell's obscure poem, "The Definition of Love," may be explicated in terms of the circle and the androgyne. I wish to argue that this puzzling lyric defines perfect love, and that perfect love implies the impossible desire for complete union in the androgynous state:

> My Love is of a birth as rare
> As 'tis for object strange and high:
> It was begotten by despair
> Upon Impossibility.   (ll. 1-4)

An explanation in terms of a merely social impossibility (high social rank) would be most unsatisfying. Also it would disagree with the title, which states that the poem presents a definition, and definitions must be universally valid. If we identify the "object strange and high" with the androgyne as an image of perfection, we avoid having to reduce the "impossibility" from its cosmic to a purely social level, and at the same time the identification increases the poetic tension by associating it with a desire to annul the effects of the Fall. This interpretation finds support in the fact that the whole poem is pervaded by cosmic imagery, while the familiarity of the idea is proved by a passage in Sir Thomas Browne's *Religio Medici* (1642). Clearly inspired by Renaissance treatises on love, Browne states that true lovers cannot be satisfied with embraces, "but desire each to be truly the other; which being impossible, their desires are infinite and must proceed without a possibility of satisfaction" (Bk. II, sec. 6). But Marvell is not content to state that the desired union is impossible: Fate is jealous to see "Two perfect Loves; nor lets them close" as "Their union would her ruine be." If Fate is connected with the structure of the universe, the consummation of the speaker's desire would induce cosmic ruin. Spenser, of course, states the same thing in the passage in *The Faerie Queene* (IV, x, 34-35, 41) where he describes love or concord as a balance between opposites, Nature alone being bisexual. It is in the nature of things that man and woman, after the Fall, must remain separate personalities. The "Iron wedges" that prevent the two halves of the "circle" from closing are the celestial signs that always separate

---

[36] Edgar Wind reproduces the portrait in his *Pagan Mysteries in the Renaissance* (New York, 1968), pl. 80; for his comments, see pp. 213 f.

the poles of the universe. Each of these signs may be viewed as a pyramid with its apex at the center of the earth, as we read in Sacrobosco's popular handbook on the structure of the universe (*Tractatus de Sphaera*).[37] Because these signs follow the movement of the sphere, their "Iron wedges" will always "crowd" themselves "betwixt." The equator, therefore, represents the meeting point only of the equinoctial line and the ecliptic, the most famous of all oblique angles. Because of their obliquity such angles were considered imperfect, and so Marvell, like Milton, could draw on this well-known geometrical concept for an image of perfection:

> As Lines so Loves *oblique* may well
> Themselves in every Angle greet:
> But ours so truly *Paralel*,
> Though infinite can never meet.
>
> Therefore the Love which us doth bind,
> But Fate so enviously debars,
> Is the Conjunction of the Mind,
> And Opposition of the Stars.   (ll. 25–32)

Love, then, may effect a temporary physical union of opposites, but the separation into male and female is as permanent as the separation of the celestial poles or (to use Spenser's examples) of air from fire and land from water. The very terms of human existence prevent lovers from achieving their desired union except in a "Conjunction of the Mind." Marvell's title shows that since the Fall our bodies remain separate entities and that a perfect love can be consummated only by what he terms a "conjunction of the mind."

Both Marvell and Milton turn to the structure of the cosmos for images of perfection or imperfection, a natural procedure, since the microcosmos of man repeats the structure of the macrocosmos. Milton's prelapsarian universe knows no division, no oblique angles, only harmony and union; and harmony means circular movements and symmetrical dispositions. Perhaps the most important impulse that Augustine received from Platonic thought was the aesthetic argument that a division into equal parts—an *aequalitas* structure—is beautiful because it reflects the unity of the Deity. Reason makes

---

[37] See the chapters of Sacrobosco included in English translation in J. J. Bagley and P. B. Rowley, *A Documentary History of England*, Vol. I: 1066–1540 (Pelican Books, 1966), pp. 138–151. I submit a fuller interpretation of "The Definition of Love" in my chapter on "Marvell and the Caroline Poets" to be published in *The Sphere History of Literature in the English Language*.

us prefer symmetrical arrangements; in all art that which pleases is harmony; harmony is a matter of equality and unity, and unity may be achieved through the imposition of the ratios given in the Pythagorean tetractys formula or in the lambda formula of Plato's *Timaeus*. This fusion between classical and Christian thought may be exemplified by Augustine's attribution of the same harmonious ratio of 2:1 (the octave proportion, or the diapason) to the Trinity, the created universe, and the scheme of redemption.[38] Bonaventura and Ficino carried this Christianized system of classical aesthetics into the Middle Ages and the Renaissance, and the many *aequalitas* structures traced in *Paradise Lost* by Gunnar Qvarnström and Alastair Fowler [39] reveal its validity also for John Milton. Milton, it seems, disposed the body of his text and the chronological scheme for his epic action in such a manner that *Paradise Lost* reflects the harmony that proves its origin is in God. In a biblical epic this technique was probably the only appropriate one. Reviewers of Qvarnström's *The Enchanted Palace* have found it difficult to accept his structural analyses, largely because the present age has forgotten the very existence of "mathematical images," let alone their symbolic import. Although unity is still a criterion of literary excellence, we have lost contact with the tradition that unity is reflected in a harmonious disposition of parts, and that the highest intellectual activity consists in the discovery of unity. The tradition upon which Milton drew therefore requires extensive documentation, unfamiliar as it is to most of us today.

It may, perhaps, become a little less unfamiliar if we consider the way it influences the subject matter of *Paradise Lost*, Book V. This book is so completely dominated by sense perception that even God is referred to in terms of the sense organs. Thus we are told that "God's own ear / Listens delighted" (V, 626 f.) and that God is envisaged as "th'Eternal Eye" (V, 711). It may be argued that Milton's concern is to show that the delights of sense perception are perfectly legitimate in an unfallen world, but his technique of description compels us to consider sense perception as such. Milton takes his readers on a conducted tour, as it were, of the "five watchful senses" (l. 104) in the course of which they are prompted to employ their rational faculty to observe exactly how the senses function. It is possible for a single sense to form its own circle of

[38] Augustine, *De Trinitate*, I, iv, 3–4 (see *Oeuvres de Saint Augustin* [Paris, 1955], XV, 356–367). This passage is followed by a section describing salvation in terms of an escape from multitude to unity through Christ.

[39] Gunnar Qvarnström, *The Enchanted Palace* (Stockholm, 1967); *Poems of Milton*, ed. Carey and Fowler.

perfection, as when taste after taste is said to be "upheld with kindliest change" (l. 336), or when the sense of touch proceeds from rough and smooth to soft and hard ("Rough or smooth rind, or bearded husk, or shell" [l. 342]). The total effect of the book, however, is of passing from one sense to another in an uninterrupted sequence or circle. The passage presenting Raphael's first visit (ll. 331–387) takes the reader from taste to touch and from smell to vision, while the preceding narrative contains the vocal tribute paid to God by Adam and Eve. The purpose of the angelic visit is of course primarily to permit Adam to listen. This systematic and extremely logical presentation of the five senses, plus the fact that Milton extends the perspective by placing sense perception among the five powers that unite in man, recalls Book II of Augustine's De libero arbitrio. Augustine teaches us that all perception of order is a mental act, and Milton presents sense perception in such a manner that we are compelled to admire what Augustine calls its numerical order. By perceiving this order we progress from the world of sense to that of pure mind and finally to the God who created this admirable order. In other words, if we read Book V in the spirit of Augustine's treatise on free will, we achieve the kind of ascent from body to mind which Milton describes at V, 469–490. Augustine explains how "Wisdom shows itself to the seeker in the guise of numbers embodied in all things of this world":

Wherever you turn, wisdom speaks to you through the imprint it has stamped upon its works. When you begin to slip toward outward things, wisdom calls you back, by means of their very forms, so that when something delights you in body and entices you through the bodily senses, you may see that it has number and may ask whence it comes. Thus you return to yourself: you know that you cannot approve or disapprove of what you touch with the bodily senses, unless you have within you certain laws of beauty to which you refer the beautiful objects that you perceive outside you.

Look at the sky, the earth, and the sea, and at whatever in them shines from above or crawls, flies, or swims below. These have form because they have number. Take away these forms and there will be nothing. Whence are these except from number? Indeed, they exist only insofar as they have number.[40]

Artists, too, organize their works by means of numbers, and when we ponder these works, they "delight the inner judge who gazes

[40] Saint Augustine, On Free Choice of the Will, trans. Anna S. Benjamin and L. H. Hackstaff (Indianapolis, 1964), p. 73. The quotation is from Bk. II, chap. 16.

upward upon numbers." And if finally we go beyond the spirit of the artist, we may perceive "eternal number" in the mind of God.

The foregoing is one of Augustine's favorite arguments, and we know that Augustine was Milton's favorite theologian, as Plato was his favorite philosopher. It is therefore without hesitation that I submit the thesis that we should consider, as an image of perfection, the abstract order displayed by the harmonious operation of the five watchful senses and the various powers in the microcosmos of man. The purpose of this order, which clearly reflects the order of Heaven as described toward the end of Book V, is to compel us to consider its source. At V, 616–657, we experience a celestial version of the delights derived from sense perception, beginning and concluding (as in Eden) with hearing. In this manner earth is indeed a shadow of Heaven, and our rational appreciation of the harmoniously organized senses and powers of man has taught us to appreciate the celestial hierarchies arranged "in orbs / Of circuit inexpressible" (ll. 594 f.).

Because of this emphasis on a rational order including all levels of being and all activities, the eating of the apple ("Greedily she engorged without restraint" [IX, 791]) becomes a shocking violation of order. No poet besides Milton has succeeded in making this action so inherently significant; Book V provides the basis for understanding this aspect of the Fall. Satan, as was to be expected from his limited understanding, sees only the ridiculous side of the apple episode: "him by fraud I have seduced / From his creator, and the more to increase / Your wonder, with an apple" (X, 485–487). For the narrative climax of Book IX to be properly felt, it is necessary to pay proper attention to Milton's discussion of sense perception in Book V; it is also prerequisite to understand the true import of the episode when Christ ascends the chariot of paternal Deity in Book VI, and, in so doing, assumes omnipotence. As Gunnar Qvarnström was the first to discover,[41] this episode is placed at the center of Milton's epic; when the ten books were organized into twelve, the central placing of Christ was made even more apparent. In an epic consisting of twelve books, Christ quite obviously "holds the middle" by appearing as omnipotent judge and victor toward the end of Book VI and as omnipotent creator at the beginning of Book VII.

For more than a thousand years readers of the Bible and of biblical commentaries had been accustomed to think of Christ as always

[41] Gunnar Qvarnström, *Dikten och den nya vetenskapen* (Lund, 1961), pp. 169–228.

being in the middle. Bonaventura, for example, felt compelled to begin his extensive commentary on the story of creation (*Collationes in Hexaemeron*) with a "collation" devoted entirely to showing the many ways in which Christ can be seen to hold the middle (*medium tenet*). By so doing Christ creates *aequalitas* structures, the most glorious of all structural images of perfection. Bonaventura adduces many biblical passages in support of his thesis that *Christus medium tenet*, one of them being Ezekiel 1 (the passage on which Milton based his own description of the chariot of paternal Deity), another Revelation 1:13. The purpose of both these prophetic visions is to show that Christ is always in the middle, the four-wheeled chariot of Ezekiel being universally considered a symbol of the created world based on groups of four. (See frontispiece.) Some exegetes must have gone too far in submitting a Pythagorean interpretation, judging from Gasparius Sanctius' refutation (*In Ezechielem*, 1619) of the theory that Ezekiel had any connection with Pythagoras. As for the view that the soul transmigrated from the one to the other, what could be more insane? Sanctius nevertheless calmly goes on to state that the four wheels teach us that nature is made of four; that these four are as one proves that multitude is capable of unity through obedience to Christ. Hence Sanctius describes the chariot as a type of obedience,[42] and so do Antonius Fernandius [43] and John Diodati, to mention only two other seventeenth-century exegetes. According to Diodati, the chariot is a "figure of the consonant harmony, which is in all the works of Gods providence," and it is also a figure of the "constancy, perseverance, simplicity and uprightness of the Angels in their service." [44]

At the center of Milton's epic, therefore, is his version of the most powerful and mysterious prophetic vision of the Old Testament, a vision interpreted by exegetes in terms of the harmony of the Pythagorean quaternion or tetractys as manifested in the 4 of the Gospels and the many groups of 4 in the created universe. This splendid image of harmony through obedience connects beautifully with the theme of man's first disobedience, since the full import of the latter is grasped only when the state of obedience has been

[42] Gasparius Sanctius, *In Ezechielem* (Loudun, 1619), cols. 31, 32.

[43] Antonius Fernandius, *Commentarii In Visiones Veteris Testamenti* (Loudun, 1617), col. 371: Angeli omne liberum suum arbitrium in solius Dei charitatem verterunt, sicque immobiles facti sunt persistentes in veritate. . . . One observes the stress placed on free will.

[44] John Diodati, *Pious and Learned Annotations Upon the Holy Bible* (3d ed.; 1651); see the annotations on Ezekiel 1, 10.

clearly visualized. The long sequence of images of perfection presented through Books III–V reaches its climax with the description of the chariot of paternal Deity and of its decisive role in the epic action. The chariot would have been readily recognized by Milton's contemporaries as a visual enactment of the state of obedience which alone ensures perfect harmony. By themselves, the angels have no inherent power; power follows solely as a consequence of complete union with God through love freely given, and it is because He represents perfect union that Christ is invested with omnipotence.[45]

The powerful image of the chariot is the best possible clue to the presence in the epic of structures based on the number 4 and on the mathematical ratios formed by the first four numbers. As these structures have been presented with admirable clarity by Alastair Fowler in his edition of *Paradise Lost*, they are not summarized here. Instead, I draw attention to the way in which the material presented here supports the theory that Milton's *Nativity Ode*, by incorporating in its structure the key numbers of the lambda formula, 8 and 27, enacts the harmony that it praises.[46] Although the history of patristic, medieval, and Renaissance syncretism still remains to be written, it is possible to perceive the main outlines of an exegetical tradition that expressed the harmony of creation and the scheme of redemption through mathematical images in the manner of Pythagoras and Plato, images that permit the accommodation to our world of sense of that perfection of which the created universe is but a dim and shadowy reflection. Even as a young man, then, Milton revealed his familiarity with the aesthetic theory of

[45] The symbolic import of the chariot helps to solve the problem of whether Christ pursues Satan and his hosts into the "utter deep" alone, or accompanied by His faithful angels. On one occasion Christ is described as "sole victor" and His angels as mere eyewitnesses (VI, 880–884), while on another Chaos describes how Heaven "poured out by millions her victorious bands / Pursuing" (II, 996–998). See Fowler's comments (*Poems of Milton*) on the relevant passages (including VI, 809–810) and Qvarnström, *Enchanted Palace*, pp. 20–23. Because the chariot symbolizes "the Angels about Christ his throne," to use John Diodati's phrase, there is no real contradiction. After the creation the chariot will also typify the universe in a state of union with God. Since, therefore, the chariot represents multitude in a state of union through obedience freely given, both versions of the victory are true. Christ is sole victor because he is the unifying force, but the "millions" of the faithful are also present through their symbolic representation in the chariot (see VI, 845–852).

[46] I have presented this theory in "The Hidden Sense: Milton and the Neoplatonic Method of Numerical Composition," in M.-S. Røstvig et al., *The Hidden Sense and Other Essays* (Oslo, 1963), pp. 1–112. Further evidence in support of this theory may be found in my essay, "Structure as Prophecy."

numerical decorum posited by biblical exegesis from the days of Augustine.

Milton could have studied the application of this aesthetic theory in the works of Edmund Spenser. Scholars like A. Kent Hieatt[47] and Alastair Fowler[48] have traced the presence of highly complex mathematical images in the structure of the *Epithalamion* and *The Faerie Queene*, and I have myself indicated the presence of simpler structures in Spenser's minor poems.[49] To this list of examples can be added *The Shepheardes Calender*. As I show elsewhere, Spenser's first publication presents a calendar for all of time (as stated in the envoy) and, in so doing, incorporates in its poetic structure the temporal structure attributed to the history of man by exegetes. And since the structure of time imitates that of eternity (like the structure of the created universe), we are again confronted by mathematical images of this highest perfection. The circular nature of time is brought out by attributing to the December and January eclogues the same theme, the same narrative technique (monologue), and the same stanza pattern (six lines rhyming *a b a b c c*). Because the ratio created by the number of stanzas (26 and 13) is that of the octave or diapason (2:1), and because the octave denotes the closing of the circle,[50] time is seen to return to that eternity whence it issued. An analysis of the themes distributed among the various eclogues shows that Spenser followed Augustine in dividing human history into two ages in a state of Nature (the four first eclogues), two ages under the Law (the second set of four eclogues), and two under Grace (the last four eclogues). At the center of this temporal sequence (i.e., in eclogues VI and VII) has been placed the person who must always be shown to hold the middle—Christ. The June eclogue shows Christ through its description of paradise regained (an image of Christ, or the Church); the July eclogue, through its sequence of Old Testament types of Christ. In this manner Spenser, like the exegetes, shows Christ arriving *in medio annorum* to impose harmony.

[47] A. Kent Hieatt, *Short Time's Endless Monument* (New York, 1960).

[48] Alastair Fowler, *Spenser and the Numbers of Time* (London, 1964). See also two studies by S. K. Heninger, Jr., "Some Renaissance Versions of the Pythagorean Tetrad," *Studies in the Renaissance*, VIII (1961), 7–33, and "The Implications of Form for *The Shepheardes Calender*," *ibid.*, IX (1962), 309–329.

[49] *Hidden Sense*, pp. 80–92.

[50] Because the last note returns to the first, albeit in a higher key. This well-known argument was often applied to the scheme of redemption, since the eighth age returns man to his first state of perfection, just as Christ rose on the eighth day.

Whereas the lambda numbers 2, 4, 9, and 8 can be traced in the structure of the various "staffes" or stanza patterns, the last number, 27, must necessarily be found, if at all, only in the number of stanzas. The fact that the cycle actually concludes with a sequence of 27 identical stanzas and that it does so in a rather clever way therefore indicates that Spenser wanted his poetic cosmos to incorporate the ratios productive of the most perfect harmony. The December eclogue has only 26 stanzas, but analysis of the November eclogue reveals that its last six lines anticipate the December "staffe," which means that the *Calender* concludes with an uninterrupted sequence of 27 identical stanzas. Barring the lay of Dido, November consists of groups of 8 as indicated by the rhyme scheme and the dialogue, so that 8 and 27 are the chief structural numbers of the last two eclogues. Thus Spenser saw to it that his calendar of universal time contained the appropriate mathematical images of perfection.[51]

Students of iconography are familiar with geometrical images of perfection like the circle or the equilateral triangle, and the arithmetical or mathematical images discussed here are basically of the same kind. The chief difference is that the latter represent an even higher degree of abstraction; they constitute the purest type of sign language accommodated to the world of sense. These symbols would have seemed to possess truly eternal validity. The ratio 2:1, in any age and under any system, always indicates the harmony of the diapason, as Augustine well knew when he traced this ratio in the Trinity, in the created universe, and in the scheme of redemption.[52] The fact that perception of this ratio often depends upon sustained intellectual effort was then considered as proof of its validity, but today this very circumstance is often adduced as an indication of its doubtful character. It is to be hoped that increasing familiarity with the traditions involved will conduce to a better understanding of these more abstract images of perfection sometimes employed by Renaissance poets.

[51] See my essay, "*The Shepheardes Calender*—A Structural Analysis," *Renaissance and Modern Studies*, XIII (1969), 49–75.
[52] See n. 38.

II
DONNE'S MICROCOSM

Toshihiko Kawasaki

The early seventeenth century shows an increasing tendency toward introversion, agoraphobia, and preoccupation with the small: a number of poets and writers shy away into a cozy nook and cherish small, precious objects. To be sure, we find in some contexts an outgoing spirit, a claustrophobia, and a macroscopic vision, but they no longer dominate the poetic scene.[1] Georges Poulet characterizes the whole tendency as the "shrinking of the circle of existence"; to him it is part of the baroque sensibility, and "a happy process, the recalling of forces dispersed in a too-vast space, the concentration on a nearby object that can be possessed." [2] Increasing social tensions, moreover, must have accelerated the shift of emphases.

This is not the place to wrestle with the elusive term "baroque," or with the complex social background of the age; but at least we recognize that Donne, baroque or not baroque, was a precursor of the "shrinking" process. "The good-morrow" may be quoted as an example:

> . . . love, all love of other sights controules,
> And makes one little roome, an every where.
> Let sea-discoverers to new worlds have gone,

[1] Marjorie Hope Nicolson, *Science and Imagination* (Ithaca, 1956), traces the vicissitudes of the shift from macroscopic to microscopic interests which took place during the seventeenth century. Her *Breaking of the Circle* (rev. ed.; New York, 1960) is also relevant to my thesis. Kitty W. Scoular, *Natural Magic* (Oxford, 1965), though arguing for a different thesis, quotes many poems of the age which deal with minute objects.

[2] Georges Poulet, *The Metamorphoses of the Circle*, trans. G. Dawson and E. Coleman (Baltimore, 1966), p. 19.

Let Maps to others, worlds on worlds have showne,
Let us possesse one world, each hath one, and is one.

(ll. 10–14)

The repudiation of the "sea-discoverers," who were, after all, char-
acteristic of the spirit of the age, may yet have been a heritage from
the preceding age.[3] But the lovers' yearning for a small, private, and
self-contained world surely smacks of the early seventeenth cen-
tury. Above all, we must observe that the important word,
"world," is repeated: what the pair of lovers jointly possess is
thought to be one "world." That is to say, it is the lovers' world in
a commonly figurative sense, but it refers more specifically to their
"one little roome." What each of them possesses individually—
his or her beloved—is, then, another "world." Finally, each of them
is still another world to the other.[4] The lovers' world excludes the
"worlds" that appear in the preceding line and refers to realms out-
side the "little roome" currently occupied by the lovers. The room
itself, deemed to be a universe ("an every where"), is completely
self-contained. On the other hand, the "new worlds" mean Amer-
ica par excellence, but not exclusively. They signify values that
worldlings desire; they are gross and incomplete in comparison
with the "one [small] world" of the initiated lovers. The plural
form of "worlds" and "new worlds" should be noted. Faithful to
the so-called Platonic tradition, Donne regards the One as categori-
cally superior to the Many.[5]

This contrast between the larger exterior world and the smaller
interior world obviously falls into the traditional scheme of con-
trast between the macrocosm and the microcosm, which is part of
the Hermetic or Neoplatonic concept of universal correspondences.
What is singular with Donne, however, is that his microcosm and

[3] E.g., Spenser, *Amoretti*, XV. Cf. also Sir John Davies, *Nosce Teipsum*; George
Herbert, "Vanitie (I)."

[4] Helen Gardner's controversial new edition (John Donne, *The Elegies, and
The Songs and Sonnets* [Oxford, 1965]) reads the line as "Let us possesse our
world, each hath one, and is one," and comments (pp. 198–199): "The 'world' of
each is the other. Since they are 'one' they possess one world which is 'ours,' but
there are also four worlds, since each 'hath one and is one.'" In *The Complete
Poetry of John Donne*, ed. John T. Shawcross (Garden City, N.Y., 1967), the
word "our" is also used. I prefer "one" because of its "microcosmic" connotation.

[5] E.g., "Obsequies to the Lord Harrington," ll. 67–68: "for a point and one /
Are much entirer then a million." See also *The Sermons of John Donne*, ed.
George R. Potter and Evelyn M. Simpson (Berkeley and Los Angeles, 1953–
1962) (hereafter cited as *Sermons*), II, 247: "how great a number soever a man
expresse in many figures, yet when we come to number all, the very first figure
is the greatest and most of all."

macrocosm not only correspond to each other as two entities and symbolically reflect each other, but also that they represent a definite system of relative values: the smaller world is more valuable than the larger. In this respect Donne was fairly consistent throughout his life. The only difference between his earlier and later uses of the figure is that in his love poetry the microcosm refers most frequently to the lovers' private room, or to the lover and/or his beloved, or to his or her eye or teardrop, each of which is considered more valuable than the outside world; on the other hand, in Donne's religious works the microcosm often refers to man, who should be esteemed because he is God's creature:

It is too little to call *Man* a *little World;* Except *God,* Man is a *diminutive* to nothing. Man consistes of more pieces, more parts, then the world; then the world doeth, nay then the world is. And if those pieces were extended, and stretched out in Man, as they are in the world, Man would bee the *Gyant,* and the Worlde the *Dwarfe,* the World but the *Map,* and the Man the *World.*[6]

Here the correspondence between the microcosm and the macrocosm is not only that between something small and something large, but also that between the ectype and the prototype, represented, respectively, by the "Map" (the global map) and the "World." Donne reverses the accepted order, however, and argues that man is the prototype and the world is his copy.

A second characteristic of Donne's microcosm figure is that it is structurally multilevel. In other words, not only does Donne refer to the universe (or sometimes to the globe, which more specifically should be termed the "geocosm") as the macrocosm, and to man as the microcosm, but he is also fully conscious of the existence of continuing dimensions of a (so to speak) macro-macrocosm above and a micro-microcosm below, and of other extensions. In many instances the entire structure is neatly systematic and looks as if it were a great chain whose links extend methodically from the largest to the smallest. It seems evident, therefore, that Donne's microcosm figure functions in concert with another Hermetic or Neoplatonic traditional concept of universal correspondence, the Great

---

[6] *Devotions Upon Emergent Occasions,* ed. John Sparrow (Cambridge, 1923), pp. 15–16. Cf. also "Letter to Mr. R. W." ("If, as mine is, thy life a slumber be"), ll. 29–32; "To Sir Edward Herbert, at Julyers"; *The First Anniversary,* ll. 235–237; *Sermons,* IV, 104, 228. Otherwise Donne employs microcosm figures in order to show how small and insignificant man is in his fallen state (e.g., *Holy Sonnet,* V; *Sermons,* I, 308–309). In Donne's religious works, therefore, the figure functions either to augment or to diminish the status of man.

Chain of Being. In "The good-morrow" the chain descends from the outside world to the "little roome" the lovers occupy, then to the pair conjointly, then to each party of the pair, and finally

> My face in thine eye, thine in mine appeares,
> And true plaine hearts doe in the faces rest,
> Where can we finde two better hemispheares
> Without sharpe North, without declining West? (ll. 15–18)

Thus the eye that reflects the other party becomes the micro-microcosm. If the chain of correspondences is complete, each link must unfailingly reflect the entity of the link immediately above it and in its turn be mirrored by the link immediately below, so that the entity of the highest and largest link (the macro-macrocosm) is transferred downward, link by link, and eventually is "contracted" into the lowest and smallest (the micro-microcosm). Furthermore, since the smaller world is invariably the more valuable in Donne's secular macrocosm-microcosm symbolism, it is natural that the lowest and smallest link of the chain of cosmos earns the poet's deepest sympathy. This ever-diminishing order of macrocosm-microcosm correspondences is surely a variant of the "shrinking of the circle of existence" mentioned by Poulet.

Donne is fastidiously consistent in his metaphor when he calls the two eyes of each of the lovers "two hemispheares," meaning that the eyes of one lover jointly make up one perfect "world" because they mirror the other lover who is herself a small "world." Yet the eyeballs, since only half of each one is visible, are as it were one micro-microcosm split into halves and juxtaposed as "two hemispheares." [7] This fastidious consistency may encourage us further to suppose that more detailed correspondences are implied in the stanza, although they are syntactically undeveloped. For example, man's face or head is often regarded as one microcosm because of its roundness, and it is naturally reflected in the eye, which is a micro-microcosm. The heart, on the other hand, symbolically stands for the sun, and it may subsequently correspond to the face and then to the eye, just as the heliocosm corresponds to the geocosm and then to the microcosm.

[7] I take it, therefore, that the line means: "Where can we find two better hemispheres than your eyes or my eyes?" Grierson and Gardner, however, believe the "two hemispheres" consist of the four eyes of the two lovers. Cf. Gardner, *The Elegies* . . . , p. 199: "*two . . . hemispheares.* Presumably, as Grierson says, looking in each other's eyes each beholds only a hemisphere, since the whole world cannot be at once visible."

"The Sunne Rising" depicts a situation of lovers similar to that in "The good-morrow." Again the lovers' room is a microcosm because it is private and self-contained, categorically excluding the outer world. This poem, however, has a pattern of concentric double circles, because the room-microcosm contains within itself a miniature reproduction of the Ptolemaic cosmic structure. In this image pattern, the room is a macrocosm rather than a microcosm, and its walls constitute the "spheare" of the sun; the bed in which the lovers lie is a geocosm, with the sun going around it ("This bed thy [the sun's] center is"); the lovers who lie in the bed are of course a microcosm ("In that the world's contracted thus"). The room-microcosm of this poem, therefore, seems intended to be a paradoxical kind of mini-macrocosm.

A third characteristic of this microcosm imagery is that Donne is acutely conscious of the transference of identity by each link in the chain. "A Valediction of weeping" may illustrate Donne's use of the chain of cosmos as the figure of identity transferences:

> Let me powre forth
> My teares before thy face, whil'st I stay here,
> For thy face coines them, and thy stampe they beare,
> And by this Mintage they are something worth,
>   For thus they bee
>   Pregnant of thee;
> Fruits of much griefe they are, emblemes of more,
> When a teare falls, that thou falls which it bore,
> So thou and I are nothing then, when on a divers shore.
>
> On a round ball
> A workeman that hath copies by, can lay
> An Europe, Afrique, and an Asia,
> And quickly make that, which was nothing, *All*,
>   So doth each teare,
>   Which thee doth weare,
> A globe, yea world by that impression grow,
> Till thy teares mixt with mine doe overflow
> This world, by waters sent from thee, my heaven dissolved so.
>
> (ll. 1–18)

The global map is of course a microcosm in a most literal, almost prosaic, sense. The poem says that the way the beloved lady's teardrop reflects the lover is analogous to the way the global map contracts the entity of the globe into itself. In either instance, the identity of the prototype is wholly transferred to its ectype. Only within this framework does the teardrop imagery escape being absurd and grotesque; instead it manifests its precisely structured beauty. The poem argues that if the lovers cry excessively, serious consequences will ensue: the roundness of the teardrop (the micro-microcosm) will be disfigured by too much water, and the reflected image of the lover will be blurred and destroyed. Excessive weeping will symbolize destruction of the man, or of the man and the lady together (the microcosm), and will subsequently allude to the macrocosmic cataclysm, the Flood. "Therefore," exhorts the lover in effect, "you must stop crying, or you will hasten my death, which will be equivalent to the destruction of the world."

The concluding stanza also contains abundant allusions to macrocosmic functions of the microcosm, namely, of the beloved lady:

> O more then Moone,
> Draw not up seas to drowne me in thy spheare,
> Weepe me not dead, in thine armes, but forbeare
> To teach the sea, what it may doe too soone;
> Let not the winde
> Example finde,
> To doe me more harme, then it purposeth;
> Since thou and I sigh one anothers breath,
> Who e'r sighes most, is cruellest, and hasts the others death.
>
> (ll. 19–27)

The trite Petrarchanism of the lady-moon, the tear-sea, and the sigh-wind has thus become powerfully Donnean, mainly because the scheme of universal correspondence is strikingly consistent throughout the poem.

The macrocosm-microcosm correspondences in the poem are accompanied by such symbolic terms as "coines," "stampe," "beare," "Mintage," "pregnant," and "emblemes." Donne frequently uses these terms, in both his poetry and his prose. They signify a transposition, of which he seems particularly fond, of value from a prototype to a copy.[8] In "A Valediction of weeping" they of course refer to the transference of identity which takes place at each step of descent along the chain of cosmos. And within the structure of the chain, the most extreme of the identity transferences is the one

[8] For outstanding examples, cf. "The Canonization," ll. 7–8; "The Dreame"; *The Second Anniversary*, ll. 223 f.; *Devotions*, XII: Prayer; *Essays in Divinity*, ed. Evelyn M. Simpson (Oxford, 1952), p. 80; *Sermons*, III, 103–104. This concept derives from the Neoplatonic theory of *signatura rerum*, as well as from that of *liber creaturarum*.

that takes place at the smallest link at the very end of the chain. Instead of the eye micro-microcosm of "The good-morrow," here it is the tear micro-microcosm. In either event, the micro-microcosm contracts the microcosm in the metaphorical realm, just as the eye or the teardrop mirrors the man in the physical realm.

This sort of radical metaphor is highly characteristic of Donne, in the sense that the most metaphorical meaning is endorsed by the most literal meaning. Witness also the imagery of twin compasses. It is likely that these metaphors have their roots in a Hermetic mentality that believed in universal analogies. The reflected image in the eye or the teardrop should, as a physical transference of identity, exemplify with reason a metaphorical transference of identity. It is small wonder that Donne returns to the reflected image time and again in his poetry.

We seem to have grounds, moreover, to believe that Donne is ultimately interested in dissolution rather than in transference of identity. Many microcosmic images in his love poetry are accompanied by the Hermetic or Neoplatonic metaphysics of the unity of the two, or the absorption of one's self into the entity of the beloved, and vice versa. "The good-morrow," for instance, in which the lover traces the chain of cosmos from the outside world step by step down to the eye micro-microcosm, feeling more and more at home at each step of the descent, concludes:

> What ever dyes, was not mixt equally;
> If our two loves be one, or, thou and I
> Love so alike, that none doe slacken, none can die. (ll. 19–21)

The microcosm figure of the poem as a whole sounds almost like a poetic rendering of a passage in Ficino:

. . . whenever two people are brought together in mutual affection, one lives in the other and the other in him. In this way they mutually exchange identities; each gives himself to the other in such a way that each receives the other in return; . . . each has himself and has the other too. A has himself, but in B; and B also has himself, but in A.[9]

The evidence that Donne was obsessed by the metaphysics of the unity of lovers is so omnipresent in his poetry[10] that further

[9] *Commentary on Plato's Symposium*, ed. and trans. Sears Reynolds Jayne (Columbia, Mo., 1944), pp. 144–145.
[10] Aside from the poems discussed, cf. "The Extasie," ll. 35–36: "Love, these mixt soules, doth mixe againe, / And makes both one, each this and that"; "A

illustration may be superfluous, but "The Canonization" may profitably be discussed in passing. Its third stanza is a famous celebration of the metaphysics of the Two becoming One:

> The Phoenix ridle hath more wit
> By us, we two being one, are it.
> So, to one neutrall thing both sexes fit.
> Wee dye and rise the same, and prove
> Mysterious by this love.   (ll. 23–27)

Donne is working here within the Hermetic tradition of androgynism. The "one neutrall thing" certainly refers to the mode of synthesized existence which was regarded in the tradition as more complete than either of the two sexes. It embodies the almost mythical quality of unity in duality, or *coincidentia oppositorum.* In the Platonic and Neoplatonic tradition, the One is always pure and complete, whereas the Two is impure and incomplete.

The fourth stanza, on the other hand, is an unforgettable manifestation of the lovers' preference for tiny precious things and small confined places:

> . . . if unfit for tombes and hearse
> Our legend bee, it will be fit for verse;
> And if no peece of Chronicle wee prove,
> We'll build in sonnets pretty roomes;
> As well a well wrought urne becomes
> The greatest ashes, as halfe-acre tombes,
> And by these hymnes, all shall approve
> Us *Canoniz'd* for Love.   (ll. 29–36)

It is significant that the self-contained lovers give precedence to the "sonnet" and the "well wrought urne" over the "Chronicle" and the "halfe-acre tombe." [11]

The final stanza brings further homage to the lovers' microcosm:

Valediction forbidding mourning," l. 21: "Our two soules therefore, which are one"; "Loves infiniteness," ll. 31–33: "But wee will have a way more liberall, / Then changing hearts, to joyne them, so wee shall / Be one, and one anothers All."

[11] This fact may suggest that Donne's (and other seventeenth-century poets') preference for small things may also have governed his (and their) means of literary expression. In other words, his elliptical songs and sonnets may have been an outcome of the same microcosmic mentality. In this context the possible "stanzas = rooms" pun (from Italian, *stanza* meaning "room") becomes more meaningful. Donne's was the kind of mind that declared: "as some *Abridgements* are greater, then some other authors, so is one man of more dignity, then all the earth" (*Sermons*, IV, 227).

> You whom reverend love
> Made one anothers hermitage;
> You, to whom love was peace, that now is rage,
> Who did the whole worlds soule contract, and drove
> Into the glasses of your eyes
> So made such mirrors, and such spies,
> That they did all to you epitomize,
> Countries, Townes, Courts. (ll. 37–44)

The word "hermitage" clinches the agoraphobic nature of Donne's microcosm. To "contract" the "whole worlds soule" is of course the function traditionally expected of any microcosm.[12] The "glasses of your eyes" is another eye micro-microcosm; characteristic of Donne, it is accompanied by symbolic imagery like "such mirrors, . . . such spies, . . . epitomize." It seems evident, therefore, that in Donne's love poetry the lovers' preoccupation with small things, with the microcosm concept, and with the unity of the two are all inseparable parts of the whole.

"The Flea" enjoyed a degree of fame among Donne's contemporaries which may seem excessive today, but the poem is in many ways highly characteristic of Donne. First of all, it dwells on a tiny, homely creature, which functions as a micro-microcosm, partly because the flea transfers to itself the most vital part of the microcosm ("It suck'd me first, and now sucks thee, / And in this flea, our two bloods mingled bee"), and also because the flea metamorphoses entities into an agoraphobic closed chamber ("w'are met, / And cloystered in these living walls of Jet"). The underlying paradox that little is large and large is little ("How little that which thou deny'st me is") is of course a commonplace adjunct to Donne's macrocosm-microcosm conceit, and he employs it here with tongue-in-cheek preciosity. The flea, which has sucked the the blood of the lover and then that of the girl and mixed them within itself, is a parodic embodiment of the Neoplatonic philosophy of love that the two become one ("one blood made of two").[13] Just as the eye or teardrop micro-microcosm—an extreme

[12] Gardner's and Shawcross's editions read "extract" for "contract," which works well if the line is related to an alchemical background, another Hermetic tradition operating in Donne's mind. I prefer "contract" because of its microcosmic connotation.

[13] Some of Donne's poems represent the other extreme, mostly the poems included in the first of the two divisions established by Dame Helen Gardner in her new edition. They portray more extroversive lovers who act on the principle of the many and variety, instead of the one and unity; "The Indifferent" may be the best example. Gardner attributes these poems to Donne's immature days, but I am more inclined to regard them as negative images of his great "Neoplatonic" poems.

example of physical transference of identity—achieved the most poignant expression of metaphorical transference of identity in such poems as "The good-morrow," "The Sunne Rising," and "A Valediction of weeping," so here the flea, because of the physiological unity it accomplishes within itself, works as an excellent embodiment of the metaphorical unity of the lovers. The transference of identity is deliberately overdone, however, so that the whole poem becomes a parody of the serious versions presented by the other poems mentioned.

"The Flea" is also an elaborate play on the Trinity ("Oh, stay, three lives in one flea spare"). This mock religiosity gives a distinct flavor to the poem, which may ultimately include a parody of the sacred rites of matrimony:

> . . . wee almost, yea more then maryed are.
> This flea is you and I, and this
> Our mariage bed, and mariage temple is.   (ll. 11–13)

"The Flea" also has an undertone in which Eros and Thanatos are subtly combined, but I shall have more to say about that later. Such witty gymnastics make the poem an Alexandrian *jeu d'esprit* in erotics. But it contains, though in caricature, the kind of truth that meant much to Donne, such as the small containing the large, the lower mirroring the higher, the one becoming another, the two becoming one, and so forth.

That "The Flea" parodies the rites of holy matrimony suggests that Donne's microcosm figure is part of the broad traditional symbolism of the Western world, including even the doctrines of the Eucharist and the Incarnation. The following passage from Donne's *Devotions* seems to demonstrate a kinship between the microcosm and the Eucharist: "O Eternal! and most gracious *God,* who hast made *little things* to signifie *great,* and convaid the *infinite merits* of thy *Sonne* in the *water* of *Baptisme,* and in the *Bread* and *Wine* of thy other *Sacrament,* unto us . . ." (p. 132).

Donne's figures, however, are not simply more pointed variants within the traditional symbolism. They seem rather to derive from his efforts to exploit traditional symbolic concepts for the sake of novel intellectual and emotional effect. Such efforts gave a special role to his use of the doctrine of universal correspondence, of which the microcosm is an eminent example. He no longer seems to take the doctrine at face value, but to employ it in such a way that its repeated and exaggerated use as a poetic figure may satisfy his deeper psychological needs. The poems quoted afford proof that such a figure as the perfect unity of himself and the beloved lady in the closed chamber was more than a conceited exaggeration of a Neoplatonic cliché. It must have represented a kind of love that was truly significant for him, and the microcosm figure was a perfect means for its expression.

The consistency of Donne's sensibility has been acknowledged by his critics, and the same consistency characterizes his use of the microcosm figure. There may be alterations in tone. As Dame Helen Gardner has pointed out, Donne's love poetry shows the poet's ecstasy and displays his unfettered brilliance, but his religious poetry is a product of conscience and effort of will and therefore shows the poet in a more sober aspect.[14] A scrutiny of his prose works, however, discloses a side more familiar in his love poetry—the ecstatic bent of his mind. Notably, in the prose his microcosm imagery continues his preoccupation with the possibility of identity transference and ego dissolution.

One sermon, for instance, is characteristic for its mention of "a death of rapture, of extasie." In it Donne contemplates "a Transfusion, a Transplantation, a Transmigration, a Transmutation into him [Jesus]," and he speaks about the dissolution in these terms: "for good digestion brings alwaies assimilation, certainly, if I come to a true meditation upon Christ, I come to a conformity with Christ." [15] The following passage from another sermon enunciates a similar concept: "As my meat is assimilated to my flesh, and made one flesh with it; as my soul is assimilated to my God, and *made partaker of the divine nature*, and *Idem Spiritus*, the same Spirit with it; so, there [in Heaven] my flesh shall be assimilated to the flesh of my Saviour, and made the same flesh with him too" (III, 112–113). We may infer from these examples that Donne, who in his love poetry was obsessed by an Eros-oriented dissolution, is now preoccupied with an agape-oriented dissolution.[16] In his theology, human love and divine love share the transmutative

[14] Donne, *Divine Poems*, ed. Helen Gardner (Oxford, 1952), pp. xvi–xvii, xxxiv–xxxvii.

[15] *Sermons*, II, 212. Cf. also p. 210, where Donne mentions the Pauline *"mortem raptus*, a death of rapture, and of extasie," and states that the "contemplation of God, and heaven, is a kinde of buriall, and Sepulchre, and rest of the soule." The sentence that follows is one of the most beautiful ever written by Donne.

[16] The following passage (*Sermons*, I, 164) is evidence that Donne is after the same sort of "unity" in his religious works as in his love poetry, though differently oriented: "then come we to that transmutation, which admits no re-transmutation, which is a modest, but infalible assurance of a final perseverance, so to be joyned to the Lord, as to be one spirit with him; for as a spirit cannot be divided, so they who are thus changed into him, are so much His, so much He, as that nothing can separate them from him." Cf. also *Sermons*, VIII, no. 3.

powers and, at their highest manifestation, aspire to "*caro una,* two shall be one" (*Sermons,* I, 199).

As the Eros-oriented dissolution was a commonplace of the Neoplatonic metaphysics of love, the agape-oriented dissolution is the Neoplatonic part of Johannine and Pauline theology.[17] Donne is explicit about it: "I forbid thee not S. *Pauls* wish, *Cupio dissolvi,* To desire to be dissolved, therefore, *that thou mayest be with Christ*" (VII, 140). The problem with Donne, however, is, as always, not what tradition he has recourse to, but how, and with what sort of personal intensity, he utilizes it. It sometimes appears, moreover, as if his desired dissolution is more directly oriented by Thanatos. We need not enter into detail here about his death wish because, aside from his own famous pronouncement in *Biathanatos,* a strong case has already been made for it.[18] The way in which Donne is obsessed by death seems to testify to his fascination as well as to his horror. After all, his Eros sometimes looks suspiciously akin to Thanatos, perhaps more seriously so than it was for many of his contemporaries. In one of his sermons Donne gives commonplace equations of Eros and Thanatos, death and procreation, and juxtaposes the "excrementall jelly that thy body is made of at first" and the "jelly which thy body dissolves to at last" (III, 105) as the most noisome and putrid thing to be found in nature. It is apparent that he is repelled, but fascinated, by both.

The most outstanding example in this category is Donne's endless harping upon the worm. Again, this theme is nothing but a recapitulation of a medieval cliché this time that of *memento mori.* Donne's worm, however, has a peculiar connotation of its own as a means for the dissolution of identity. Here the tone of personal intensity exceeds even that of Donne's youthful obsession with erotic dissolution. His last sermon, "Deaths Duell," comes to mind as almost a pat example. It first dwells upon the posthumous dissolution as follows: "we must al passe this *posthume* death, this *death* after *death,* nay this death after buriall, this *dissolution* after *dissolution,* this *death* of *corruption* and *putrifaction,* of *vermiculation* and *incineration,* of *dissolution* and *dispersion* in and *from* the grave" (X, 238). Then the worm is introduced as the powerful agent to complete the dissolution because it achieves the most complete infusion of human identities we can imagine: "When

17 Cf. John 17:20–23; Rom. 12:4–5; 1 Cor. 12:27; Gal. 3:28.
18 D. R. Roberts, "The Death Wish of John Donne," *Publications of the Modern Language Association of America,* LXII (1947), 958–976. Cf. also "The Calme," ll. 41–42: "the thirst / Of honour, or faire death, out pusht mee first."

those bodies . . . must say . . . *to corruption thou art my father,* and *to the Worme thou art my mother and my sister. Miserable riddle,* when the *same worme* must bee *my mother,* and *my sister,* and *my selfe. Miserable incest,* when I must bee *maried* to my *mother* and my *sister,* and bee both *father* and *mother* to my *owne mother* and *sister, beget,* and *beare* that *worme* which is all that *miserable penury"* (*ibid.*). The fierce ingenuity with which Donne handles this fantastic paradox of identity dissolution is reminiscent of his juvenile gymnastics of wit in "The Flea." The parallelism goes beyond that of ingenuity: with grim humor both the sermon and the poem deal with the serious matter of matrimony, although the worm's orgy is a feverish carousal of Eros and Thanatos together.

There are in Donne's writings dozens of deeply preoccupied references to the worm. Each time the important point is that the worm in its seamy tininess accomplishes the most thorough dissolution of the identity of man. It administers the extreme rites to the body, just as the flea administers the matrimonial rites to the oddly sorted couple. Donne's worm, in this sense, may be the reincarnation of the flea. It may be, in other words, the most degenerate and deformed descendant of the poet's beautiful micro-microcosm. Donne is horrified at, but fascinated by, its deformity.

Donne's microcosm dies hard—and for good reason. Fundamentally his microcosm, it seems to me, has its roots deep in his formidable ego. Only an extraordinary egotist can be so deeply and constantly engrossed in the reflection of his own figure in the pupil of his beloved's eye, or, as a matter of fact, in the process of his flesh being assimilated into the worm. One critic has cogently pointed out that throughout his life Donne was "unable to find any window that would not give him back the image of himself." [19] This comment applies very well to Donne's microcosm imagery.

Nevertheless, we should admit that Donne the religious writer does show a different face to the audience. It is, as Dame Helen Gardner has defined it apropos of his devotional poetry, the face of a "practical moralist," and it represents the more characteristic side of Donne as a religious man. In the following passage from a sermon, for instance, he emphasizes man's moral responsibility to God and argues to the effect that, although his body may be dissolved in the worm and ultimately become dust, the soul will not be: "after a surfet of sin there's no such retiring, as a dissolving of

[19] J. E. V. Crofts, "John Donne: A Reconsideration," in *John Donne,* ed. Helen Gardner (Englewood Cliffs, N.J., 1962), p. 82.

the soul into nothing; but God is from the beginning the Creator, he gave all things their being, and he is still thy Creator, thou shalt evermore have that being, to be capable of his Judgments" (II, 248). More than once Donne refers with unmistakable gusto to such complete posthumous physical dissolution as would result from a sort of universal atomism, but only to emphasize that man after all cannot afford to lose his identity before God:

One humour of our dead body produces worms, and those worms suck and exhaust all other humours, and then all dies, and all dries, and molders into dust, and that dust is blowen into the River, and that puddled water tumbled into the sea, and that ebs and flows in infinite revolutions, and still, still God knows in what *Cabinet* every *seed-Pearle* lies, in what part of the world every graine of every mans dust lies.   (*Sermons*, VIII, 98)

Other sermons (e.g., III, 109–110; IV, 53; VI, 156; VII, 71; X, 240 f.) provide distinguished examples of this vein of Donne's thought. In such utterances he is more sober than ecstatic, more moral than mystical, more controlled than fervent. Obviously he is fulfilling his duty as a conscientious Anglican minister, trying hard to save his congregation through his preaching, rather than indulging in private contemplation.

Most significant here is the fact that the agoraphobic and self-contained microcosm has little place in this side of Donne's religious mind. This fact has already been suggested in the passage just quoted, which states that "every seed-Pearle" in a supposedly secret "Cabinet" is, in fact, envisioned by the eye of God. But the microcosm figure is even more explicitly belittled in, for example, the following passage from an earlier sermon:

if thou wilt think thy selfe a little Church, a Church to thy selfe, because thou hast heard it said, That thou art a little world, a world in thy selfe, that figurative, that metaphoricall representation shall not save thee. Though thou beest a world to thy self, yet if thou have no more corn, nor oyle, nor milk, then growes in thy self, or flowes from thy self, thou wilt starve; Though thou be a Church in thy fancy, if thou have no more seales of grace, no more absolution of sin, then thou canst give thy self, thou wilt perish.   (VII, 232–233)

To be brief, in his sermons Donne holds the position in which "that figurative, that metaphoricall" microcosm will no longer save him.

We may account for the change as a shift of stress from *verba* to *res*, as attested by Donne's own remarks in his sermons: "Language must waite upon matter, and *words* upon *things*" (X, 112); and "The eloquence of inferiours is in words, the eloquence of superiours is in action" (VI, 227). Donne is aware of the fact that a private self-consolation through metaphorical eloquence, in poetry or prose, will lead to nowhere in the practical—or the spiritual— world. But the change should also be attributed to the fact that, while his love poetry is essentially "private" in nature, his religion is "social" and "public," in accordance with the tradition of the Church of England.

We can trace fairly clearly how Donne has moved from his earlier microcosmic symbolism through middle-aged complexity to the final flat denunciation. The lines quoted below exemplify the agoraphobic use of the self-contained microcosm:

> A way thou fondling motley humorist,
> Leave mee, and in this standing woodden chest,
> Consorted with these few bookes, let me lye
> In prison, 'and here be coffin'd, when I dye.
>
> (*Satyre* I, ll. 1–4)

This passage is not only agoraphobic, but also slightly thanato-philous, which makes it seem all the more characteristic of the earlier Donne.

In the "Ecclogue" dated 26 December 1613 Donne dramatically employs the microcosm symbolism. First, Idios (derived, significantly, from the Greek word meaning "private person" as well as "ignoramus") tries to justify his own unsociableness (and, at the same time, Donne's absence from his patron's wedding) by an overserious exposition of the microcosm philosophy:

> As man is of the world, the heart of man,
>   Is an epitome of Gods great booke
>   Of creatures, and man need no farther looke;
> So is the Country'of Courts, where sweet peace doth,
>   As their one common soule, give life to both,
> I am not then from Court.   (ll. 50–55)

But this presentation is promptly undermined by the brutal realism of Allophanes (or "the other self") as follows:

>   Dreamer, thou art.
>   Think'st thou fantastique that thou hast a part
>   In the East-Indian fleet, because thou hast
>   A little spice, or Amber in thy taste?   (ll. 55–58)

Indeed, the "epitome" does not save the situation.

Finally, in a later sermon, Donne accurately diagnoses the metaphorical self-consolation derived from the self-contained microcosm:

> If he take up another Comfort, that . . . he can content himselfe with himselfe, he can make his study a Court, and a few Books shall supply to him the society and the conversation of many friends, there is another worme to devoure this too, the hand of divine Justice shall grow heavy upon him, in a sense of an unprofitable retirednesse, in a disconsolate melancholy. (IX, 293)

We have already seen that the "one little roome" or the "sonnets pretty roomes" played an important role in Donne's microcosmic love poetry, and that the figure of the room was closely related to his inveterate penchant for the oneness of the two. The following passage from a sermon presents a striking contrast, sounding characteristically macrocosmic because of its commendation of the "house" at the expense of the "room," as well as its advocacy of the Many:

> God . . . loves holy meetings, he loves the *communion of Saints*, the *houshold of the faithfull:* . . . the Church is not a *grave:* it is a *fold,* it is an *Arke,* it is a *net,* it is a *city,* it is a *kingdome,* not onely a house, but a house that hath *many mansions* in it: still it is a *plurall* thing, consisting of *many:* . . . so sociable, so communicable, so extensive, so derivative of himself, is God, and so manifold are the beames, and the emanations that flow out from him. (VI, 152)

This passage seems to illustrate the ascending scheme of the chain of being, which, though not too precise in structure, starts from a small link and climbs up to larger links, rather than vice versa. It is obvious that this passage, unlike Donne's love poetry, which heavily drew upon the doctrine of the One, is wholly dependent on the other half of the Neoplatonic philosophy of universal correspondence—the half that emphasizes the Many, or the doctrine of plenitude.

In the following passage from a sermon the house metaphor exemplifies an expanding rather than a contracting movement of imagery: "Be comforted then, sayes Christ to them, for This, which is a House, . . . A House of Mansions, a dwelling, not a sojourning, And of many Mansions, not an Abridgement, a Modell of a House, not a Monastery of many Cells, but an extension of many Houses, into the City of the living God" (VII, 139). Donne's shift of emphasis from room to house is significant when we compare his love poetry with his religious works.

The passage from *Devotions* beginning "No man is an Iland" is so famous that to quote it here would be supererogatory. We should, however, realize that the island is a microcosm, whereas the continent stands for the macrocosm which the religious Donne has come to propound. The island-continent imagery clearly has an outgoing connotation. To take a differing example, Donne's well-known sermon preached to the Virginia Company in 1622 refers to England as a small island, not as a happy microcosm in which we might sit snugly, but as a sort of base camp from which we should start capitalistic expansion toward "new worlds." Here Donne clearly renounces his earlier disposition toward "one little roome." The island imagery is significant as another variant of the microcosm.[20]

Social and public religion as illustrated by Donne's works was part of the tradition of the Church of England. He does his best as James's and Charles's favorite minister.[21] He acts, for instance, as a strong advocate for public worship observed by many in church, although he does not categorically denounce private worship. This attitude is certainly in concert with Richard Hooker's exhortation in *Of the Laws of Ecclesiastical Polity*.[22] Donne counsels us in a sermon (VII, no. 11) to relinquish the "Chamber-prayers" so that we may join the "Congregation" (p. 292), which is of course another variation on the theme "from room to house." Stylistically, too, the passage is noteworthy for its outgoing and augmenting imagery, such as: "he that hath a handfull of devotion at home, shall have his devotion multiplyed to a Gomer here [in the Church]" (*ibid.*).

In another sermon (X, no. 10) Donne sets up a clear distinction between "Monasterie, and Ermitage, and Anchorate," on the one hand, and "*Concio, Coetus, Ecclesia, Synagoga & Congregatio*" on the other (p. 219). The former group of words he characterizes as "such words of *singularitie*"; the latter, as "those *plurall* words" (italics mine). The preference is unequivocally given to the plural:

[20] Phineas Fletcher's *Purple Island* contains the most eloquent expression of the seventeenth-century island microcosm. Marjorie Nicolson (*Breaking of the Circle*, p. 58) is probably correct in suggesting that the British were particularly interested in this imagery because they were islanders.

[21] Kaichi Matsuura, *A Study of the Imagery of John Donne* (Tokyo, 1953), is excellent on this aspect of Donne's literature.

[22] Cf. Bk. V, xxiv, "Of public Prayer."

"in which [plural] words God delivereth himselfe to us" (*ibid.*). Evidently Donne has come a long way from his earlier love poetry in which the One predominated. In yet another sermon (VI, no. 10), moreover, he explicitly rejects agoraphobia [23] in warning us against "living in a corner" or "retiring into a Monastery" (p. 215).

Finally, in the following house-room metaphor Donne's eternal delight in the diminishing order from the largest to the smallest may be detected:

Let the whole world be in thy consideration as one house. . . . Let this Kingdome, where God hath blessed thee with a being, be the Gallery, the best roome of that house, and consider in the two walls of that Gallery, the Church and the State, the peace of a royall, and a religious Wisedome; Let thine owne family be a Cabinet in this Gallery, and finde in all the boxes thereof . . . the peace of vertue, . . . and then lastly, let thine owne bosome be the secret box, and reserve in this Cabinet, and find there the peace of conscience, and truelie thou hast the best Jewell in the best Cabinet. (*Sermons*, IV, 49)

It is obvious that the same mentality revealed by Donne's love poetry is at work here. The "best Jewell in the best Cabinet" may therefore be regarded as a micro-microcosm; nevertheless, it is neither agoraphobic nor self-contained. It is happily incorporated into an authentic Anglican framework.[24]

Thus there are two Donnes in Donne's religious writings: the one microcosmic, the other macrocosmic. The former seems to represent the man who withdraws into his private chamber in order to contemplate his dissolution into the Godhead; the latter is he who steps forth and tries to save the congregation in the Church. It is the "room" Donne versus the "house" Donne, the "singular" Donne versus the "plural" Donne. It is the latter, however, that dominates. Even some of the passages quoted above to show Donne's desire for ego dissolution are heavily qualified within

[23] Cf. *Sermons*, VII, 397: "Corner Divinity, clandestine Divinity are incompatible termes; If it be Divinity, it is avowable. . . . Publication is a fair argument of truth."

[24] Joan Webber has made the highly useful suggestion that the one image characteristic of the Anglicans is the microcosm, while that of the Puritans is the pilgrim (*The Eloquent "I"* [Madison, Wis., 1968], pp. 7-8, 23-24, 41, 44). She analyzes Donne's *Devotions* as the representative exposition of his Anglican position, but, as a book of private meditations, that work should be taken as representing no more than one religious facet. Donne's sermons, on the other hand, shed a different light because they are more public and because they emphasize action. In short, they have less to do with the microcosm figure.

the same sermons by an orthodox Christian belief in the Resurrection.

This kind of dichotomy in a religious mind is by no means peculiar to Donne. Jesus' life clearly testifies to these two mutually conflicting and mutually complementary impulses. Richard Hooker's Church of England was not incompatible with Nicholas Ferrar's Little Gidding Society. Both the introversive and extroversive aspects of religion are indispensable to any established church, although the emphases do vary from church to church and from time to time. Donne's emphasis was fundamentally in accord with that of his Church in his time, and, as in his secular poetry, in his religious poetry the microcosmic imagery served as a proper vehicle for expressing his fervent beliefs.

III

DONNE'S POETRY OF COMPLIMENT: THE SPEAKER'S STANCE AND THE TOPOI OF PRAISE

Barbara K. Lewalski

Donne's epicedes and obsequies and certain of the verse letters can most profitably be studied in terms of their evident purpose, to compliment and praise. In Renaissance poetics, as O. B. Hardison has shown, all the poetic genres could be related to the purposes of praise or blame, but the occasional forms praising particular persons upon particular occasions formed a special category, one closely aligned with, and usually approached in terms of, the classification of epideictic kinds of rhetoric.[1] Donne, however, does not respect the precise distinctions made by rhetoricians and writers of the *artes poeticae*, prescribing the form and the decorum of a poem of praise according to the specific occasion and the social status of the person: encomium, epigram, panegyric, epitaph, epicede, elegy, and so on. Rather, if we set aside Donne's anniversary poems, which are altogether more complex in conception and treatment, the epithalamia, which are concerned to celebrate the occasion of a marriage rather than an individual, and those verse letters that offer advice on moral conduct or poetry in the forthright tones of manly friendship, Donne's remaining poems of compliment— almost all of them written in the period 1605–1614[2]—display a

[1] O. B. Hardison, Jr., *The Enduring Monument: A Study of the Idea of Praise in Renaissance Literary Theory and Practice* (Chapel Hill, N.C., 1962), esp. pp. 68–122.

[2] I adopt here the dates ascribed to the verse letters in W. Milgate, ed., *John Donne: The Satires, Epigrams, and Verse Letters* (Oxford, 1967) (hereafter cited as Milgate), and use the same text for all quotations from the verse letters. The

remarkable stylistic similarity, whoever the person praised. They are analytic, epistolary addresses, studded with extravagantly hyperbolic tropes. They are alike also in the responses they have evoked from critics: general neglect or else castigation as inordinate flattery intended merely to curry favor with patrons.[3]

Donne's poetry of praise impresses the reader as radically different from the epideictic poetry of his contemporaries, and the impression is not a mistaken one. The difference is not that Donne is more outrageously hyperbolic than other poets. In fact, he develops his praises from topics thoroughly conventional in the period: praise of the subject as an exemplar of the virtues appropriate to his station and role; praise of the subject as the perfection of certain virtues or of Virtue itself, or as the "image" or "pattern" of Virtue in the Neoplatonic sense; praise of a lady as a celestial being, the *donna angelica* of *stilnovisti* and Petrarchan convention; praise of an individual in Christian theological terms as regenerate soul, saint, or heir to scriptural promises; praise of a monarch or prince in typological terms as correlative with some notable Old Testament ruler or judge, or as a recapitulation of Christ, or because he is God's vicegerent, an "image" of God.[4]

dates of the funeral elegies are based upon evidence supplied in H. J. C. Grierson, ed., *The Poems of John Donne* (2 vols.; Oxford, 1912, 1966) (hereafter cited as Grierson); in John T. Shawcross, ed., *The Complete Poetry of John Donne* (Garden City, N.Y., 1967) (hereafter cited as Shawcross); and in Edmund Gosse, *The Life and Letters of John Donne* (2 vols.; New York, 1899). Quotations from the funeral elegies are from Grierson's text unless otherwise indicated. Only one poem of the type with which I am concerned here falls outside the dates given: *An hymne to the Saints, and to the Marquesse Hamylton* (1625). The letter "To Mrs. M. H." (Magdalen Herbert) which begins "Mad paper stay" does fall within my period (1608), but it is much more familiar in tone than the poems to the other great ladies. It is less a poem of compliment than a genial, witty tribute in quasi-Petrarchan terms to a good friend on the occasion of her impending marriage.

[3] Milgate's introduction to his edition of the verse letters is an honorable exception to this generalization, as is the article by Laurence Stapleton, "The Theme of Virtue in Donne's Verse Epistles," *Studies in Philology*, LV (1958), 187–200. Both these critics, however, center too exclusively upon the moral dimensions of the letters, scanting the metaphysical and theological hyperbole that so sharply separates these poems from, for example, the verse epistles of Ben Jonson.

[4] These topoi have been identified through an examination of several kinds of contemporary epideictic poems: praises and elegies celebrating Queen Elizabeth, some of which have been excerpted and collected in E. C. Wilson's *England's Eliza* (Cambridge, Mass., 1939); the elegies upon the death of the young prince Henry (d. 1612), several of which were published by Joshua Sylvester along with his own and Donne's contributions in *Sundry Funeral Elegies, on the Untimely Death of the Most Excellent Prince, Henry* ([London], 1613); and a variety of praises addressed to members of the nobility and gentry during the period defined by the publication date of *Astrophel* (1595), the collection of elegies for Sir Philip Sidney titled from Spenser's contribution, and the publication date of Ben Jonson's folio (1616) which includes many epideictic verse letters, epigrams, and epitaphs.

Moreover, Donne is at one with some of his contemporaries—Ben Jonson, Samuel Daniel, Sir Walter Ralegh, Henry Lok, Cyril Tourneur, Henry Goodyere, among others—in promoting certain new trends in epideictic verse: the Horatian verse letter which compliments obliquely as it explores a general moral or social topic; the Christian emphasis on grace and regeneration as the source of merit in the person praised; and the movement toward tight logical organization of poems.[5] The uniqueness of Donne's poems of compliment arises, rather, from the speaker's stance and from the symbolic value discovered in the person addressed, both of which have profound implications for the ways in which the conventional topoi are developed. In Donne's practice the poem of praise undergoes a sea change, becoming, for all its audacious wit, a metaphysical inquiry into the bases of human worth.

The characteristic stance of Donne's speaker is one of studying, or meditating upon, or contemplating the person he addresses or elegizes. The meditation may be presented as peculiarly the speaker's, or, more commonly, the speaker may involve "us"—the sympathetic audience—in the experience. This stance is taken occasionally in Henry Lok's poems,[6] but no contemporary poet approaches Donne's consistent use of it. The meditational stance is also significantly different from the more or less logical analysis of a person or a concept which occurs in some of Jonson's poems and in certain of the elegies on Prince Henry.[7] In Donne's poems the speaker is in the position of seeking to discover or understand something about the nature of reality by means of, or through, the person praised. Accordingly he proposes to study Lucy, Countess of Bedford, through her friends in an effort to reach the divinity

[5] E.g., Jonson, "XII. Epistle. To Elizabeth Countesse of Rutland," in "The Forrest," in *The Complete Poetry of Ben Jonson*, ed. William B. Hunter, Jr. (Garden City, N.Y., 1963), pp. 102–105; Daniel, "To the Ladie Margaret, Countesse of Cumberland," and "To the Ladie Anne Clifford," in A. B. Grosart, ed., *The Complete Works in Verse and Prose of Samuel Daniel* (5 vols.; London, 1885–1896), I, 203–216; Ralegh, "An Epitaph upon the right Honourable sir Phillip Sidney," in J. C. Smith and E. De Selincourt, eds., *The Poetical Works of Edmund Spenser* (Oxford, 1950), pp. 558–559; Lok, "Sonnets of the Author to Divers," in *Ecclesiastes, etc.* (1597), reprinted in *Miscellanies of the Fuller Worthies' Library*, ed. A. B. Grosart (4 vols.; London, 1871), II; Tourneur, "A Griefe on the Death of Prince Henrie," in *Three Elegies on the Most Lamented Death of Prince Henrie* (London, 1613); Goodyere, "Elegie on the untimely Death of the incomparable Prince, Henry," in *Sundry Funeral Elegies*, sigs. F3–F4.
[6] Sonnets to Lady Anne Russell, Lady Rich, and Lady Carey in Grosart, *Miscellanies*, II, 373–374, 377, 385.
[7] E.g., Jonson, "LXXVI. On Lucy Countesse of Bedford," in "Epigrammes"; "XIII. Epistle. To Katherine, Lady Aubigny," in "The Forrest," in Hunter, ed., *Complete Poetry*, pp. 32, 106–110; Tourneur, "A Griefe," in *Three Elegies*.

in her; elsewhere he declares that he finds in her "all record, all prophecie." [8] In another poem Donne finds Edward Herbert to be "All worthy bookes." [9] He offers on different occasions to tell the Countess of Salisbury and the Countess of Huntingdon what he has learned "by daring to contemplate" them.[10] In the elegy on Prince Henry he recounts how we can understand the near relation of reason and faith by "contemplation of that Prince." [11] In "Obsequies to the Lord Harrington" Donne rejoices that he has grown good enough "that I can studie thee, / And, by these meditations refin'd, / Can unapparell and enlarge my minde." [12] And, by a nice reversal, in an "Epitaph on Himselfe" he offers his (dead) self as an object of meditation to everybody, so that each one can "In my graves inside see what thou art now" and, by contemplation of the changes wrought in the speaker's soul and body by death, can "mend thy selfe." [13]

This meditational stance does not require use of the Ignatian or any other method of meditation. It means simply that the speaker —often explicitly and always in practice—undertakes to explore religious or philosophical truth by writing the praises of an individual. The conventional topoi of praise are therefore not used as counters, but are subjected to intensive analysis to force them to yield their essential meanings. Also, the speakers constantly employ the theological language and imagery appropriate to conventional religious meditation, thereby evoking in the reader expectations of seriousness and sincerity. As a result Donne's praises have created a critical furor which most other epideictic poems escape, precisely because Donne's are not simply the conventional small change of polite social intercourse, but are presented as a means of arriving at profound spiritual truths.

The second major difference is in the symbolic conception of the person praised, which permits Donne consistently to apply to any individual those extreme formulations of the conventional topoi which most contemporary poets applied (and then with circumspection) only to royalty. Donne's topics are framed so as to

[8] "Reason is our Soules left hand," ll. 9-10 (Milgate, p. 90); "You have refin'd mee," l. 52 (Milgate, p. 93).

[9] "To Sir Edward Herbert, at Julyers," l. 48 (Milgate, p. 81).

[10] "Man to Gods image," l. 46 (Milgate, p. 87); "Faire, great, and good," l. 32 (Milgate, p. 108).

[11] "Elegie upon the untimely death of the incomparable Prince Henry," l. 18 (Sylvester, ed., *Sundry Funeral Elegies*, sigs. E-E2v).

[12] Ll. 10-12 (Grierson, I, 271).

[13] Ll. 10, 21 (Milgate, p. 103).

insist that Virtue, or Goodness, or Divinity, is incarnate in the in-
dividual praised or mourned: the All is persistently conflated in
the particular example. Robert Ellrodt has rightly observed that
this impulse is contra-Platonic:

This [unity] is not, one can see, an ideal, mathematical, intelligible
unity of the Platonic or Plotinian One, the One beyond Being. The
effort of Donne to seize the totality of being in the individual being is
oriented on the contrary according to the Christian perspective of the
Incarnation. This is easily done when the All means precisely Christ,
the Man God. . . . More remarkable is the instance that shows the
author of the *Anniversaries* and the *Epicedes* "incarnating" the All in
the person who is the object of his praises.[14]

The human individual is symbolic in a particular way for Donne,
not as an image or reflection of an ideal Platonic form or idea, but,
more precisely, as an image of God; on that ground the individual
can be said to embody, restate, or incarnate divine reality or the
entire Book of the Creatures in himself. This symbolic perspective
is not casually assumed by Donne, and, although it is applied to
one patron or patroness after another, it is also not meaningless
hyperbole. Of course these propositions are developed with a good
deal of wit, and part of that wit inheres in the social manner that
exalts the particular subject at hand over all other persons, some
of whom Donne may have praised as highly in other poems. This
procedure is apt to strike us as the shallowest social posturing, how-
ever amusing it may be. But behind these gestures of witty compli-
ment is a conception of the source of human worth which is hinted
in many of the poems and made explicit in one of the most hyper-
bolic of them, the verse letter "To the Countesse of Salisbury":
"Faire, great, and good, since seeing you, wee see / What Heaven
can doe, 'and what any Earth can be." [15] These compliments are
not praises judiciously evaluating the specific virtues and charac-
teristics of the individual, as Ben Jonson's often are,[16] but meta-
physical praises of the possibilities of the human spirit acted upon
by God. Yet these possibilities are never treated abstractly, but

14 Robert Ellrodt, *Les Poètes Métaphysiques Anglais* (3 vols.; Paris, 1960), I,
137 (my translation).
15 Milgate, p. 107.
16 E.g., "LXXIV. To Thomas Lord Chancelor," "XCV. To Sir Henrie Savile,"
and "LXXVI. On Lucy Countesse of Bedford," in "Epigrammes"; "XIII. Epistle.
To Katherine, Lady Aubigny," in "The Forrest"; "52. An Epigram. To the
Honour'd [Elizabeth] Countesse of [Rutland]," in "Underwood," in Hunter, ed.,
Complete Poetry, pp. 31, 42–43, 32, 106–110, 206–207.

only as they may inhere in a particular human individual. And they may inhere in any particular individual whom Donne wishes or needs to praise at any given time. The patrons and patronesses may be substituted one for another, since the hyperbolic topoi do not belong to any individual as such: they are recognitions of what Heaven can make of any piece of human clay, of what we can study and discern through any good Christian life, of the "God" in the Countess of Bedford, or in any other person.

Some of Donne's verse letters and funeral elegies resemble Jonson's verse letters in that the subject is a general proposition relating to virtue, or religion, or death, or sorrow, and the poem takes the form of an analytical argument demonstrating the proposition or exploring its implications. In these poems Donne takes the occasion of a verse letter to explore a subject whose ramifications extend far beyond the particular occasion, yet the person addressed or elegized is organic to the development of the argument. The nonpersonal but incarnational focus means that the person praised is not an allegory or an exemplum, or merely the recipient of the poetic argument, but is precisely the individual in whom (for the purposes at hand) the "All" may be said to inhere.

The epistle "To Sir Edward Herbert, at Julyers" (1610) develops the argument that man is capable of producing all things, good and evil, out of himself. Taking the posture of one of Herbert's "good friends" and speaking for that select group, the speaker argues in objective, analytic terms that "Man is a lumpe" that produces all beasts (passions); that he is happy only when wisdom controls those beasts but that normally (like the devils in the Gadarene swine) he incites them and makes them worse; and that he himself adds corrosiveness to the curses of God and to the punishments God sends for his good.[17] The next point is that, because our business is "to rectifie / Nature, to what she was" (ll. 33–34), we do wrong to conceive man as a microcosm since he is greater than all: "Man into himselfe can draw / All; All his faith can swallow, 'or reason chaw. . . . / All the round world, to man is but a pill," which is variously "Poysonous, or purgative, or cordiall" depending upon who takes it (ll. 37–42). In conclusion the speaker addresses Herbert directly as the embodiment of all that has been said: Herbert bravely and truly claims to know man and therefore knows all the world. In him (and thereby for his friends who contemplate him) this universal knowledge is cordial:

17 Milgate, pp. 80–81.

As brave as true, is that profession than
Which you doe use to make; that you know man.
This makes it credible; you'have dwelt upon
All worthy bookes, and now are such a one.
Actions are authors, and of those in you
Your friends finde every day a mart of new. (ll. 45-50)

Also of this kind is the epistle "To the Countesse of Huntington" (1605?) which begins "That unripe side of earth." [18] Here the central issue of the poem is the right definition and conduct of a worthy love. The speaker's stance is personal: he analyzes his own problem, but then expands the terms so that at the end of the poem he speaks for all "able men, blest with a vertuous Love" (l. 121). The great distance the speaker observes between himself and the exalted lady whose friendship he enjoys might seem to invite Petrarchan adoration, but the speaker, concerned to prove himself an "able" lover, satirizes and repudiates that stance—no calf-eyed Petrarchan devotion for him. Either he will win love in return or he will cease loving: "I cannot feele the tempest of a frowne, / I may be rais'd by love, but not throwne down" (ll. 27-28); "The honesties of love with ease I doe, / But am no porter for a tedious woo" (ll. 75-76). The problem of how to love worthily one so elevated in rank and merit is resolved by the transformation of the terms from Petrarchan amorous devotion to Neoplatonic admiration of perfection. The speaker affirms that when we reach our height of goodness she is still the sun above, so that her love has the bounty of light "That gives to all, and yet hath infinite" (l. 102). Such perfection evokes men's love, but the impure soul cannot reach this height " 'Till slow accesse hath made it wholy pure" (l. 105). Passion is mere profanity to this Neoplatonic love which—whether the object be near or far—is all delight, the epitome of all virtue. The general problem of identifying worthy love is, then, resolved by means of the solution of the personal difficulty: How is the lowly but self-respecting poet to love the great lady?

Some of the funeral elegies are also epistles of this variety. They pose and explore, on the occasion of a particular death, some general problem, usually the power (or paradoxical lack of power) of death or sorrow over mankind when the counterpoise is a regenerate Christian soul. To be sure, this problem is addressed in

[18] *Ibid.*, pp. 81-85. Addressed to Lady Elizabeth Hastings.

one way or another in most Christian funeral elegies: it is a donnée of the genre. But, characteristically, Donne incarnates the problem and its resolution in the particulars of the occasion, and he bases the traditional consolation of elegy less upon the departed person's happy condition in Heaven than upon the full recognition of his worth and privileges as a regenerate soul.

The "Elegie on the Lady Marckham" (d. 1609) queries the extent and limitations of death's power in that continuing conflict which exists between death and mankind.[19] The speaker, addressing a generalized audience assumed to be concerned about this death, notes that God has set bonds between man (the microcosm) and death, as between land and sea at the creation: "Man is the World, and death th'Ocean, / To which God gives the lower parts of man" (ll. 1–2). Yet death "breaks our bankes, when ere it takes a friend" (l. 6), and our grief makes us, like Noah, drown our world again. These tears of passion prevent us from seeing what we are, and what the dead woman is. The problem posed by her death is resolved by the revelation of her nature as regenerate soul. Death has no true power over that soul, now freed by corporeal death from the spiritual death of sin, or over her flesh which in the grave will be refined as in an alembic, becoming at the last day "th'Elixar of this All" (l. 28). Her worth, and its power to resolve the problem, pertain to her as regenerate soul:

> Grace was in her extremely diligent,
>   That kept her from sinne, yet made her repent.
> Of what small spots pure white complaines! Alas,
>   How little poyson cracks a christall glasse!
> She sinn'd, but just enough to let us see
>   That God's word must be true, All, sinners be.
>
> (ll. 39–44)

She wept for her imperfections (as common natures do) and seemed to climb to Heaven by repentance, though in fact she was already there. At length the speaker, having resolved in general terms the problem of death's power, composes his elegy so that it is itself a force in man's continuing conflict with death. He affirms his willingness to testify "How fit she was for God" so that Death may repent his vain haste, but also declares his unwillingness to show "How fit for us . . . How Morall, how Divine," lest this add to Death's triumphs (ll. 53–62).

[19] Grierson, I, 279–281. The subject is Lady Bridget Markham, cousin of Lucy, Countess of Bedford.

The "Elegie on Mistress Boulstred" (d. 1609) also analyzes the power of death and its paradoxical defeat in taking the souls of the just.[20] As many have recognized, the poem begins with a recantation of the "Death Be Not Proud" sonnet, the speaker throughout addressing Death in personal terms but also as spokesman for "us," her friends: "Death I recant, and say, unsaid by mee / What ere hath slip'd, that might diminish thee" (ll. 1–2). The speaker then describes vividly—by means of a nature-reversed topos taken as actual fact, rather than in the more usual sense as the speaker's grief-induced aberration—the whole world as a universe of death. All life, not only creatures of the earth but also the fishes of the sea and the birds of the air, is served at Death's table and devoured by him. At first the countervailing power of the regenerate soul looks slight in this perspective: Death must indeed lay all he kills at God's feet, but God reserves only a few creatures, leaving most to Death. Yet meditation on Mistress Boulstred as one of the regenerate few reveals that Death has achieved no triumph here: her soul is in Heaven, her body waits only to go there where it will be "almost another soule," for this privilege belongs to her as one of the elect, secure in grace:

> Death gets 'twixt soules and bodies such a place
> As sinne insinuates 'twixt just men and grace,
> Both worke a separation, no divorce. (ll. 43–45)

By his haste Death has lost what chance he might have had of winning Mistress Boulstred by the vices of later age—ambition, covetousness, spiritual pride—or of winning others to sin by thinking evil of her or desiring her wrongfully. Death still has the opportunity to provoke others to sin through immoderate grief for her, but the speaker proposes that her "knot of friends" counter that opportunity by weeping only because we are not so good as she is.

The elegy "Death," which begins "Language thou art too narrow" (also assumed to be occasioned by the death of Cecilia Boulstred),[21] analyzes the problem of sorrow in relation to the death of the just. The speaker, as "our" spokesman, begins with a conventional inexpressibility topos (he is so grief-stricken that he cannot express his grief) and then undertakes a tirade against

---

[20] Grierson, pp. 282–284. Cecilia Boulstred was also related to Lady Bedford. Cf. Ben Jonson's "Epitaph" on her death (Hunter, ed., *Complete Poetry*, pp. 356–357).

[21] Grierson, I, 284–286.

Sorrow, the chief addressee of the poem, for attempting to extend his empire over all mankind by taking Mistress Boulstred. Paradoxically, however, Sorrow fails in that effort, for if we pine and die in sorrowing over her death, that is no misery after she has left us. The resolution of this problem also comes from her status as regenerate soul, embodiment of all worth:

> For of all morall vertues she was all,
>   The Ethicks speake of vertues Cardinall.
> Her soule was Paradise; the Cherubin
>   Set to keepe it was grace . . .   (ll. 33–36)

The point is reinforced by several biblical images: since Mistress Boulstred was paradise, God took her lest (like Adam and Eve) we love her above Him and His laws; her heart was a Moses' bush burning with religious fires but not consumed; she prefigured here her life in Heaven; she was of seraphic order on earth and now dwells with the seraphim next to God. Then the speaker, through a lovely image, conveys how her body and soul together are changed through death: "the tree / That wraps that christall in a wooden Tombe, / Shall be tooke up spruce, fill'd with diamond" (ll. 58–60). Through her status as regenerate soul, heir to the promises, the general problem of the ambiguities of Christian sorrow for death are resolved, and the specific "we" of the poem can be appropriately, if paradoxically, termed her "sad glad friends" (l. 61).

Another category of verse letters comprises poems primarily concerned with exploring that most common of the conventional topics of praise, the virtuous lady, in its characteristic Donnean formulation whereby the lady is regarded as the very embodiment or incarnation of Virtue. Usually the poems state explicitly that God has made her so. In these tightly unified poems, the topos is analyzed logically and seriously, and in the course of such analysis some important philosophical issue is posed and resolved: notably, How can complete virtue exist in, act in, or manifest itself to an essentially wicked world? The speaker's stance in these poems is superficially one of Petrarchan admiration, and the particular addressee is of course expected to be pleased by it, but by means of the analytic method and meditational posture the poems probe much deeper levels of significance. They suggest that by meditating upon the lady in terms of the conventional Virtue topos, taken as truth, the speaker himself and also the larger audience in-

fluenced by the lady can come to understand the weighty philo-
sophical and religious issues raised.

In the course of exploring the "perfect virtue" topic, the letter
"To the Countesse of Huntingdon" (1608–09) which begins
"Man to Gods image" [22] poses the question why virtue has em-
bodied itself in woman's weak form; the reason is to reveal perfect
virtue to weak souls. The speaker first calls attention to the tradi-
tional theological strictures against women: Eve was made to
man's image, not God's; there is some doubt whether she was given
a soul; woman may not hold ecclesiastical or civil offices; in woman
mild innocence might sometimes appear (as a seldom comet), but
active goodness is a miracle. The Countess is a miracle like the
star that led the Magi, revealing virtue both to "apt soules, and the
worst." The Countess, like all the others, is Virtue incarnate: Vir-
tue exiled by men has "fled to heaven, that's heavenly things, that's
you" (l. 22). Virtue, which gilded others, has turned the Countess
to gold and transubstantiated her into virtue itself. But she retains
the lowly roles of wife and mother to manifest herself and virtue,
"Else, being alike pure, wee should neither see" (l. 33). The refer-
ences to the Star and the Magi, and to the revelation of heavenly
things in low, fleshly form, invite us to connect her as incarnation
of Virtue with the Incarnation; continuing the analogy the speaker
finds her a far-off "revelation" to himself, concluding that he
shows some virtue in daring to contemplate her. He insists that he
does not flatter in saying these things: he had prophesied them
before and now merely records them (as prophet or apostle telling
of the Incarnation). And he makes explicit what he praises, the
source of her virtue—"God in you":

> Now that my prophesies are all fulfill'd,
>   Rather then God should not be honour'd too,
> And all these gifts confess'd, which hee instill'd,
>   Your selfe were bound to say that which I doe.
>
> So I, but your Recorder am in this,
>   Or mouth, or Speaker of the universe,
> A ministeriall Notary, for 'tis
>   Not I, but you and fame, that make this verse;
>
> I was your Prophet in your yonger dayes,
> And now your Chaplaine, God in you to praise. (ll. 61–70)

[22] Milgate, pp. 85–88.

The epistle "To the Countesse of Bedford" (1609) which be-
gins "T'have written then" [23] identifies the Countess as perfect
virtue and, in analyzing this topos, addresses the problem of true
virtue in the world from another perspective. The speaker identi-
fies himself as a "nothing," but one that might produce something
(as mines in barren ground yield coal or stone), since her virtue
acting on him has hallowed a pagan muse. She is "the worlds best
part, or all It" (l. 20); she is the home of virtue (which fled from
courtiers), or she is virtue itself which preserves one court and
ransoms one sex. But since the Countess does not understand her
own worth, the speaker invites her to meditate with him on the ills
of others, chiefly that our bodies taint our minds and souls, that our
bodies which are able to produce all things out of themselves pro-
duce only vicious things, and that we grudge to make ourselves fit
for Heaven. In such a world her complete virtue poses a problem:
Can it exist as unalloyed virtue or is there some perverseness or
tincture of vice in the facts that she is unaware (and hence un-
believing) of her own worth and that her ignorance of vice may
lessen her compassion for others? The conclusion is that virtue can
remain unalloyed in her; in others the aspersion of vice or vice itself
may play a role in counteracting another vice, but in her it has no
such office. Cordial virtue is appropriately her sole nourishment.

Another epistle to Lady Bedford (1608–1612) beginning
"Honour is so sublime perfection" [24] asks how the Countess's perfect
virtue can be properly manifested to, or praised by, the unworthy.
The first argument relating to this issue is that all honour, even to
God himself, comes from inferiors. The second is that radiation
from the Countess can subdue the clouds of the speaker's darkness
and give him light to contemplate her. A hyperbolic figure pro-
vides the terms for resolving the problem: she teaches the speaker
(and his audience) "the use of specular stone, / Through which all
things within without were shown" (ll. 29–30). That is, her ex-
ternal behavior fully reveals her inner state:

> You, for whose body God made better clay,
> Or tooke Soules stuffe such as shall late decay,
> Or such as needs small change at the last day.
>
> This, as an Amber drop enwraps a Bee,
> Covering discovers your quicke Soule; that we
> May in your through-shine front your hearts thoughts see.
>
> (ll. 22–27)

---

[23] Milgate, pp. 95–98.
[24] "To the Countesse of Bedford" (*ibid.*, pp. 100–102).

In the Countess, therefore, virtue can be revealed or manifested, since she gives equal care to being and seeming, to religion (the internal state) and to wit or discretion (external actions). Not content to make wit and religion colleagues, she transmutes wit into religion and thereby resolves the problem of the revelation of virtue in the wicked world. Accordingly, the speaker urges her to continue in this path, "great and innocent" (l. 54).

Yet another verse letter "To the Countesse of Bedford At New-yeares Tide" (1610) [25] explores the topos celebrating Lady Bedford as the embodiment of perfect virtue by focusing upon a problem personal to the speaker: How is he as poet to praise her in such a way as to gain credence from his audience? He desires, "since these times shew'd mee you," to "show future times / What you were" (ll. 10–12), for it is appropriate that verse embalm virtue. One problem is his own nothingness, but another is that she, as the embodiment of virtue, is a miracle; the audience may not believe in her now that faith is so scarce, or at least not believe that so low a thing as he could truly express her. Here the resolution of the problem is left to God, Who will teach her appropriate discretion in manners so that her virtue will be apparent to all, and Who will so exercise her with doubts, temporary absences of His comfort, and involvement with others' weaknesses that she will become comprehensible to weaker mortals. Finally, the speaker declares that Lady Bedford's merit is the result of God's grace proclaming the "private Ghospell" of her enrollment among the elect:

> From need of teares he will defend your soule,
>   Or make a rebaptizing of one teare;
> Hee cannot, (that's, he will not) dis-inroule
>   Your name; and when with active joy we heare
>   This private Ghospell, then 'tis our New Yeare. (ll. 61–65)

Yet another verse letter of this kind to Lady Bedford (1608–1612) beginning "You have refin'd mee, and to worthyest things" [26] develops from the topos defining the lady as the embodiment or essence of both beauty and virtue. Her virtue manifests itself chiefly at court where this quality is rare, her beauty chiefly in the country where beauty is similarly rare. Since she is now in the country, the speaker determines to praise her beauty, which is a light producing there a new world and new creatures. The problem

[25] Milgate, pp. 98–100.
[26] *Ibid.*, pp. 91–94.

is simply whether, and how, it is appropriate to praise beauty instead of virtue, given the consensus of classical and Renaissance rhetoricians that praises ought to be directed primarily to virtue. The resolution of the problem begins with the praise of her beauty as "vertues temple":

> Yet to that Deity which dwels in you,
> Your vertuous Soule, I now not sacrifice;
> These are *Petitions,* and not *Hymnes;* they sue
> But that I may survay the edifice.   (ll. 31–34)

The speaker therefore seeks to go on "pilgrimage" to a temple (to behold her beauty), praising her "not as consecrate, but merely'as faire" (l. 49). There is a further justification of this procedure in that Neoplatonic identity of beauty and goodness which is somehow realized in her:

> If good and lovely were not one, of both
> You were the transcript, and originall,
> The Elements, the Parent, and the Growth,
> And every peece of you, is both their All:
>   So'intire are all your deeds, and you, that you
>   Must do the same thing still: you cannot two. (ll. 55–60)

The speaker then discounts this argument as logic-chopping school divinity; the testimony of the senses themselves leads to the Neoplatonic intuition. "Senses decree" confirms her "The Mine, the Magazine, the Commonweale, / The story'of beauty," and to the speaker it is evident that whoever has seen that beauty would also wish to see her virtue: "As, who had bin / In Paradise, would seeke the Cherubin" (ll. 69–72).

A related category includes poems centering on a conventional topos but one that is more hyperbolic than the Virtue topos. Also, instead of posing and resolving a problem, these poems analyze the terms of the topic (as pertaining to the person praised) to arrive at a precise and complete definition. Given Donne's incarnational focus, the assumption in poems of this kind is that meditation upon a particular person in the terms of such a topos, defined precisely and taken as truth, will reveal something about the nature of things, to the speaker in the first instance but also to the audience joining him in the analysis-meditation.

Of this kind is the verse epistle or elegy addressed to the Countess of Bedford, probably on the occasion of the death of Lady

Markham (1609), beginning "You that are she and you, that's double shee." [27] The central topos is a conventional Neoplatonic definition of friendship, "they doe / Which build them friendships, become one of two" (ll. 3–4); both ladies are praised by means of an analysis of this figure. At first the praise seems to center upon the departed: Lady Bedford is defined as "double shee," and the topos "one of two" is first explained by analogy to the unity of soul and body, with Lady Markham as the heavenly soul and the Countess (because of her grief) as the "dead" body to whom the mourners pay tribute as if to the whole person: "She like the Soule is gone, and you here stay, / Not a live friend; but th'other halfe of clay" (ll. 13–14). Then the terms are pressed further, and the particular unity of the friends is defined as an entity subject to decay in some parts but not in its elements (virtues), which being pure cannot decay. The speaker accordingly observes that though her soul is fled to Heaven and her flesh to death, her virtues "as to their proper spheare, / Returne to dwell with you, of whom they were" (ll. 29–30). This deft turn associates the Countess of Bedford with God as source and end of all good: all Lady Markham's virtues are said to be contracted in the Countess who (again like God) cannot by taking additions of this sort be diminished or changed in any way. Lady Bedford is advised, finally, that she cannot replace Lady Markham with another friend; only a faithful book, indeed only the Book of Judith, can be such a "book of virtues" as she. In this poem, analysis of the topic "one of two" in regard to this particular friendship leads, although the conclusion is not stated explicitly, to a metaphysical intuition about the "conservation of good" in the world operating, in the economy of faithful friendship, to prevent the loss of any dram of virtue.

The "Letter to the Lady Carey, and Mrs. Essex Riche" was written in 1611–12, when Donne was abroad with Sir Robert Drury;[28] it is nearly contemporaneous with *The Second Anniversary* and may have been occasioned by rumors Donne heard that some of his noble patronesses were displeased by his hyperbolic praise of Elizabeth Drury.[29] Now a conventional Petrarchan topos affords the focus—Lady Carey is a "Saint"—the precise definition of the term "Saint" being carried forward in serious

[27] "To the Lady Bedford" (Milgate, pp. 94–95). The friend is probably Lady Markham, although possibly Cecilia Boulstred. Both these ladies, as noted above, were relatives of Lady Bedford; they died at Twickenham within three months of each other, in 1609.

[28] Milgate, pp. 105–107.

[29] *Ibid.*, p. 273 (Commentary).

Christian terms, albeit with whimsical wit. The speaker, located in idolatrous France where all saints are invoked, refuses to be a schismatic by separating himself from the common practice, nor yet a heretic by addressing any saint other than Lady Carey. Moreover, to redress the "low degree" of faith in that place he undertakes to tell what he has understood of her sainthood by the only means able to produce such understanding—by faith: "I thought it some Apostleship in mee / To speake things which by faith alone I see" (ll. 11–12). By this means the speaker sees that her sainthood is not a collection of individual virtues as papist devotees of saints might think, or as obtains with those whose virtues are "But in their humours, and at seasons show" (l. 18). Rather, true virtue is a unity; it is "our Soules complexion" (l. 32), or, yet more precisely, "True vertue'is Soule, Alwaies in all deeds All" (l. 36). Virtue, so defined, could not work upon Lady Carey's soul, "For, your soule was as good Vertue, as shee" (l. 39), and therefore it wrought upon her beauty, transforming that beauty to virtue also, so that her beauty moves others to virtue. Her sister is identified as worthy of praise in the same terms, being virtue and beauty of the same stuff. At length the speaker reaffirms his stance as one rendering "true devotion" to true saints, declaring that he has written what "in this my Extasie / And revelation of you both I see" (ll. 53–54). The poem intimates the metaphysical insight that true goodness (sanctity) is not a balance sheet of virtues but the total transformation of the self; the pervasive language (apostleship, faith alone, ecstasy, revelation) indicates that the cause of the transformation (like the object of the speaker's devotion) is the indwelling presence of God.

The letter to the Countess of Bedford (1608–1612) beginning "Reason is our Soules left hand, Faith her right / By these wee reach divinity, that's you," [30] is in some ways the most outrageously hyperbolic of all these poems. It focuses upon the conventional Petrarchan topos, the celestial (or divine) lady, and in analyzing that topos with theological precision appears (for a while at least) to conflate Lady Bedford with God Himself. The speaker declares his concern to "reach" (that is, to love) divinity—identified as Lady Bedford—and he proceeds by the theologically recognized means of reaching God: reason and faith. Those "who have the blessings of your sight" (like those who dwell with God) love her by reason; the speaker being distant loves by faith, and so is presumably heir to the biblical promises here echoed: "blessed are they

[30] "To the Countesse of Bedford" (Milgate, pp. 90–91).

that have not seen, and yet have believed"; "faith is the . . . evidence of things not seen." [31] Nevertheless, reason plays a role in relation to faith, not "to'encrease, but to expresse" it, that is, to clarify it to the understanding. Therefore the speaker undertakes rationally to seek the traces, the evidences, and the effects of Lady Bedford's divinity in the world: "Therefore I study you first in your Saints, / Those friends, whom your election glorifies, / Then in your deeds . . ." (ll. 9–11). Finally, as the reasons for loving her grow infinite (as God is infinite), the speaker is thrown back upon "implicite faith" in that overarching attribute of divinity acknowledged by all, "That you are good" (l. 17). At this point the divinity topos begins to be restricted and further clarified: her goodness is said to be preserved because her birth and her beauty are as a balm (inborn preservative) to keep it fresh, and also because she makes of learning and religion and virtue a mithridate (curative against poisons) to keep off or cure ill, her share in the mortal condition being acknowledged by the need of such medicine. She is praised as the "first good Angell" to appear in woman's shape and as "Gods masterpeece, and so / His Factor for our loves" (ll. 31–34). Here the topos is revealed as something other than witty blasphemy. The Countess is divine because, being good, she preserves and manifests the image of God, and in doing so she becomes God's "Factor"—that is, His agent or deputy—attracting our loves to that divinity in herself. The final lines return to the issue of the speaker's reaching (loving) divinity. The speaker urges Lady Bedford to concern herself before all else (even before benefiting him by being the object of his contemplation or his patroness) with her "returne home" to Heaven and with making that return "gracious," that is, fraught with grace for others (in imitation of Christ, the primary factor for God in this role). For the worst that can happen to a man is to "misse" the divine in Heaven: "For so God helpe mee, 'I would not misse you there / For all the good which you can do me here" (ll. 35–38). Meditation on the topos of the divine lady in relation to Lucy, Countess of Bedford, yields the insight that the good soul as image of God can manifest Him to others and lead the meditators to God.

The poems in the final category—the longest and most complex of the verse letters and funeral elegies—fuse the various methods of development we have noted: a problem is posed and resolved by study of the person praised, and a conventional topos is closely analyzed for whatever problems or metaphysical insights it may

---

[31] *Ibid.*, ll. 3–4. Cf. John 20:29, Heb. 11:1.

yield. But the focus shifts; in these poems it is squarely upon the person praised as an object of contemplation and upon the speaker's concern with the analytic and meditative process itself. These poems directly address the issue of what the speaker can understand by meditating upon a human person and what it is that he praises in such an exercise. In a sense, then, these are poems about themselves and about Donne's conception of the poetry of praise. It is no accident that all these poems were composed within two years of the two *Anniversaries*, reflecting, perhaps, Donne's need to explain what he had attempted in those complex, much misunderstood poems, but more probably indicating that the challenge of writing the *Anniversaries* had markedly increased his capacity to articulate the premises of his poetry of praise.

The letter "To the Countesse of Salisbury," dated August 1614,[32] undertakes to determine exactly what the speaker (and we are sharing the exercise with him) can come to know and understand by meditating upon the Countess—"daring to contemplate you" (l. 32). First, she manifests what "Faire, great, and good" really are, given their absence from the decaying world; she becomes, indeed, the embodiment of these qualities, which have the force of Platonic ideas. Now that the sun is grown stale and little valued, she comes "to repaire / Gods booke of creatures, teaching what is faire" (ll. 7–8). Also, now that all is "wither'd, shrunke, and dri'd," now that the world's frame is "crumbled into sand," now that "Integritie, friendship, and confidence, / (Ciments of greatnes)" are vaporized, and now that men by love of littleness seek to "draw to lesse, / Even that nothing, which at first we were," the speaker by contemplating her greatness learns that one must be great in order to get "Towards him that's infinite" (ll. 9–24). Also, in an age so evil that all are guilty of crimes and a good person seems a monster, the Countess manifests what goodness is. The speaker learns further that he and others also can have a share in the qualities she embodies and manifests as absolutes. This principle affords the speaker an excuse for having praised others (Elizabeth Drury?) in similar terms. One justification is that, like the praises of one who would acclaim God's works of creation as they occurred, day by day, the speaker's praises of each person are true when given, although the next day may reveal something better to him. More important, he insists that he praises the same qualities in all these persons:

[32] Milgate, pp. 107–110. The addressee is Lady Catherine Howard.

> I adore
> The same things now, which I ador'd before,
> The subject chang'd, and measure; the same thing
> In a low constable, and in the King
> I reverence; His power to work on mee:
> So did I humbly reverence each degree
> Of faire, great, good; but more, now I am come
> From having found their *walkes,* to finde their *home.*
>
> (ll. 57-64)

Lesser manifestations of fair, great, and good in other women have enabled the speaker now to "read" these Platonic absolutes in her, and he can do so despite residing in Plato's "darke Cave" or in the "Grave" of human mortality because she does "illustrate" those who study her. Despite his blindness and unworthiness (deprived as he is of physical means to see her at court), he believes that by contemplating her with his inner vision "I shall . . . all goodnesse have discern'd, / And though I burne my librarie, be learn'd" (ll. 83-84). Since the Countess is the present subject she is taken as the embodiment, the incarnation, of these Platonic absolutes, and other ladies are images or imitations to lead the speaker to her. This hyperbole is placed in perspective by the opening couplet, "Faire, great, and good, since seeing you, wee see / What Heaven can doe, 'and what any Earth can be." This statement reveals that the praise is directed primarily to the qualities themselves, where-ever resident, and that the speaker celebrates what Heaven can make of any human clay, any good Christian.

In the elegy on Prince Henry (d. 6 Nov. 1612) the central topos is the customary identification of Henry as Christ figure.[33] The problem of the poem, developed by means of a Nature-re-versed topos taken as fact, is the dislocation of reason and faith in the world caused by the death of the expected savior. Again the chief focus is upon the speaker as meditator, seeking to discover what contemplation of this prince may mean. As Ruth Waller-stein has noted, analytic meditation fuses with devotion as the

[33] Shawcross, pp. 257-260. In Sylvester, ed., *Sundry Funeral Elegies,* sigs. E-E2v. As a "young saviour," Prince Henry was expected by the Protestants to thrust back the encroachments of papist and Spanish power and influence; his death in his hopeful youth was commonly interpreted as God's punishment upon the sinning nation or else as that sacrifice of an innocent which would redeem the nation's sins. On all these grounds he was presented as a type of Christ. See Sylvester, "Lachrymae Lachrymarum," in *Sundry Funeral Elegies,* sigs. C-C2v; Thomas Heywood, "A Funerall Elegie," in *Three Elegies,* sig. B4.

speaker begins with a plea for the preservation of his faith—"Look to Me *Faith;* and look to my *Faith,* GOD"—and ends by imagining himself an *"Angel singing."* [34]

The speaker first defines for himself, and also for "us," the respective roles of reason and faith as the two centers of man. Reason is concerned with "All that this naturall World doth comprehend" (l. 6), faith with the enormous greatnesses (divine things) that are beyond the world. Yet (in scholastic terms) reason and faith almost meet, and contemplation of Prince Henry offers "us" our best opportunity to experience their congruence: "For, All that *Faith* could credit Mankinde *could,* / *Reason* still seconded that This PRINCE *would*" (ll. 19–20). Now that he is gone "Wee see not what to beleeve or know" (l. 24). It was believed that the Prince would fulfill the Christ-type–savior role: he awed neighboring states, he "Was His great *Father's* greatest Instrument, / And activ'st spirit to convey and tye / This soule of *peace* through *Christianitie*" (ll. 32–34). His peace, an emblem of the millennial peace, was expected to last until the millennium. But now this faith is heresy; God's curse on us is not death but a life that is "As but so manie *Mandrakes* on his Grave" sustained by "his *putrefaction*" (ll. 54–56), and the soul of our world is now grief. Moreover, as a Logos figure he was also the object of reason, the "only *Subject* REASON wrought upon" (l. 70); now that reason is gone "Wee / May safelier say, that Wee are dead, then *Hee*" (ll. 79–80). At this point Henry's value as object of the meditation is stated precisely: as a type of Christ he is "Our *Soule's* best Bayting and Mid-*period* / In her long *Journey* of *Considering* GOD" (ll. 85–86). Since Henry is a type of the Logos, the object of reason and faith, his absence causes the dislocation of both these centers in macrocosm and microcosm. Just as God cannot be understood in His essence, so the speaker despairs of contemplating Henry in himself—"as *Hee* is HEE" (l. 84)—but concludes that if he cannot "reach" him by reason and faith he may do so through love, "As *Hee* embrac't the *Fires* of *Love* with us" (l. 88). The speaker might understand Henry through love by contemplating "That *Shee-Intelligence* which mov'd This Sphear" (l. 90). The allusion may be to Henry's devoted sister Princess Elizabeth who was often mentioned in contemporary elegies as chief mourner for him, but the identification is deliberately vague: "Who-e'r thou

[34] Ruth Wallerstein, *Studies in Seventeenth-Century Poetic* (Madison, Wis., 1950), pp. 70–71, discusses a number of the Prince Henry elegies in their stylistic aspects and reprints several of them.

bee / Which hast the noble *Conscience*, Thou art *Shee*" (ll. 91–92). "Conscience" here surely carries the Latin sense of sharing private knowledge with another.[35] The speaker accordingly pleads that whoever had such a relationship of love and fidelity and communion of souls with Henry may let the speaker know their histories, their oaths, their souls, so that thereby he can reach Henry. This understanding achieved through love will make him an angel: "So, much as *You Two mutual Heavens* were *here*, / I were an *Angel singing* what *You* were" (ll. 97–98). As Ruth Wallerstein has noted, the poem itself testifies that the speaker has attained his wish. In this poem the individual praised is a recognized Christ-type whom the speaker takes as an appropriate midpoint in the "long *Journey* of *Considering* GOD" (l. 86). The object of the meditation is the divine manifested in the individual.

The "Obsequies to the Lord Harrington," brother to Lady Bedford (d. 27 Feb. 1614),[36] is the longest of these poems of compliment. The praise of Harington is conducted in terms of the Platonic topos of the soul as harmony and the Virtue topos; his death poses the problem of the uses of good men to the world and its loss by their death. The speaker focuses sharply upon his own meditative purposes and his endeavor to see God in the good person praised, but "we"—the audience—are permitted to share in this very personal formal meditation, conducted at the wholly appropriate hour of midnight. Invoking Lord Harington, as he might invoke God in another kind of meditation, the speaker observes that Harington has retained his soul's infused harmony and, accordingly, now bears a part in God's cosmic organ. He invites Harington to rejoice that the speaker himself has

> to that good degree
> Of goodnesse growne, that I can studie thee,
> And, by these meditations refin'd,
> Can unapparell and enlarge my minde,
> And so can make by this soft extasie,
> This place a map of heav'n, my selfe of thee.   (ll. 9–14)

As he pursues his meditation, the speaker sees Harington as a sun illuminating him so that he is enabled to see all things in and through Harington: "I see / Through all, both Church and State, in seeing thee; / And I discerne by favour of this light, / My selfe, the hard-

---

[35] "Conscience ... L. *conscientia*, privity of knowledge (with another)" (*OED*).
[36] "Obsequies to the Lord Harrington, brother to the Lady Lucy, Countesse of Bedford" (Grierson, I, 271–279).

est object of the sight" (ll. 27–30). He does so because he sees God in Harington, by reason of his virtue:

> God is the glasse; as thou when thou dost see
> Him who sees all, seest all concerning thee,
> So, yet unglorified, I comprehend
> All, in these mirrors of thy wayes, and end.
> Though God be our true glasse, through which we see
> All, since the beeing of all things is hee,
> Yet are the trunkes which doe to us derive
> Things, in proportion fit, by perspective,
> Deeds of good men; for by their living here,
> Vertues, indeed remote, seeme to be neare.   (ll. 31–40)

Next, he comes to understand more about Virtue by meditating on Harington; he sees that it cannot be divided into separate virtues but grows "one intirenesse" (l. 62), one compound, instantly discerned. This truth is especially obvious in short-lived good men like Harington, forced "to bee / For lack of time, his owne epitome" (ll. 77-78). Then the problem posed by Harington's death is engaged directly. Harington has set an example of living virtuously in youth and an example of a pious death; but the world also needs examples relating to other ages and circumstances. Since Harington was like a true clock constantly controlled by God, he ought to have stayed here as "a generall / And great Sundyall, to have set us All" (ll. 153–154). Now that he has died, Death "else a desert" is "growne a Court," and the churchyard is the suburbs of the New Jerusalem, the place from which Harington begins his triumph. The speaker now claims a right analogous to the prerogative of the Roman citizen, to chide the person accorded a triumph. Since by Roman custom triumphs were given only to those who enlarged a kingdom, and since Harington by conquering himself only renders back his own soul and body "as intire / As he, who takes endeavours, doth require" (ll. 211–212), his triumph is premature. He should have stayed to enlarge God's kingdom "By making others, what thou didst, to doe" (l. 214). He had such a charge, for "the Diocis / Of ev'ry exemplar man, the whole world is" (ll. 225–226). Yet the speaker cannot chide the sovereign, God, for permitting the early triumph, and he must agree that "It was more fit, / That all men should lacke thee, then thou lack it" (ll. 245–246). Indeed, the speaker by implication has undercut his complaint, for he has testified to his own advance in goodness through contemplating Harington, who thereby is shown to be able after death to enlarge God's kingdom. To the world he is an exemplar man; to the meditator he is more: he is a glass to see God and all else besides, because he is a regenerate soul whose perfections arise not of himself but of God, "who takes endeavours" as perfected actions.

What has been said should not obscure the fact that witty praise is of the essence of Donne's poetry of compliment, or that the addressee and the broader audience are expected to enjoy the witty figures, the deft turns of phrase and thought, the extravagant postures, for their own sake. And yet this wit is compatible with —indeed it is the very vehicle for—serious metaphysical explorations of the bases of human worth. The precise theological ground for these poetic explorations is itself a matter for investigation,[37] but it is clear now that the praises are not directed to the specific moral qualities of particular individuals (as with Ben Jonson), but to the potentialities of the human soul as image of God. As so often with Donne, in these extravagantly hyperbolic poems of compliment wit and high seriousness have fused so completely as to become indistinguishable. Donne's observation to the Countess of Bedford defines his method in this poetry of compliment with precision: "nor must wit / Be colleague to religion, but be it." [38]

---

[37] I explore this matter in a forthcoming book on Donne's *Anniversaries*.
[38] "Honour is so sublime perfection," ll. 44–45 (Milgate, p. 102).

IV
LANGUAGE, NOISE, AND NONSENSE: *THE ALCHEMIST*

Ian Donaldson

Comedy conventionally ends with a celebration of things won: feasts and dances signal the arrival of a legacy or a once-lost relative, the imminence of a marriage or the conclusion of a quarrel. Ben Jonson's comedy, on the other hand, rarely ends on this note of happy achievement; the expected prizes tend instead to disappear or to prove worthless. A silent wife turns out to be no wife, a legacy turns out to be no legacy, and elixir fails to materialize, a project comes to nothing, a bride deserts her husband on their wedding day. The comic action is insistently negative. Such prizes as are won—Sir Dauphine's legacy in *Epicoene*, for example, or Celia's trebled dowry in *Volpone*—seem finally less conspicuous than these major, central losses.

What the characters in Jonson's plays are left with at the end of the fifth act is often worthless trash. In *The Devil is an Ass*, Meercraft tells Fitzdottrel of the ease with which money may be made:

> I'le never want her! Coyne her out of cobwebs,
> Dust, but I'll have her! Raise wooll upon egge-shells,
> Sir, and make grasse grow out o' marro-bones,
> To make her come. (II, i, 7–10)

Needless to say, money does not come, and all that remains (so to speak) is small and random items of rubbish: cobwebs and dust, eggshells and marrow bones, quite untransmuted and worthless. Images such as these recur throughout Jonson's dramatic and nondramatic work. The world itself is described in one of Jonson's poems as "a shop / Of toyes, and trifles," [1] an image that returns in a familiar passage of his *Discoveries* (ll. 1437–1444):

What petty things they are, wee wonder at? like children, that esteeme every trifle; and preferre a *Fairing* before their Fathers: what difference is betweene us, and them? but that we are dearer Fooles, Cockscombes, at a higher rate? They are pleas'd with Cockleshels, Whistles, Hobby-horses, and such like: wee with Statues, marble Pillars, Pictures, guilded Roofes, where under-neath is Lath, and Lyme; perhaps Lome.

"Trifles" such as these form the lure in *Bartholomew Fair* to draw the curious to Smithfield: puppets and pears and gingerbread—"trash," like its vendor's name. Could one but explore the inside of Bartholmew Cokes's head, remarks his tutor Humphrey Waspe, doubtless one would find the same worthless trifles there as in the fairground itself: "cockleshels, pebbles, fine wheat-strawes, and here and there a chicken's feather, and a cob-web" (I, v, 95–97).

In Jonson's world people are drawn magnetically to a "Center attractive" [2]—a fairground, a house, a "fountain of self-love"—not so much out of any feelings of real concord as out of common folly and greed. Fundamentally such people are divided and alone: "the great heard, the multitude; that in all other things are divided; in this alone conspire, and agree: To love money" (*Discoveries*, ll. 1450–1452). The separateness of person from person is suggested by another (and closely related) kind of imagery in Jonson's work, which may be called the imagery of division. It takes many forms, one of which may be seen in this description by Crites in *Cynthia's Revels* (III, iv, 75–80) of the way in which a new gallant's appearance is appraised at court:

> . . . you shall heare one talke of this mans eye;
> Another, of his lip; a third, his nose;
> A fourth commend his legge; a fift his foot;
> A sixt his hand; and every one a limme:
> That you would thinke the poore distorted gallant
> Must there expire.

Such piecemeal and minute opinions seem positively to rend the new courtier limb from limb; the cumulative effect of the passage is to suggest the larger fragmentation of the whole society of the

---

[1] "To the World," ll. 17–18. All quotations are taken from *Ben Jonson*, ed. C. H. Herford and Percy and Evelyn Simpson (11 vols.; Oxford, 1925–1952).
[2] Induction to *The Magnetic Lady*, ll. 108–109.

court. Similar imagery of dismemberment, as Christopher Ricks has shown, is also to be found extensively in *Sejanus*, where the final destruction of the protagonist and the disintegration of the body politic are each hinted at by the constant mention throughout the play of distinct parts of the body: eyes, tongues, hands, knees, arms, ears.[3] In *Epicoene*, too, the constant casually humorous talk of physical mutilation and collapse helps create a similar sense of social fragmentation: Captain Otter reveals that his wife "takes her selfe asunder still when she goes to bed, into some twentie boxes; and about next day noone is put together againe, like a great Germane clocke" (IV, ii, 97–99); Truewit threatens to lop a leg or an arm, a thumb or a finger from Sir John Daw (IV, v, 122–139), and Morose despairingly wishes he might redeem his rash act of marriage "with the losse of an eye (nephew) a hand, or any other member" (IV, iv, 8–9). The play ends, not, as many comedies do, with a marriage, a symbolic act of union, but with a divorce, a symbolic division.[4]

Imagery of this kind is of quite a different order from the imagery of a play like (let us say) *The Merchant of Venice*, where images of bonds and rings and musical harmony suggest at once the cohesiveness of the social group and the value of the objects that most of its members pursue. Jonson's imagery, like the larger action of his plays, tends instead to suggest the vanity of human wishes and the fragmentation of the social group, picturing a world in which "Things fall apart; the centre cannot hold."

In some obvious ways the action of *The Alchemist* is not so self-defeating as that of, say, *Volpone* or *The Devil is an Ass*. Lovewit, after all, gets his rich widow, and Face is allowed to keep his loot; the play ends with master and servant united in a pact that is somewhat firmer than the original pact among Subtle, Face, and Dol. Yet for the majority of characters in the play, action proves circular and frustrating in much the way I have described above; riches exist only in the imagination, nothing is finally won. "Action," indeed, does not seem quite the word to describe what these characters do; most of them, frankly, do very little. Even Surly, apparently one of the more vigorous visitors to the house,

[3] Christopher Ricks, "*Sejanus* and Dismemberment," *Modern Language Notes*, LXXVI (1961), 301–308.

[4] The association of dismemberment and divorce is found in Matthew 5 : 27–32. For a further discussion of this play as a "comedy of disunity" see my essay, " 'A Martyrs Resolution': Jonson's *Epicoene*," *Review of English Studies*, n.s., XVIII (1967), 1–15.

gets bogged in the execution of his counterplot and is finally dismissed by Lovewit as one who, having had the opportunity to act, "did nothing" (V, v, 54). Characters such as Sir Epicure Mammon and Tribulation Wholesome similarly do virtually nothing—nothing, that is, except talk. *The Alchemist* is often praised for the vigor of its action, yet it is also the most verbal of plays, a play in which talking becomes a substitute for doing and achieving.

In *Discoveries* (ll. 1881–1883) Jonson traditionally describes speech as "the only benefit man hath to expresse his excellencie of mind above other creatures," adding that speech "is the Instrument of *Society*." The word "instrument" is carefully chosen: speech puts society in tune and joins man to his fellows as other creatures may not be joined.[5] It is a natural corollary of Jonson's lofty view of language that he should also consider corruptions of language as evidence of an untuning of the individual mind and of a wider disturbance in society as a whole:

Neither can his mind be thought to be in tune, whose words doe jarre; nor his reason in frame, whose sentence is preposterous; nor his Elocution cleare and perfect, whose utterance breakes it selfe into fragments and uncertainties. 　　　　　　　　　　　　　　(*Discoveries*, ll. 2142–2146)

Wheresoever, manners, and fashions are corrupted, Language is. It imitates the publicke riot. The excesse of Feasts, and apparell, are the notes of a sick State; and the wantonnesse of language, of a sick mind. 　　　　　　　　　　　　　　(*Discoveries*, ll. 954–958)

For all Jonson's obvious delight in chronicling the exact notations of linguistic extravagance, he views language soberly as an index of moral and intellectual health: "*Language* most shewes a man: speake that I may see thee" (*Discoveries*, ll. 2031–2032).[6] One of the recurring figures in Jonson's plays is the interminable and inconsequential talker whose discourse seems to consist of nothing more than noise or wind. Crispinus in *Poetaster*, Lady Wouldbe in

[5] This passage in *Discoveries* is taken almost entire from Juan Luis Vives, *De Ratione Dicendi*, i (*Opera* [1555], I, 85) (see *Ben Jonson*, ed. Herford and Simpson, XI, 265). Vives's *instrumentum* does not permit of a musical sense, but the context of Jonson's passage suggests he may be thinking of the "instrument" (either the caduceus or the flute) of Mercury, the god of music as well as of eloquence. In *Cynthia's Revels*, V, v, 10–17, "HERMES wand" is seen as having power to charm follies that are "like a sort of jarring instrument, / All out of tune." Cf. also *Discoveries*, ll. 1753–1754: "For as in an Instrument, so in style, there must be a Harmonie, and concent of parts."

[6] Such a proposition is ably explored in relation to Jonson's prose comedies by Jonas A. Barish in *Ben Jonson and the Language of Prose Comedy* (Cambridge, Mass., 1960).

Volpone, and the Collegiate Ladies in *Epicoene* all talk powerfully, unceasingly, and often nonsensically, using language as an instrument not of reason or of concord but of crude aggression. Moria in *Cynthia's Revels* is described as a "lady made all of voice, and aire, talkes any thing of any thing" (II, iv, 14–15), and Saviolina in *Every Man out of His Humour* as one whose talk is "nothing but sound, sound, a meere *eccho;* shee speakes as shee goes tir'd, in cob-web lawne, light, thin: good enough to catch flies withall" (II, iii, 208–210). "Air," "flies," "cob-web lawne": such delicate and insubstantial images as these—like Humphrey Waspe's straws and feathers and cobwebs in *Bartholomew Fair*—perfectly convey the vapidity of the characters to which they refer.

Similar images are also found in *The Alchemist,* a play in which language is constantly modulating into parody, rant, and cant, into mock-heroic, foreign, and nonsensical speech, and finally into mere noise; in which language, instead of drawing people to one another, splits them asunder. The play opens in the midst of a violent quarrel: *"Face.* Beleev't, I will. *Subtle.* Thy worst. I fart at thee." Language, from the start, is equated with mere wind and noise; Subtle's first action at once belies his name (later in the play Mammon is to express an interest in a poet "that writ so subtly of the *fart"* [II, ii, 63]):

> *Face.* You might talke softlier, raskall. *Subtle.* No, you *scarabe,*
> I'll thunder you, in peeces. I will teach you
> How to beware, to tempt a *furie'*againe
> That carries tempest in his hand, and voice.   (I, i, 59–62)

The images are again worth noticing; for Subtle, language is like thunder and tempest, a windy and destructive force. (Later, as Lovewit knocks at the door, Face ironically observes to Subtle, "Harke you, thunder" [V, iv, 137]). Jonson has Ovid use the same phrase while fooling in the banquet scene in *Poetaster* ("We tell thee, thou anger'st us, cot-queane; and we will thunder thee in peeces, for thy cot-queanitie" [IV, v, 124–125]; Ovid is playing Jupiter), and in *Volpone* Mosca speaks in similar terms while counseling Voltore how to destroy their opponents with his rhetoric:

> MERCURY sit upon your thundring tongue,
> Or the *French* HERCULES, and make your language
> As conquering as his club, to beate along,
> (As with a tempest) flat, our adversaries.   (IV, iv, 21–24)

Language is pictured as a weapon more than once in *The Alchemist*; Mammon warns Surly that Subtle will "Pound him to dust" and "bray you in a morter" with his arguments (II, iii, 142, 178), and later Lovewit speaks to Kastril about quarreling as one might speak about dueling:

> Come, will you quarrell? I will feize you, sirrah.
> Why doe you not buckle to your tooles?   (V, v, 131–132)

Conversely, Lovewit speaks to Ananias of weapons as one might speak of a rhetorical argument: "I shall confute you with a cudgell" (V, v, 108). Language is used several times like grapeshot; in IV, vii, for instance, Surly is actually forced out of the room by the strong blasts of Kastril's and Ananias's talk. Like any other weapon, language can also injure the user; it would "burst a man," says Surly, to try to repeat the alchemical language used by Subtle (II, iii, 198).

The notion of "bursting" is of major interest in the play, and to understand it, it is helpful to return to one of the topics raised in the quarrel that opens the play, namely the question of identity:

> *Face.*   Why! who
> Am I, my mungrill? Who am I?   (I, i, 12–13)

The question remains poised throughout the play: Who, indeed, is Face? He slips quickly from one role to another, and Lovewit's final words to him, "Speake for thy selfe, knave," do not resolve the problem. Is the speaker of the epilogue Face, or Jeremy, or the actor playing the role of Face-Jeremy? In the opening exchange of the play Subtle claims that Face simply did not exist before Subtle met him:

> *Subtle.*   Slave, thou hadst had no name——— . . .
> Never beene knowne, past *equi clibanum,*
> The heat of horse-dung, under ground, in cellars,
> Or an ale-house, darker than deafe-JOHN's: beene lost
> To all mankind, but laundresses, and tapsters,
> Had not I beene.   (I, i, 81, 83–87)

Subtle is doing no less than claim responsibility for having created Face as a character; Face, however, claims that things may be the other way about:

> *Face.*   Why, I pray you, have I
> Beene countenanc'd by you? or you, by me?
>
> (I, i, 21–22)

Throughout the play there is talk of characters being "made": "Come, I was borne to make thee, my good weasell," says Mammon to Face (II, iii, 328), and Surly later announces to Dame Pliant that "Your fortunes may make me a man" (IV, vi, 13). The sustained metaphor—and on this matter Edward Partridge is perceptive [7]—is that of an alchemical experiment that brings a new being into existence. Continually, however, the opposite is threatened, the explosion or dispersal of personal identity: "Doe you flie out, i' the *projection?*" (I, i, 79). Later in the play Mammon ponders the possibility of having his mirrors cut in subtle angles "to disperse, / And multiply the figures," and of having mists of perfume "vapor'd 'bout the roome, / To loose our selves in" (II, ii, 46–47, 49–50). Such images as these, like those of dismemberment noted above, further suggest the potential fragmentation and dissolution of personal identity.

The image of vapor has other cognates in the play. Adapting a passage from Martial (I.xcii.7–10), Jonson describes how Face first saw Subtle at Pie Corner, "Taking your meale of steeme in, from cookes stalls" (I, i, 26). A "meale of steeme" is, indeed, all that Subtle, along with most of the characters of the play, is finally to get. In any production of the play smoke drifts out across the stage from Subtle's laboratory fire, a suitable visual symbol both of the insubstantiality of the hoaxers' promises and of the densely obfuscating nature of their language, a "sweet smoke of rhetoric" made literally manifest. Jonson was later to use the same visual symbol in *Bartholomew Fair,* where quarrelsome vapors are accompanied by clouds of steam and tobacco smoke.[8] (The idea is foreshadowed, perhaps, in the tobacco-taking scene of *Every Man in His Humour* [III, ii], and in the "Mist made of delicate perfumes" from which Truth and Opinion emerge to argue their cases in the Barriers of *Hymenaei* [ll. 681 ff.].) Other, verbal images of insubstantiality are freely used in *The Alchemist:* the "drum" with which Dol will keep the Spanish don awake (III, iii, 44–45), the hollow bouncing balls to which Subtle and Face liken

---

[7] Edward Partridge, *The Broken Compass: A Study of the Major Comedies of Ben Jonson* (London, 1958), chap. vi. I am indebted to this admirable account of the play.

[8] See James E. Robinson, "*Bartholomew Fair:* Comedy of Vapors," *Studies in English Literature, 1500–1900,* I, no. 2 (1962), 65–80.

themselves (IV, v, 98–99), the "puck-fist" (puffball) to which
Face compares Subtle (I, ii, 63). Mammon's fantasies are likewise
gossamer-light: he dreams of shirts "of taffata-sarsnet, soft, and
light / As cob-webs," and eunuchs to

> . . . fan me with ten estrich tailes
> A piece, made in a plume, to gather wind.
> We will be brave, *Puffe*, now we ha' the *med'cine*.
>
> (II, ii, 89–90, 69–71)

Wind, plume, puff, perfume, mist, vapor, steam, smoke, fume, fart
—such words return throughout *The Alchemist*, hinting at the
imminent vaporization of wealth, language, and personality itself.

Language is a subject of compelling interest to most of the
characters in the play. Mammon vows he has a treatise penned
by Adam "O' the *Philosophers stone*, and in high-*Dutch*. . . .
Which proves it was the primitive tongue" (II, i, 84–86). Ananias
champions Hebrew against all other languages of the world; and
on this point, as Jonson's editors have remarked, he resembles many
Puritans of the day who believed Hebrew (as well as "*high-
Dutch*," apparently) to be the original language spoken by Adam,
and handed down to the Jews after the confusion of Babel. While
Mammon and Ananias, in their contrary ways, are occupied with
speculations about the language spoken in paradise, the languages
spoken in the play are more likely to remind one of Babel itself.
High Dutch and Hebrew are not the only languages of which we
hear. Dapper speaks words of Turkish, and Face, snatches of
Dutch; Subtle speaks in Latin and in the deeply obscure language
of alchemy; Surly, dressed as the Spanish don, speaks (somewhat
inaccurately) in Spanish, a language that Kastril takes to be
French; Kastril himself has come up to London to learn the
difficult "*Grammar*, and *Logick*, / And *Rhetorick* of quarrelling"
(IV, ii, 64–65) as practiced by the roaring boys. All these people
use language to impress and bewilder others. Language does not
unite them; it divides them. It is a vehicle not so much of sense as
of nonsense.

The more eccentric a man's linguistic habits, the easier (in this
play) it proves to gull him. When Surly as the Spanish don arrives,
he looks a pushover, and Face confidently instructs Dol how to
treat him:

> Firke, like a flounder; kisse, like a scallop, close:
> And tickle him with thy mother-tongue. His great

VERDUGO-ship has not a jot of language:
So much the easier to be cossin'd, my DOLLY.

(III, iii, 69–72)

As Edward Partridge points out, "mother-tongue" is an obscene pun: sex is the common language, a language that is nonrational and nonverbal. Mammon, too, wants Dol to "talk" with him, "to give a man a tast of her——— wit——— / Or so" (II, iii, 259–260). Talk, for Mammon, becomes confused both with the sexual act and with his imagined Midas touch:

> *Mammon.*   Now, EPICURE,
> Heighten thy selfe, talke to her, all in gold; . . .
> She shall feele gold, tast gold, heare gold, sleepe gold:
> Nay, we will *concumbere* gold. I will be puissant,
> And mightie in my talke to her!   (IV, i, 24–25, 29–31)

Such a confusion of activities finally devalues them all: speech, "the only benefit man hath to expresse his excellencie of mind above other creatures," is reduced to sex, an activity man shares with the beasts; yet Mammon is so concerned with making pompous speeches to Dol that he never actually achieves the physical contact of which he dreams. Sex becomes a substitute for language; language becomes a substitute for sex.

The "Queen of the Fairies" scene with the blindfolded Dapper at the end of the third act continues a similar process of linguistic reduction. Speech is broken down into nonsensical fragments of sound: "*Ti, ti do ti, ti ti do, ti da.*" The gibberish spoken to Dapper proves merely the first stage of a descent to more profound depths of linguistic obscurity. The fourth act begins with Sir Epicure Mammon's "talk" with Dol and proceeds to the interview in broken Spanish between Subtle, Face, and the disguised Surly; then, as Subtle takes Kastril off to practice his violent quarreling at the end of the scene, language undergoes an even more violent fragmentation: the fifth scene of Act IV presents Dol "*In her fit of talking.*"

The subject of Dol's dislocated and nonsensical speech is, appropriately, the history of language since the beginning of the world; like Mammon and like Ananias, Dol professes a concern for "the primitive tongue." Jonson is borrowing freely from the Puritan Hugh Broughton's turgid work, *A Concent of Scripture* (1590):

Dol.   *For, as he sayes, except*
We call the Rabbines, and the heathen Greekes——
Mammon. Deare lady. *Dol. To come from Salem, and from Athens,*
And teach the people of great Britaine—— Face. What's the matter,
    sir?
Dol. To speake the tongue of EBER, *and* JAVAN—— *Mammon.* O,
Sh'is in her fit. *Dol. We shall know nothing——* Face. Death, sir,
We are un-done. *Dol. Where, then, a learned Linguist*
Shall see the antient us'd communion
Of vowells, and consonants—— Face. My master will heare!
   Dol. A wisedome, which PYTHAGORAS *held most high——*
   Mammon. Sweet honorable lady. *Dol. To comprise*
All sounds of voyces, in few markes of letters.   (IV, v, 12–23)

'All sounds of voyces": as the speech reaches its climax, the side-
note reads, *"They speake together"*; Dol, Face, and Mammon all
talk wildly and at once, while offstage the voice of Subtle—inter-
rupted in the middle of the lesson in quarreling he is giving to
Kastril—is also heard. Jonson is fond of such moments as these,
when language becomes a mere tangle of sound: there is a similar
moment at the end of the second act of *Bartholomew Fair* ("*They
speake all together . . .*"), and another in the courtroom scene
at the end of *The Devil is an Ass*, where Fitzdottrel speaks rapidly
in several different languages, and still another in the fifth act of
The Alchemist when all the neighbors speak to Lovewit simultane-
ously ("Fewer at once, I pray you" [V, v, 21]).

    Dol's wild harangue on the ways of achieving universal linguistic
understanding runs as a lunatic counterpoint to this noise and non-
sense; "the instrument of *Society*" has become untuned, and in a
moment, as a final climax, comes *"A great crack and noise within."*
The scene may be viewed as a parody of the Pentecostal miracle
when the apostles "began to speak with other tongues, as the Spirit
gave them utterance" (Acts 2 : 4). But instead of universal com-
prehension, there is here universal obscurity; instead of union,
there is division; instead of the "sound from heaven as of a rushing
mighty wind" (Acts 2 : 2) there is merely the (artificially manu-
factured) blast from the laboratory. The New Testament account
of the Whitsun gift of tongues was often considered to be the typo-
logical counterpart of the Old Testament account of the destruction
of the Tower of Babel and the consequent fragmentation of lan-
guages. Hugh Broughton, in the work from which Dol Common
quotes in this scene, had written of the Pentecostal happenings in
these terms: "In this Citie they received power in a strong wind, in

fiery cloven tongues, were filled with the holy Ghost, and could speake to every one his owne language. So the *Jerusalem* from above was to be buylt, that all nations might woorke in it, as contrariwyse by tongues not understood, the worke was but *Babylon* a confusion." [9] *The Alchemist* seems to reenact the Babel story, showing people violently split among themselves, driven further from a common language and from common sense as they attempt to fulfill their private fantasies.

The explosion itself comes as a fitting culmination to the earlier talk of bursting and of vaporization. Its symbolic suggestiveness is comparable to that of the explosion that occurs in Newgate in the last act of *The Devil is an Ass* at the disappearance of Pug to hell, and to the description of the dissolution of the staple in *The Staple of News:*

> *Thomas.* Our *Staple* is all to piéces, quite dissolv'd! . . .
> Shiver'd, as in an earth-quake! heard you not
> The cracke and ruines? we are all blown up!
> Soon as they heard th'*Infanta* was got from them,
> Whom they had so devoured i' their hopes,
> To be their *Patronesse*, and sojourne with 'hem;
> Our *Emissaries, Register, Examiner,*
> Flew into vapor . . .   (V, i, 39–46)

The explosion in *The Alchemist* prefigures a similar disappearance of both rogues and fools:

> *Face.* O sir, we are defeated! all the *workes*
> Are flowne *in fumo:* every glasse is burst.
> Fornace, and all rent downe! as if a bolt
> Of thunder had beene driven through the house.
> *Retorts, Receivers, Pellicanes, Bolt-heads,*
> All strooke in shivers! . . .
> *Mammon.* Is no *projection* left? *Face.* All flowne, or stinks, sir.
>   (IV, v, 57–62, 89)

"All flowne": soon Mammon is to discover that not only the projection but the projectors themselves have dispersed: "The whole nest are fled!" (V, v, 58); ". . . *it, and they, and all in* fume *are gone*" (argument, l. 12). The fume in which Face is said to work (II, ii, 21; III, i, 19), the fume of which Dapper complains in Lovewit's privy (V, iv, 5), seems finally to blow the house apart

[9] Hugh Broughton, *A Concent of Scripture* (London, 1595), sig. H4.

and its occupants with it. What is finally left in the house is elo-
quently noted by Lovewit on his return:

> Here, I find
> The emptie walls, worse then I left 'hem, smok'd,
> A few crack'd pots, and glasses, and a fornace,
> The seeling fill'd with *poesies* of the candle:
> And MADAME, with a *Dildo*, writ o' the walls. (V, v, 38–42)

Shards, smoke, obscene graffiti—it is to such valueless fragments
and trifles that the play finally returns us. Nothing has been
created. The rubbish mentioned throughout the play—cobwebs,
hollow coal, feces, ashes, dust, scrapings, horse dung, "pisse,
and egge-shells, womens termes, mans bloud, / Haire o' the head,
burnt clouts, chalke, merds, and clay" (II, iii, 194–195)—remains
untransmuted still.

One further association is worth observing here. Surly speaks
of the explosion of *"sublim'd Mercurie,* that shall burst i'the heate"
(IV, vi, 44). The classical figure of Mercury had, among his many
other offices, an especial guardianship over language. In *Dis-
coveries* Jonson writes of Mercury as "the President of Language,"
"Deorum hominumque interpres" (ll. 1883–1884), and in *Cynthia's
Revels* Crites characterizes Mercury as the "sacred god of wit" (V,
iv, 612). In *Mercurie Vindicated from the Alchemists at Court,*
the figure of Mercury is finally saved from those who persecute
him with their art (including those who afflict him with "a huge
deale of talke" [l.167]). In *The Alchemist* language is like mercury,
highly volatile, capable of rising to "wit" of the kind Lovewit
praises in Face (V, v, 150), capable also, under the pressure of ex-
treme "art," of exploding out of sense into nonsense.

Jonson is the first known user of the word "nonsense." He uses
the word twice, once in the explanatory sidenote to the game of
vapors in *Bartholomew Fair* (*"Here they continue their game of
vapours, which is* non sense. *Every man to oppose the last man that
spoke: whether it concern'd him, or no"* [IV, iv]), and again in
Discoveries ("Many Writers perplexe their Readers, and Hearers
with meere *Non-sense.* Their writings need sunshine" [ll. 1868–
1870]). Sense and nonsense are opposed as sunshine to vapor.
Dryden was later to chance upon the same obvious enough antith-
esis when describing his monarch of nonsense, whose "rising Fogs
prevail upon the Day" (*Mac Flecknoe*, l. 24). Later in *Discoveries*,
Jonson uses another fine analogy which helps explain what he un-

derstood by the word "sense": "In all speech, words and sense, are as the body, and the soule. The sense is as the life and soule of Language, without which all words are dead. Sense is wrought out of experience, the knowledge of humane life, and actions, or of the liberall Arts, which the *Greeks* call'd Ἐγκυκλοπαιδείαν" (ll. 1884-1889). Although Jonson is drawing freely on Vives here, the definition of "sense" is one that he makes very much his own. His "Expostulation with Inigo Jones" (to take a single instance) is fired largely by a contempt for the kind of mechanistic thinking that allows dead things, the products of carpentry and paint, to dominate over the living things of the "sense":

> . . . O Showes! Showes! Mighty Showes!
> The Eloquence of Masques! What need of prose
> Or Verse, or Sense t'express Immortal you?　　(ll. 39-41)

> Oh, to make Boardes to speake! There is a taske[!]
> Painting & Carpentry are the Soule of Masque.　　(ll. 49-50)

In his fierce contempt for those who neglect the lively "sense" of language, Jonson stands in a humanistic tradition that runs (to take only a short view of the matter) from Vives to Pope. There is an obvious kinship, indeed, between Jonson and Pope, in the way each writer, with great linguistic lucidity and inventiveness, imaginatively re-creates in his satire the total breakdown of language into a "mass of Nonsense," civilized speech giving way to "the wond'rous pow'r of Noise" (*Dunciad*, I, 241; II, 222). Pope, like Jonson, shows a fascination with images of small, lightweight, absurdly disconnected objects: silkworms, eggshells, dust, parchment scraps, fungus, hairs, pores of the skin, fleas. Like Jonson, too, he excels at suggesting in a multitude of ways the fragmentation of the society he portrays. "Joy to great Chaos! let Division reign," says the phantom-harlot of Italian opera in the fourth book of *The Dunciad* (l. 54), and the words might with equal aptness serve for an induction to *The Alchemist*.

I have described *The Alchemist* as a highly verbal play, and it might be asked whether the play, for all its deft theatricality, does not in the last estimate seem to live too exclusively in the realm of words: "Words are Man's province, Words we teach alone." In ridiculing those who make matters of language their obsession, a writer runs the risk of appearing a little obsessed with matters of language himself. Shakespeare successfully avoids this risk, even in so linguistically self-conscious a play as *Love's Labour's Lost,* for there the action of the comedy is largely a process of discovery; fantasticated words are simply beside the point when one is faced with the bare facts of love, or sickness, or death. Shakespeare has the great power to make silence eloquent of happiness or comprehension of something gained: the silence of Leontes surveying the statue of Hermione, or (a lighter moment) the silence Benedick enforces upon Beatrice with a kiss: "Peace! I will stop your mouth." Although Jonson leaves us in no doubt as to his attitude to wanton talk ("*How* much better is it, to bee silent; or at least, to speake sparingly!" [*Discoveries,* ll. 1602–1603]), the garrulous characters in his plays tend to have silence forced upon them as a harsh and often violent punishment: Crispinus in *Poetaster* is given an emetic; Carlo Buffone in *Every Man out of His Humour* has his lips forcibly sealed up; the prattling Sir Politic Wouldbe is subjected to a practical joke, and takes silent refuge in his tortoiseshell; Zeal-of-the-Land Busy (like many other Jonsonian characters) is shamed into final silence. The typical antithesis—talkativeness versus enforced silence—is starkly presented, in a way that (despite the comic context) could be felt to be inhumane. "Sense is wrought out of experience, the knowledge of humane life, and actions, or of the liberall Arts": this statement is not often enacted in the comedies themselves. *The Alchemist,* so centrally concerned, as it is, with questions of language, is particularly susceptible to an objection of this kind; superbly organized the action is, yet the range of "humane life" it presents is also arguably rather thin. The arrival of Mercade at the end of *Love's Labour's Lost* radically alters the tone of that comedy in a way that the arrival of Lovewit does not radically alter the tone of *The Alchemist;* victory in the latter play goes to those with "wit," a word that denotes, in the main, a dexterity with language. Right to the end the play retains its slight sense of having been a complex rhetorical tournament or flyting. Yet when all the reservations have been made, *The Alchemist* remains one of the great comedies of the world.

V

REASONS THAT IMPLY THEMSELVES: IMAGERY, ARGUMENT, AND THE READER IN MILTON'S *REASON* OF CHURCH GOVERNMENT

Stanley Fish

Recently K. G. Hamilton has noted the presence in Milton's prose of a "strong figurative element, a continual exploitation of the full emotional as well as intellectual potential of words." [1] While the figurative element in itself is hardly a matter for concern, Hamilton finds that at times it "ceases merely to give an imaginative coloring to the argument and becomes the means by which the argument is being carried on" (p. 326). In that event there is a danger, especially if a sentence is long, "that the emotional overtones of the language, the piling up of images and of powerfully evocative associations, will eventually swamp altogether the purely logical statement" (p. 327). In fact, Hamilton continues, at his worst Milton offers us images and evocative associations in place of a logical statement, using the amplificatory rhetoric that characterizes his prose to conceal a basic "ratiocinative emptiness," "a lack of real intellectual content" (pp. 327, 329), not only in single sentences, but in whole works:

We can be carried along for a time by the apparent closeness of the argument, by the rhetoric, or by the imaginative force of the words

---

[1] *Language and Style in Milton*, ed. R. D. Emma and J. T. Shawcross (New York, 1967), p. 324. Hamilton's phrases of course summarize what have been critical commonplaces since Raleigh.

and images; but, because of Milton's method which depends so much on the development of argument within the individual sentence rather than on a strong ratiocinative progress through the whole work, when a relative emptiness of dialectical content becomes characteristic of the sentence the reader inevitably begins to get the impression that nothing is being offered him beyond words, that he is getting nowhere, gaining no real illumination. Milton, as a dialectician, is at times given to jumping up and down in one place—what appears structurally to be a dynamic progress may resolve itself finally into a complex but static expression of the strength of his own conviction, rather than either a reasoned statement or an imaginative apprehension of the basis of that conviction. (p. 329)

As a description of what happens in Milton's prose, this assessment is perfectly accurate, but as an evaluation it is, I believe, wrong, if only because Hamilton assumes a failure according to standards Milton would not have acknowledged. I refer of course to the standards of expository prose: a series of carefully reasoned arguments, simply and plainly presented, and tied together in a larger logical framework by numbered chapters and books, the whole rising toward a grand and triumphant *quod erat demonstrandum.* In the following pages I argue that Milton's purposes commit him to producing a prose displaying none of these characteristics (although they sometimes appear to be present) and, moreover, that their absence is very often a large part of his objective. In other words, the reader who "begins to get the impression . . . that he is getting nowhere" is exactly where Milton wants him to be. Hamilton reserves his harshest words for a passage from *The Reason of Church Government,* a tract that will, I trust, more than any other, provide a basis for turning his criticism into praise.

Let us begin by examining a passage in which "the figurative element ceases merely to give an imaginative coloring to the argument and becomes the means by which the argument is being carried on":

And thus Prelaty both in her fleshly supportments, in her carnall doctrine of ceremonie and tradition, in her violent and secular power going quite counter to the prime end of Christs comming in the flesh, that is to revele his truth, his glory and his might in a clean contrary manner then Prelaty seeks to do, thwarting and defeating the great mistery of God, I do not conclude that Prelaty is Antichristian, for what need I? the things themselves conclude it.[2]

This sentence from the third chapter of the second book has two structures, the one the reader is allowed (encouraged) to anticipate, and the one that reveals itself when the other has aborted. The first structure is logical and argumentative; it is a structure of expectations, based on the words "thus Prelaty both" and exhibiting the form, "A, because of B and C, is D." That is to say, it promises a conclusion that will follow naturally upon the identification of the two salient attributes of Prelaty. But the anticipated rhythm of the sentence is not carried through; rather than two attributes, we are given three, and before we have time to consider exactly what this means in relation to the very specific "both," the weight of the sentence shifts to the explanatory clause beginning "that is." The focus of attention shifts, too, from Prelaty to the "end of Christs comming"; it is at this point, when the control afforded by a linear and directing syntax is relaxed (or abandoned), that a new principle of organization comes to the fore. The pivotal point of the sentence is now the word "that," and on either side of it a series of opposites face each other in a kind of confrontation: "Prelaty," "fleshly," "carnall," "ceremonie," "tradition," and "secular" versus "Christ," "revele," "truth," "might," and "clean." Whatever meaning the sentence finally has is the product of this confrontation rather than of any sustained argument. Indeed so strong is the "figurative element," or at least the attracting power of associatively linked phrases, that individual words convey meaning independently of the syntax in which they are supposedly embedded. Technically, "clean" is an adverb, and should be glossed "wholly"; but the proximity of "truth," "glory," and "revele" (which here retains its root meaning, *revelare*, "to unveil" or "to uncover") pressures us to read "clean" as "clear" or "unsullied," a reading that has the advantage of providing a nice counterpoint to the combined suggestiveness of "ceremonie," "tradition," and "fleshly." In a very real sense, the words on either side of the dividing "that" become interchangeable; together, they form a single pair of words and a single large opposition which is the sum of the associations they share: on one hand all the false appearances and fleshly coverings of the earthly perspective, and on the other the simplicity and clarity of unadorned truth.

It is too little to say that in this example the "purely logical statement" is "swamped"; rather it is dismissed, not only implicitly by the movement of the prose, but overtly by Milton himself when he breaks off his still verbless sentence (so unimportant has syntax

2 *Complete Prose Works of John Milton*, ed. Don M. Wolfe et al. (New Haven, 1953-), I, 850.

become that the omission is hardly noted) to tell us that the chain of inferences we had been led to expect is superfluous: "I do not conclude that Prelaty is Antichristian, for what need I? the things themselves conclude it." These final words are a perfect description of what has happened in the sentence. The responsibility for "concluding" has passed from the logically based syntax, which is left incomplete, to a series of single words whose argumentative force is immediate and (self-) sufficient; and this shift from rational discourse to figurative purpose is reflected by the response of the reader, who does not wait for a formal conclusion to determine the truth about prelacy. In effect, the reader has been made to exchange one way of knowing for another: he begins by withholding judgment pending the marshaling of evidence, but in the end he is judging simply by reading or seeing and without the intermediary interposition of any evidentiary process.

What is particularly significant about this sentence is the self-consciousness it both evidences and induces. Not only does Milton obviously intend the effect I have described, he intends it to be noticed. It is almost as if he were daring the reader to disagree with him. There is a submerged question here—"You do see, don't you?"—and along with it a submerged implication that if you do not see, well, so much the worse for you. In some sense, then, the reader is a central figure in the "plot" of this sequence, as he is, I believe, in the whole of *The Reason of Church Government*. His larger role is clarified in another passage that makes the same point in very nearly the same language:

Let others therefore dread and shun the Scriptures for their darknesse, I shall wish I may deserve to be reckon'd among those who admire and dwell upon them for their clearnesse. And this seemes to be the cause why in those places of holy writ, wherein is treated of Church-government, the reasons thereof are not formally, and profestly set downe, because to him that heeds attentively the drift and scope of Christian profession, they easily imply themselves.   (I, 750)

Here again ratiocination (reasons formally set down) is opposed to intuition (they easily imply themselves), and in this instance the opposition is clearly a way of distinguishing between two classes of reader-observers. The sentence acts as a "multiple-choice examination," [3] pressuring the reader to place himself in one of two

[3] I borrow this phase from Joan Webber who uses it to characterize Burton's sentences in her brilliant study of seventeenth-century prose, *The Eloquent "I"* (Madison, Wis., 1968), pp. 101–102.

categories, those who have recourse to reason and those who do not. The choice, however, is no choice at all, at least as the sentence offers it: either agree that the truth of the matter is self-evident, or admit that you have not heeded "attentively the drift and scope of Christian profession." (Heads I win, tails you condemn yourself.) This brilliant piece of strategy (one might call it the "emperor's clothes" ploy) has the effect of subsuming the question of record —whether prelacy or Presbyterianism is the better form of church government—in a question of personal "honor"; for in the context of the larger argument, agreeing that the truth is self-evident is equivalent to allying oneself with the Presbyters, a decision that is here made an almost accidental by-product of a self-defensive gesture ("Of course I see!"). Not only does the reader concede the major point, he "preconcedes" all subsequent points, since he has acquiesced in the devaluing of the very faculty—reason—from which later counterarguments might be expected to arise. Reason is dismissed, as it is again in chapter iii, Book II, but in neither place does it wholly disappear; rather it is linked, if only by a process of elimination, with prelacy, a union that grows ever firmer with each succeeding page. Thus even while Milton is busily discrediting one kind of logic (reasons formally set down), he is using, and using very effectively, another—a logic of association whose arguments are made by the pairs of coordinate terms which emerge if one glances down the printed page:

darknesse　clearnesse

reasons formally set down　reasons that imply themselves

those who have not heeded the drift and scope of Christian profession　those who have

prelacy　Presbyterianism

These opposing pairs together form one large opposition which turns outward to face the reader, asking him, in effect, "Where do *you* stand?" (Milton gives *his* answer very loudly.) The reader is again in the very center of the "action," poised somewhat uneasily between the contending parties, their modes of apprehension, and their indigenous patterns of imagery; and this position he occupies quite literally in the concluding sentences of chapter iii (emphasis mine):

If the religion be *pure, spirituall, simple,* and *lowly,* as the Gospel most truly is, such must the face of the ministery be. And in like manner if the forme of the Ministery be *grounded* in the *worldly* degrees of autority, honour, *temporall* jurisdiction, we see it with our eyes it will turne the *inward* power and *purity* of the Gospel into the *outward carnality* of the *law;* evaporating and exhaling the *internall* worship into empty conformities, and *gay shewes.*   (I, 766)

In this excerpt the syntax does not even pretend to do anything more than hold in place the words I have italicized; *they* carry the argument, moving in a kind of dance from one pattern of rela- tionships to another, first ranging themselves formally in lines of battle, "pure," "spirituall," "simple," "lowly" against "grounded" (the metaphor becomes literal in the company of its fellows), "worldly," "temporall," and then separating into opposing pairs which engage each other in a hand-to-hand combat: "inward" versus "outward," "purity" versus "carnality," "internall" versus "gay shewes." These smaller oppositions operate to flesh out the more abstract opposition of the Gospel to the Law which in turn feeds into the ever-present opposition of prelacy to Presbyterian- ism. And exactly in the middle of the sentence, and therefore in the middle of the smaller and larger coordinates, stands the reader, or more properly his eyes, which are declared responsible ("we see it with our eyes") for judging between the "faces" of the two ministries. But the responsibility is limited, of course, since the judgment is already embedded in the imagery and the reader can only approve it or, alternatively, become its object. For this sen- tence, too, pressures us to choose between alternatives that are immediately self-revelatory. Are your eyes "pure," "spirituall," "inward," or are they "carnal," "worldly," and "outward"? Are they answerable to that which "most truly is" or to "gay shewes"? And again a reader's response (he can hardly withhold it) not only places him in a hierarchy of vision but commits him to a whole series of attendant positions: for the Presbyters and against prelacy, for the inner light and against priestly ceremony, for the immediate validation of illumined eyes and against the worldly machinery of reasons formally set down.

Insofar as these excerpts are representative, they suggest that *The Reason of Church Government* is one continuing and elabo- rate "eye test." Milton in fact says as much when he declines to argue a point, declaring it to be "for the plainnesse thereof a matter of eye sight, rather then of disquisition" (I, 775). This remarkable statement is, in its implications, decidedly subversive, for if the competing claims of the prelates and the Presbyters are to be evaluated independently of disquisition, much of *The Reason of Church Government*, and especially its logical superstructure, must be dismissed as window dressing. There is some evidence for this view in the sentences we have already examined, and it is I think confirmed in those places where Milton directs our attention specifically to the operative word—reason. This word appears on nearly every page of the tract, as one might expect it to, but what one does not expect is to find it used in such a way as to take from it much of the force it usually carries.

"Reason" appears seven times in the introduction alone, where it is allied closely with the idea of persuasion. Milton begins by rehearsing a distinction first made by Plato. Human laws ought not to be set forth "barely" or with only "a lordly command"; rather, persuasion, in the form of "native colours and graces of speech," should be used to "incite, and in a manner, charme the multitude into the love of that which is really good" (I, 746). This conventional opening seems to place the author firmly on the side of rhetoric in its ancient quarrel with philosophy. Within a few sentences, however, the clear opposition of lordly commands barely set forth to a "winning" persuasion begins to blur:

Moses therefore the only Lawgiver that we can believe to have been visibly taught of God, knowing how vaine it was to write lawes to men whose hearts were not first season'd with the knowledge of God and of his workes, began from the book of Genesis, as a prologue to his lawes; which *Josephus* right well hath noted. That the nation of the Jewes, reading therein the universall goodnesse of God to all creatures in the Creation, and his peculiar favour to them in his election of *Abraham* their ancestor, from whom they could derive so many blessings upon themselves, might be mov'd to obey sincerely by knowing so good a reason of their obedience.   (I, 747)

Within the syntactic unit that begins with "*Moses* therefore" and ends with "obedience" there coexist, in a rather uneasy relationship, two ways of accounting for the fact that the Jews do obey: one that assumes a visible and chartable pattern of cause and effect, and another that equates persuasion with a knowledge of God, given by God. The distance between the two is the distance between the word "therefore," with its promise of a series of related propositions tied to one another by the ligatures of logical thought, and the word "obedience" with its suggestion of something immediate and intuitive. The attentive reader will not be unaware of the tension between these two anatomies of persuasion. In the context of what has preceded it, he would expect "knowing how vaine it was to write lawes" to be followed by still another testimonial to the power of rhetoric to "charm"; instead he finds the effectiveness of laws tied not to the manner of their presentation but to the a priori condition of the heart that is to receive them, "first season'd with the knowledge of God." This reference to God, parenthetical and almost casual, complicates the terms of a discussion that had been proceeding on the level introduced by "humane lawes, which for the most part aime not beyond the good of civill society" (I, 746). On that level the usefulness of rhetoric as a means of persuasion is defensible; but on the level of "the knowledge of God" the place of rhetoric is less secure. What exactly happens when the heart is seasoned with such knowledge? Who does the seasoning? What part, if any, is played by human arts?

In this sentence the participle "season'd" is tenseless and agentless, indicating an action already completed by the time the reader comes upon it; but the agent who effects the action is not identified, nor are the time and manner of its effecting specified. (Certainly neither Moses nor the law he has not yet written has anything to do with it.) Paradoxically, the only direction afforded us is given by the syntactical ambiguity that makes it possible to substitute "God" for Moses as the referent of "knowing": "taught of God, knowing how vaine it was to write lawes to men whose hearts were not first season'd with the knowledge of God." In this reading, of course, God plays all the parts: He perceives the natural obdurateness of the heart; He softens (seasons) it by infusing into it a knowledge of Himself; and then He presents Himself to it in the form of "his lawes." There is no room in the sequence for any agency apart from God, especially not for the native "colours" and graces of speech. Indeed, at this point the values attached in the opening lines to winning persuasion ("persuasion certainly is a more winning . . .") and lordly commands barely set down ("to set them barely forth . . . as it were a lordly command") are being reversed; and this reversal is complete at the end of the sentence, when reason, another form of persuasion, is, in effect, absorbed into obedience: "That the nation of the Jewes, reading therein the universall goodnesse of God . . . might be mov'd to obey sincerely by knowing so good a reason of their obedience." The "reason" that moves the Jews to obey is the goodness of God, hardly a reason in the conventional sense and certainly not one provable by a syllogism or by any other logical process.

When "reason" next appears, we find it is first "requir'd" and then it will "demand":

If then in the administration of civill justice, and under the obscurity of Ceremoniall rites, such care was had by the wisest of the heathen, and by *Moses* among the Jewes, to instruct them at least in a generall reason of that government to which their subjection was requir'd, how much more ought the members of the Church under the Gospell seeke to informe their understanding in the reason of that government which the Church claimes to have over them: especially for that the church hath in her immediate cure those inner parts and affections of the mind where the seat of reason is; having power to examine our spirituall knowledge, and to demand from us in Gods behalfe a service intirely reasonable.   (I, 747–748)

Again two epistemological models jostle against each other within the confines of a syntactic unit, as the status of the reader undergoes a series of progressive diminutions. First we are being "instructed" (with Milton's Jews) in a "generall reason," and presumably in any situation to which those terms would be appropriate our participation would be important; "government" is a slight dissonance, moving, as it does, almost imperceptibly in the direction of a reason imposed, or no reason at all; with "subjection" we are rudely and unceremoniously (the adverb is carefully chosen) shown our true position vis-à-vis the government God would have us accept; and "requir'd" takes away any suggestion that the initiative, or for that matter the choice (for reason is but choosing), is ours. Only fifteen words separate "instruct" and "requir'd," but the reader who has negotiated the distance between them has exchanged one way of looking at the world for another, moving from a context in which rational processes have some place in the consideration of matters spiritual to another in which reason and the assent of a reasoning mind are somehow superfluous. And this journey is retraced when the reader is brought from the circumlocutory blandness of "seeke to informe their understanding" to the nakedness of "demand." The phrase "intirely reasonable" is finally mocking.

The pattern of these two sentences can be found on every page of *The Reason of Church Government*, and always the effect is to discredit reason and reasonings, even when the word itself does not appear: "Whether therefore discipline be all one with doctrine, or the particular application thereof to this or that person, we all agree that doctrine must be such only as is commanded" (I, 761). Here the very form of the syntax generates all the expectations raised in other places by the direct invocation of "reason." The juxtaposition of "whether" and "therefore" generates two sets of related expectations: "whether" leaves us awaiting an "or," and of course with this kind of construction the alternatives are assumed to be something on the order of contradictories. "Therefore" reinforces the promise of logicality without delimiting it. Whatever the "content" of the sentence, we feel that it can be organized and "placed" (that is, explained) within the rational framework of which this syntax is one manifestation. "Discipline," with its strong suggestion of order and regularity, does nothing at all to upset the reader's complacency, while the nicely lilting alliteration of "discipline" and "doctrine" lends a slight, but not unfelt, stylistic support to the assumptions the sentence has been encouraging. In the next clause two new and complementary contexts are alluded to: the opposition of "all" to "particular" is faintly scholastic, and the rather stiff formality of "thereof to this or that person" is decidedly legalistic. (The echo of "therefore" in "thereof" makes its own small contribution.) When the sentence begins its downward motion with "we all agree," we anticipate a conclusion that accords perfectly with what has gone before. Instead we are brought up hard against "commanded" (the impetus of the rhythm virtually deposits us on it), and with that word whatever claims had been made, silently, in the names of reason, logic, and law, are peremptorily swept away by a lordly command. The "whether . . . or" construction must now be read as "it doesn't matter which"; the force of "therefore" is blunted by a verb that overrides all "therefores"; and the illusion of choice projected by "we all agree" fades before the acknowledgment of a power whose commands make agreement unnecessary.

To this point we have two sets of sentences, more or less randomly chosen: in one the "logical statement" is "eventually swamped" by "the piling up of images and of powerfully evocative associations"; in the other, the logical statement completes itself, but is finally revealed to be either circular or self-defeating. What is common to both is the experience they give, or force upon, the reader, the experience of discarding discursive structures and moving in toward a direct confrontation with the object, whether it be God's command or the nakedly exposed faces of the two ministries. That is, the choice-but-no-choice these sentences proffer in their different ways amounts to saying (again and again), "For God's sake (and your own) see things as they really are" without the mediating and distorting screen of "coverings," "outsides," and "reasons formally set down," all of which are finally equivalent. Rather than content, these sentences offer a strategy, a strategy designed to realize the hope Milton expresses in the sixth chapter of the first book: "But my hope is that the people of England will not suffer themselves to be juggl'd thus out of their faith and religion by a mist of names cast before their eyes, but will search wisely by the Scriptures, and look quite through this fraudulent aspersion of a disgracefull name into the things themselves" (I, 788).

Looking *through* the mists (of names, reasons, "gaudy glisterings") and *into* things is exactly the motion Milton's prose encourages, indirectly in some places and with immediate and spectacular force in others:

We shall be able by this time to discern whether Prelaticall jurisdiction be contrary to the Gospell or no. First therefore the government of the Gospell being economicall and paternall, that is, of such a family where there be no servants, but all sons in obedience, not in servility, as cannot be deny'd by him that lives but within the sound of Scripture, how can the Prelates justifie to have turn'd the fatherly orders of Christs houshold, the blessed meeknesse of his lowly roof, those ever open and inviting dores of his dwelling house which delight to be frequented with only filiall accesses, how can they justifie to have turn'd these domestick privileges into the barre of a proud judiciall court where fees and clamours keep shop and drive a trade, where bribery and corruption solicits, paltring the free and monilesse power of discipline with a carnall satisfaction by the purse. Contrition, humiliation, confession, the very sighs of a repentant spirit are there sold by the penny. That undeflour'd and unblemishable simplicity of the Gospell, nor she her selfe, for that could never be, but a false-whited, a lawnie resemblance of her, like that aire-born *Helena* in the fables, made by the sorcery of Prelats, instead of calling her Disciples from the receit of custome, is now turn'd Publican her self; and gives up her body to a mercenary whordome under those fornicated arches which she cals Gods house, and in the sight of those her altars which she hath set up to be ador'd makes merchandize of the bodies and souls of men. Rejecting purgatory for no other reason, as it seems, then because her greedines cannot deferre but had rather use the utmost extortion of redeemed penances in this life. But because these matters could not be thus carri'd without a begg'd and borrow'd force from worldly autority, therefore prelaty slighting the deliberat and chosen counsell of Christ in his spirituall government, whose glory is in the weaknesse of fleshly things to tread upon the crest of the worlds pride and violence by the power of spirituall ordinances, hath on the contrary made these her freinds and champions which are Christs enemies in this his high designe, smothering and extinguishing the spirituall force of his bodily weaknesse in the discipline of his Church with the boistrous and carnall tyranny of an undue, unlawfull and ungospellike jurisdiction.

(I, 848–850)

We begin with a clearly defined three-dimensional situation, a speaker about to make a point by appealing to his audience's reason: an "I," a "thou," and an "it." With "First therefore" the reader girds himself for a rigorous mental exercise; the mode of discourse will be logical and the argument quite lengthy, moving, presumably, from first to second to third and so on. The expectation of logical rigor is strengthened by the speaker's apparent concern to define his terms; there is a progressive clarification of the phrase "economicall and paternall," first by "that is" and the clause it introduces, and then by the "but . . . not" pattern within the clause itself. This is, apparently, the proposition that will be the basis of the conclusion, and the care Milton takes with it validates his claim to the reader's (rational) attention.

With "how can the Prelates," however, we experience the first of two shifts in the direction of the syntax; the sudden introduction of the interrogative mode forces a revision in our expectations of what is to come. The dislocation is momentary, however, and the adjustment is made easily; the logic of the sequence will be less formal than had been anticipated, perhaps an enthymeme rather than a complete proof, but logically based it will presumably be. The repetition, within a few lines, of the "how can they" formula serves to settle the syntax in its new track and we fall easily into the anticipatory rhythm of a question. It is at this point that the sentence shifts again, breaking away entirely from its syntactical and logical moorings. The key word is "where"; ostensibly the occasion of a slight detour in the journey toward the awaited question mark, the "where" construction instead takes over the sentence, and its influence is extended to the sentences (if they are sentences) that follow. The question mark is never reached; nor do we continue to expect it, since the force of the interrogative is less and less felt. In its place we have the thrust of a series of suspended clauses, all ruled by "where." Nor is it long before these clauses break free even of "where" and present themselves to the reader directly, without sponsor and without a mediating discursive framework. For as the organizing and directing pressure of the syntax is relaxed, the sense of a voice, and of a temporal and spatial context enclosing both the voice and its audience, fades. "Where" has become "here and now" and there is suddenly no distance at all, physical or epistemological, between the reader and the truth. Things no longer come to him through the medium of a structured and structuring syntax, but in their essence, as they are in the structure of reality, to which he now has access; he is literally immersed in the words (and things) on the page. Now and here, not in a sentence spoken by an identifiable voice, are contrition, humiliation, and confession sold by the penny; now and here, the false semblance of the true Gospel sets herself up to be adored. And the reader sees and interprets these things himself; he is, in the truest sense of the word, an eyewitness, and because he is an eyewitness, the sentence that ends the sequence, the sentence with which we began, is, as it was meant to be, an anticlimax:

And thus Prelaty both in her fleshly supportments, in her carnall doctrine of ceremonie and tradition, in her violent and secular power going quite counter to the prime end of Christs comming in the flesh, that is to revele his truth, his glory and his might in a clean contrary manner then Prelaty seeks to do, thwarting and defeating the great mistery of God, I do not conclude that Prelaty is Antichristian, for what need I? the things themselves conclude it.   (I, 850)

"What need I conclude?" In the light of what I have been saying about *The Reason of Church Government*, this question might be rephrased to read, "What need I write?" For if the reason of church government is the command of God, and if the command of God is discovered not by rational investigation but by illumined eyes (a matter of eyesight rather than of disquisition), and if illumination is in turn the gift of that same God, there would seem to be no place for a tract that assays to "prove" the right of one of the contending parties to be the "faithfull feeders" of the Christian flock. And indeed there is not, nor has Milton written such a tract; in the sense suggested by "prove" and other related words, he has not written anything at all. For, as we have seen, in the sentences that fill up his pages the discursive framework either abdicates its responsibility to the imagery or resolves itself into a tautology (goes nowhere) or, as in this last example, simply falls away, leaving the reader with the firm, but antirational, exhortation, "open your eyes." Lest this conclusion seem paradoxical, let me point out that it merely confirms, from a different direction, the judgments of Hamilton, who complains of a "ratiocinative emptiness," and of Don Wolfe, who finds *The Reason of Church Government* "a weak presentation of Presbyterian claims," an "almost irrelevant document." [4] It could be nothing else, given the principles Milton espouses; the only things the work finally proves or "declares" are its own insufficiency and irrelevancy to the proposed task. This is the effect, as we have seen, of individual sentences, and it is also the effect of the whole, which displays, on a much larger scale, the pattern of individual sentences.

The reader perhaps has noted that the passages analyzed in the preceding pages are very much like one another, not only in form and movement, but even in their phrasing; and yet they were chosen at random from different sections and chapters of the pamphlet. What the similarities suggest is that there is no progressive advancement in the argument, merely the unceasing repetition of a few key words—"fleshly," "pure," "clear," "carnal," "spiritual," and so on—which are themselves implicated in a limited number of set relationships. Rather than reason or reasoning, we have resonance. Of course these repetitions are embedded in a surface rhetoric that displays (rather ostentatiously) all the signs of a logical structure: the division into two books, separated by an openly (and seemingly ingenuously) labeled digression; the further divisions into chapters, complete with opening and concluding sentences and summarizing headings. But even here, Milton gives the game away. The headings for chapters i and ii read as follows: "*That Church-governement is prescrib'd in the Gospell, and that to say otherwise is unsound*" (I, 750); "*That Church governement is set downe in holy Scripture, and that to say otherwise is untrue*" (I, 756). The similarities in form are obvious and revealing. An assertion of the proposition to be proved is followed by what would appear to be an anticipatory refutation of the opposing party's position; the rising rhythm of "that to say otherwise" leads us to expect that what follows will be equal in length (and force) to the clause controlled by the first "That." Instead we are met by the sudden abruptness of the conclusion, "is unsound," "is untrue." All the force generated by the sequence is concentrated in the final words. Those words are what we carry away with us, and they prejudice us against the "otherwise" before it is even heard. In still another way, then, the proffered illusion of reasonable and rigorous argument is subverted from within.

[4] *Complete Prose Works*, ed. Wolfe et al., I, 199.

Even more destructive of that illusion, however, is the inter-changeability of the two chapter headings. In Milton's lexicon "unsound" and "untrue" are synonyms; "Gospell" and "holy Scripture" are synonyms in anyone's lexicon, as are "set downe" and "prescribe." The rhythms are the same, the number of syllables is more or less equal, and the force of the constructions, as we have seen, is identical. The reader who moves from chapter to chapter has not really moved at all, except perhaps in a circle, back to the point of origin; although time is consumed and distances, in print and pages, are negotiated, there is no substantive advance in the argument. Chapter vii of the first book is another case in point. The heading reads, "*That those many Sects and Schismes by some suppos'd to be among us, and that rebellion in* Ireland, *ought not to be a hindrance, but a hastning of reformation*" (I, 794). In the first sentence we are told, in effect, that the problem itself is a fabrication of those who see sects and schisms where there are none: "As for those many Sects and divisions rumor'd abroad to be amongst us, it is not hard to perceave that they are partly the meere fictions and false alarmes of the Prelates, thereby to cast amazements and panick terrors into the hearts of weaker Christians." (Once more, the "emperor's clothes" ploy; you, not being one of these weaker Christians, perceive this, don't you?) Having dismissed the issue as a fiction, Milton proceeds to the inevitable conclusion, not really a conclusion at all: "And thus I leave it as a declared truth, that neither the feare of sects no nor rebellion can be a fit plea to stay reformation, but rather to push it forward with all possible diligence and speed" (I, 800). By "declared truth" Milton means a truth not proven, one not requiring proof. This final sentence is nothing more than a reformulation ("stay" for "hindrance," "push it forward" for "hastning") of the point originally made by the chapter heading, a point beyond which we have not advanced at all. Of course, *something* must be going on in the interim—there are some five pages between the opening and the closing of the chapter—but whatever it is (and we shall return to it), it is not the chain of inferences one might expect to find in a work entitled *The Reason of Church Government*.

In a very real sense, then, *The Reason of Church Government* is a grotesquely huge parody of one of its self-cannibalizing sentences. Outwardly it presents itself as a series of carefully reasoned arguments, complete with propositions, proofs, and conclusions, and tied together in a larger logical framework by numbered chapters and books, the whole rising toward a grand and triumphant *quod erat demonstrandum.* But actually—that is, in terms of what the reader actually experiences while he is inside the tract—these highly visible ligatures have no determining force at all (just as the syntactic ligatures of individual sentences have no determining force), and the divisions supposedly marked out by them have only a physical existence. Doors keep opening in *The Reason of Church Government,* and the reader keeps passing through them only to find himself in the room he has just left. The silent claim made by the logical superstructure is that it processes truth, but in fact its machinery merely marks out areas within which the reader, or at least one kind of reader, experiences a series of recognitions (or rememberings) of what he has always known to be true; and these recognitions occur independently of the pressure exerted by numbered chapters, divisions into books, first or second reasons, "thuses" and "therefores." Of course this pressure does exist, and it reasserts itself each time a chapter begins or ends; but for the reader whose responses are answerable to Milton's vision, these moments are merely occasions for the taking of a mental breath and not, as the surface rhetoric implies, signposts marking another stage in the building of a rational structure.

In effect, *The Reason of Church Government* has two structures (as do many of its sentences): an outer structure that promises rational argument, progressive clarification, and encapsulated knowledge; and an inner structure whose points are made at the expense of the other's promises. And these two in their relationship add still another coordinate pair to the opposing and interchangeable correspondences that constitute the tract's only true argument:

darknesse	clearnesse
reasons formally set down	reasons that imply themselves
those who have not heeded the drift and scope of Christian profession	those who have
prelacy	Presbyterianism
the outer form of the tract	the inner form of the tract
those readers who look to the outer form for direction and meaning	those readers who see through the outer form to the one stable meaning

"A study of the prose of Milton," writes Thomas Kranidas, "becomes in large part a study of the way things are complexly unified or related, and the dangerous ways in which they are disunified." [5] *The Reason of Church Government* not only provides support for this statement, but as an object it itself exemplifies the principle of unity which is, as Kranidas points out, one of Milton's "obsessions." The structure or structures of the tract reflect exactly the structures of the systems of church government which are its subject; and these in turn are mirror images of the minds of the two classes of readers to whom Milton continually refers, one in bondage to the fleshly world and therefore to reason and prelacy, the other illumined by the same saving faith that sustains the poet-speaker himself. It is to the latter reader that the radical unity of the piece—the illusoriness of its parts, the sameness of its argument at all points, which are finally one and the same point—is at once apparent.

To some extent, then, I agree with Hamilton when he implies that *The Reason of Church Government* does not say anything at all ("a lack of real intellectual content"), but this is not the same thing as concluding that it does not mean anything at all. It is simply that the locus of meaning is not the printed page, where quite literally nothing is happening, but the mind of the reader, where everything is happening. Recently, when I asked a group of students what they remembered from reading *The Reason of Church Government* the night before, they answered not with propositions or chains of inferences but with words, and groups of words, that came tumbling out haphazardly, and yet arranged somehow in the patterns of relationship we have observed in particular passages. I cannot re-create their response in all its associative spontaneity, but an equivalent effect is produced simply by rehearsing, in the order of their appearance, two lists of opposing phrases and images:

gross, patched, varnished, embellishings, veil, sumptuous, tradition, show, visibility, polluted, idolatrous, Gentilish, rites, ceremonies, feather, bravery, hide, deformed, plumes, pomp, flesh, outward, ceremonial law, delusions, parti-colored, mimic, custom, specious, sophistical, names, fallacy, mask, dividing, schismatical, forked, disfigurement, Egyptian, overcloud, scales, false, glitter, beads, art, sweet, dim, reflection, fleshly wisdom, garb, defaced, overcasting, copes, vestures, gold robes, surplices, adorn, corporeal resemblances, clothing, maskers, gaudy glisterings, delude, carnal, high, sensual, fermentations, worldly,

[5] *The Fierce Equation* (The Hague, 1965), p. 57.

external, flourishes, counterfeit, crafty, artificial, appearance, outward man, skin, defile, ignorance, pride, temples, carpets, tablecloth, slimy, confections, profane, faulty, false-whited, gilded, vanities, dross, scum, luggage, infection, formal outside, greasy, brazen, temporal, oil over, besmear, corrupt, shadow, darkened, obscured.

plainly, clearness, eternal, invariable, inspired, open, spiritual eye, inward, plain, clear, evident, pure, spiritual, simple, lowly, internal, faith, homogeneous, even, firm, unite, truth, steadfastness, perfection, unity, seamless, unchangeable, constancy, light, sacred, illumination, luster, inspiration, revelation, eye-brightening, inward prompting, divine, bright, belief, common sense, simplicity, clear evidence, naked, inward holiness, inward beauty, bareness, lowliness, purity of doctrine, wisdom of God, glory, enlightened, true knowledge, holy, cleansed, health, purge, God's word.[6]

What will strike the reader of these two lists at once, I think, is the presence of an argument, even in the absence of a discursive syntax. Statements of relationships form themselves unbidden simply because the words and phrases so obviously belong together. And the relationship continues to be obvious even when the words appear in a syntactical structure: ". . . however in *shew* and *visibility* it may seeme a part of his Church, yet in as much as it lyes thus unmeasur'd he leaves it to be trampl'd by the Gentiles, that is to be *polluted* with *idolatrous* and *Gentilish rites* and *ceremonies*" (I, 761). The order of the italicized words is the order of their (consecutive) appearance in the list, and the impression they make in the two contexts is remarkably similar. In one the mere fact of their contiguity suffices to generate connections; in the other, the connections supplied by the syntax are overwhelmed by the connections the words themselves generate. Were one asked to form a sentence of these words, the result would no doubt be something like this: "The show and visibility of Gentilish rites and ceremonies are evidence of the pollution of idolatry." And that is exactly the import of the sentence in which they do in fact appear. The organizing pressure of the "however . . . yet" construction makes very little difference, for the construction is finally not the agency of relationship. Its only effect is to focus attention on the indeterminate "it," a neutral counter that draws to itself the multiple and complementary associations of the surrounding words. They *are* the sentence at the same time that their interrelation-

[6] These lists record only initial occurrences; the repeated appearance of many of these words and phrases intensifies the effect analyzed below.

ships are independent of its structure. That is, the source of the fellowship they so obviously (self-evidently) share is to be found outside the framework that happens, for the moment, to contain them. What is true of these words and a single sentence is true of the full list and the entire tract.

In fact one can, in a sense, rewrite the "entire tract" by rearranging the two lists into a table of natural contraries:

carnal	spiritual	covered	naked
false	true	earthly	divine
sight	faith	veil	clear
varnished	plain	schism	unity
outer	inner	sophistical	simple
darkness	light	pride	lowliness
polluted	pure	clothing	bareness
idolatrous	holy	profane	sacred
hid	open	slimy	clean

Of course the list is by no means complete, and even if there were space enough to continue indefinitely the result would still be a distortion; for not only does each term interact with its opposing fellow, it is also, by virtue of its vertical relationships, implicated in all the other single oppositions. Obviously the entire complex of interrelationships cannot be represented on the printed page (mine or Milton's), for it is not finally linear. Its true medium, because it is the only medium flexible enough to hold in solution all the shifting patterns, is the reader's consciousness. I return, by a kind of back door, to the idea of a progress in *The Reason of Church Government:* not, of course, to the "ratiocinative progress" whose absence Hamilton deplores, but to a progressive enlargement of the understanding. Hamilton and I agree, in our different ways, that the reader who negotiates these hundred or so pages is not following an argument. Yet he must be doing something, and what he is doing, with varying degrees of self-consciousness, is accumulating and cross-referencing pairs of coordinate words and images on either side of a great divide; as these pairs succeed one another, not on the page but in the mind, they lose their discreteness and become, in the process of (reading) time, interchangeable. That is to say, at some point (and I will not specify it), one reads "Prelacy" in (not into) the word "profane" and "profane" in the word "Prelacy" and both in the phrase "fair outsides" and, conversely, "Presbyter" in the word "pure" and "pure" in the word "Presbyter" and both in "inward." The reader proceeds in space and

time and from point to point, but always to find the same un-
changing essences ("we see them with our eyes") shining through
their local manifestations. The form (of sentence, paragraph, chap-
ter, book, whole) may be linear, but the experience is finally static,
and so I come back finally to Hamilton, whose description is in the
end as accurate as his judgment was premature: ". . . the reader
inevitably begins to get the impression that nothing is being offered
him beyond words, that he is getting nowhere, gaining no real illu-
mination. Milton, as a dialectician, is at times given to jumping up
and down in one place." It is the reader, of course, as well as Mil-
ton, who is jumping up and down in one place, but as the referents
of single words and images keep expanding and coalescing, the
horizons of that place are extended until it contains in one im-
mediately available area all the other places one might have reached
discursively. The reader may be getting nowhere, but from the
vantage point provided by his enlarged understanding, nowhere is
equivalent to everywhere. In this sense *The Reason of Church
Government* can be said to participate in the great work pro-
claimed by Milton in the *Areopagitica*, the gathering up of the
scattered limbs or refracted images of Truth so that her "lovely
form" (and its opposites) can once more be perceived, whole and
entire.[7]

[7] Of course this account holds only for the reader who is already of Milton's
party. Milton makes no concession at all to the hostile reader who presumably
would complain, as Hamilton and Wolfe do, of weak arguments and circular logic.
Here at least Milton is not practicing the office of a pulpit, for he declines to
persuade. In *Paradise Lost* the net is cast more widely and the assumed in-
transigence of the reader dictates his method of procedure. See Stanley Fish,
Surprised by Sin: The Reader in "Paradise Lost" (New York and London,
1967), *passim*.

VI

MILTON ON
RAMIST SIMILITUDE

Christopher Grose

On 10 September 1802, in a well-known letter to Sotheby, Cole-
ridge declared that "Nature has her proper interest." Furthermore,

He will know what it is who believes and feels that everything has a
life of its own and that we are all *One Life*. A poet's heart and intellect
should be combined, intimately combined and unified with the great
appearances of nature, and not merely held in solution and loose mix-
ture with them, in the shape of formal similes.[1]

In making a poem's figures the measure of the poet's vision, Cole-
ridge was not speaking of *Paradise Lost*. Indeed, by the time he
wrote *Biographia Literaria* he had found an illuminating descrip-
tion of unfallen perception, and hence the antithesis of the "formal
simile," in Raphael's famous lecture on the "bright consummate
flow'r," which appeared as the epigraph for chapter xiii on the
imagination. Still, the earlier passage illuminates Milton's poem,
even in opposing the oneness of all life (or the poet's perception of
it) to that unmistakable stylistic index of Milton's supposedly dis-
sociated sensibility, the formal simile. For while we may gather
from Coleridge's chapter xiii that Raphael's metaphysics is in-
separable from the psychological and discursive tenor that only
gradually emerges from his speech,[2] in the poem that metaphysics

[1] See M. H. Abrams, *The Mirror and the Lamp: Romantic Theory and the
Critical Tradition* (New York, 1953), pp. 294, 386 n. 101.
[2] O *Adam*, one Almighty is, from whom
All things proceed, and up to him return,
If not deprav'd from good, created all

103

is less often experienced or enacted than described. We must admit that, to the extent that *Paradise Lost* images the perceptual experience of the poet rather than the more hieratic and discursive justification it claims to present, the work itself in its most characteristic passages reveals less the true Coleridgean poet than the maker of similitudes.[3]

It is interesting, therefore, to discover a similar emphasis in parts of Milton's own theory. Contained in the twenty-first chapter of his early and largely Ramist *Art of Logic*, Milton's discussion of logical similitude betrays a cautious skepticism regarding the connection of metaphysics and comparative figures. The handbook may be less interesting to students of the poetry than Raphael's tantalizing remarks about the difficulties of presenting the War in Heaven, for example. By and large, the *Art of Logic* merely demonstrates the extent of Milton's familiarity with current and fashionable theory regarding similitude, but we do find some significant independence from Ramist methods and even assumptions. As we shall see, Milton ultimately pulls back from linking "similars" with the proportion inherent in nature, only to direct the reader's attention to the maker of "formal simile," whatever the context or medium of his argument. And because a total theory of knowledge and language is involved, the similitudes of the poet are as pertinent as those of the dialectician.

> Such to perfection, one first matter all,
> Indu'd with various forms, various degrees
> Of substance, and in things that live, of life;
> But more refin'd, more spiritous, and pure,
> As nearer to him plac't or nearer tending
> Each in thir several active Spheres assign'd,
> Till body up to spirit work, in bounds
> Proportion'd to each kind. So from the root
> Springs lighter the green stalk, from thence the leaves
> More aery, last the bright consummate flow'r
> Spirits odorous breathes: flow'rs and thir fruit
> Man's nourishment, by gradual scale sublim'd
> To vital spirits aspire, to animal,
> To intellectual, give both life and sense,
> Fancy and understanding, whence the Soul
> Reason receives, and reason is her being,
> Discursive, or Intuitive. (*Paradise Lost*, V, 469–488)

Aside from ending the quotation where he did, Coleridge departed somewhat from Milton's text, notably in substituting "nature" for "matter" in the fourth line quoted. All references to *Paradise Lost* are from Merritt Y. Hughes, ed., *John Milton: Complete Poems and Major Prose* (New York, 1957).

[3] That Milton was less a Coleridgean poet than a maker of similes was virtually the complaint of the anti-Miltonists. There is a brief account of the argument, with a short bibliography, in my article, "Some Uses of Sensuous Immediacy in *Paradise Lost*," *Huntington Library Quarterly*, XXXI (1968), 211–212.

Milton's only formal theory of similitude appeared, then, in the handbook of logic entitled *Artis Logicae Plenior Institutio*.[4] The *Art of Logic*, as I shall call it, was published in May 1672, between the first and second editions of *Paradise Lost* and one year after the publication of *Paradise Regained* and *Samson Agonistes*. It is probably a mistake to assume that the *Art of Logic* embodies Milton's considered or current opinions as a literary artist, since for the most part it is a thoroughly traditional rehandling of the Ramist textbooks, in particular the *Dialectica* of Petrus Ramus himself and the *Commentarii* (1601) of the influential praelector in logic at Cambridge, George Downame, which were in all likelihood Milton's two prime sources. Even if Milton wholeheartedly embraced the system he expounds and amplifies in the *Art of Logic*— a system necessarily far more beholden to classical authors and even to Aristotle than it pretends—the evidence suggests that the work was largely composed long before its publication, perhaps between Milton's two degrees at Cambridge (i.e., between 1629 and 1632), a period of some controversy between the Ramists and the Aristotelians of that university.[5] Appearing as it did in 1672, Milton's *Art of Logic* may best be viewed as the early production of an author currently famous for epic and tragic literary works, rather than as the poetics of a practicing artist. In its manner it is patently a university product, clarifying a traditional text and seeking to make "copiously clear" a system that had too often been obscurely expounded.[6]

Some, though by no means all, of the difficulties can be set aside. We need not accept Franklin Irwin's argument for a late date, based on the anti-Trinitarian remarks *solus pater est verus deus* and on the assumption that Milton lost faith in the Trinity after 1641. The remark could easily have been interpolated.[7] More serious is the claim, advanced by G. C. Moore Smith, that by 1644 Milton

[4] See *The Works of John Milton*, ed. F. A. Patterson et al. (18 vols.; New York, 1931–1938), XI, vi (hereafter cited as *Works*) for the full title: JOANNIS MILTONI / Angli, / Artis Logicae / Plenior Institutio, / AD / PETRI RAMI / Methodum concinnata, // LONDINI, / Impensis *Spencer Hickman*, So- / cietatis Regalis Typographi, ad / insigne *Rosae* in *Caemeterio*, / D. Pauli. 1672.

[5] The date of composition is unknown (W. R. Parker, *Milton: A Biography* [2 vols.; Oxford, 1968], II, 938 n. 67).

[6] For the quite different claim that Renaissance poets thought Ramus to be "nothing if not lucid; . . . fit only for simpletons," see George Watson, "Ramus, Miss Tuve, and the New Petromachia," *Modern Philology*, LV (1957–58), 259–262.

[7] Franklin Irwin, "Ramistic Logic in Milton's Prose Works" (Ph.D. dissertation, Princeton University, 1941); see W. S. Howell, *Logic and Rhetoric in England, 1500–1700* (Princeton, 1956), p. 215.

had "lost his passion" for logic.[8] In the letter to Samuel Hartlib now known as *Of Education,* published with his *Poems* in 1673, Milton does say that in logic students should have only "so much as is usefull." [9] But Milton is discussing the crucial last phase in his educational scheme, the "organic arts" of "discourse" (one meaning of the Greek *logos*), including logic, rhetoric, and, "subsequent, or indeed rather precedent" to these, poetry. Taken together, these arts "enable men to discourse and write perspicuously, elegantly, and according to the fitted stile of lofty, mean, or lowly." [10] For Milton merely indicates here, as in the *Art of Logic* itself, that he requires only as much logic as is useful in the highest "organic arts." His attack on logic is the conventional Ramist (and Protestant) attack on syllogistic, scholastic logic, which he elsewhere associated with both a jingling verbalism and "airy visions" (*leves quaedam imagines*), and which he had distinguished, somewhat vaguely, from a "more accurate wisdom" (*rectioris sapientiae*).[11]

The likelihood that this handbook does not really represent Milton's own theory is much less important, however, than the fact, which it makes unmistakably clear, that whether or not he is a Ramist, Milton is thoroughly familiar with the schematic view of arguing by "similars," a view that, with obvious literary implications, must have been virtually a mental habit. Locating his discussion of similitude in the context of the entire Ramist *tabula generalis* of logical invention, Milton begins by distinguishing similitude from other comparative arguments which articulate relationships in quantitative terms. Things that are like have the same logical quality, for

logical quality is not merely habit, or disposition, or natural potency or impotency, or finally figure or exterior form, which are the Aristotelian species of quality, and to be treated in other arts, but is a certain affect or ratio by which things compared among themselves are said to be of a certain sort, namely, like or unlike. But there is nothing which when compared with another in quality is not either like it or unlike it.[12]

---

[8] G. C. Moore Smith, "A Note on Milton's *Art of Logic,*" *Review of English Studies,* XIII (1937), 335–340.
[9] *Complete Prose Works of John Milton,* ed. Don M. Wolfe et al. (New Haven, 1953–), II, 402 (hereafter cited as *Complete Prose*).
[10] *Ibid.,* pp. 401, 403.
[11] See Prolusion III, *Works,* XII, 166–167, 168–169.
[12] *Works,* XI, 193.

The three main points in the Ramist treatment of the subject may be summarized as follows.

1) Formal elements in the argument by similitude. We can distinguish similars from other kinds of argument first by their signs (*notae*), and, more fully, by structural elements or parts. Short signs of similitude comprised in one word are either the properties of similar things or the denial of dissimilars; the proper signs of similars may be nouns ("like," "effigy," "image," etc.), adverbs ("like," "as," "as if," etc.) or verbs ("imitate," "reproduce," etc.). In examples and in text Milton follows his sources, making clear what Addison would still claim in 1712, that metaphor is essentially a "similar," a "similitude contracted to one word without signs, which, however, are understood," [13] a formulation unacceptable to later critics.

2) Sometimes similars are fully developed and are thus recognizable from structural elements or parts as well as from the framing signs. Structurally, similars are seen to be of two basic forms, "disjunct" and "continued"; they are disjunct when two terms or distinct things in the context are compared with two terms or distinct things in the "similar" argument, and they are continued when *"as the first term is to the second, so the second is to the third."* [14] At this point Milton reveals a characteristic and important attitude in the Ramist tradition he is following: ". . . proportion not merely mathematical but also logical is common to all things." What follows from this premise is that, given a likeness in the proposition and the reddition, there is also an inverse and alternative likeness among the terms themselves. Milton illustrates both terms and practice at some length with a favorite example of Ramist writers:

As the best governors of ships oftentimes may not overcome the strength and rage of the tempest, so the most wise man may not always vanquish the invasion and violence of fortune.

. . . if they [the terms] are similar, they are also similar inversely and alternately. Inversely in two manners, obviously by inversion of the proposition and reddition, which is common to other comparatives, or of the terms, which seems proper to similars. For example, *As the pilot is to the tempest, so is the wise man to fortune;* inversely, therefore, it will be *As the wise man is to fortune, so is the pilot to the tempest.* This is inversion of the proposition and reddition. Again, *As is the*

---

[13] *Ibid.*, pp. 195, 197; see *Spectator*, no. 303 (16 February 1712).
[14] *Works*, XI, 197–201.

tempest to the pilot, so is fortune to the wise man; this is inversion of
the terms. Alternation is when the antecedent of the proposition is
compared with the antecedent of the reddition, and the consequent to
its consequent. The rule here, therefore, is that if things are similar
they are alternately similar. *As is the pilot to the tempest, so is the wise
man to fortune;* therefore, alternately, *As is the pilot to the wise man,
so is the tempest to fortune.*[15]

3) Following this revealing (if also tedious) analysis, which
should heighten our appreciation of the emblematic value in Mil-
ton's own maritime similes, Milton concludes his chapter by ex-
tending even further the scope of argument by similitude: *"The
fictitious similitude* [the apologues of Aesop and the so-called
Socratic parables serve as precedents] *has equal force in argument"*
with the similars previously mentioned.[16]

What are we to make of this brief, laborious text, which seems
to be neither original nor current in Milton's mature thinking and
writing? The only "pure" discussion of simile we have places the
argument of similitude in the matrix of logical invention, among
the "artificial" arguments—those that depend upon intrinsic ra-
tionality rather than upon *auctoritas.* None of the comparative ar-
guments is precisely equivalent to the simile with which we are
familiar in the epic tradition; nor does the comparative group as
a whole come close to describing the complexities of Milton's own
similes. Milton's chapter on similars might indeed seem to verge
on a complete treatment of simile, partly because it cites examples
of this mode of argument from literature. But as Rosemond Tuve
has said, such citation was commonplace long before Ramus; and,
for Ramist logics, it reinforced the oft repeated point that logic
was a general art. Literature was especially handy, it would seem,
to prove that logic existed (as it were) apart from particular argu-
mentative purposes.[17] Moreover, of the illustrations themselves,
only two are from epic (both from the *Aeneid,* as we might ex-

---

[15] *Ibid.,* pp. 199, 201, 203.
[16] The italics are those of the text (*ibid.,* p. 203). In *An Apology Against a
Pamphlet,* Milton discusses scriptural parable as similitude: "Doth not Christ him-
selfe teach the highest things by the similitude *of old bottles and patcht cloaths?*
Doth he not illustrate best things by things most evill? his own *comming* to be *as
a thiefe in the night* . . . ?" (*Complete Prose,* I, 898).
[17] See A. J. Smith, "An Examination of Some Claims Made for Ramism," *Review
of English Studies,* n.s., VII (1956), 348–359, esp. 351. For a useful and balanced
account of the controversial matter, see K. G. Hamilton, *The Two Harmonies:
Poetry and Prose in the Seventeenth Century* (Oxford, 1963), pp. 108–119, esp. 116.

pect), and only one of these would be recognizable as a true simile.[18] Milton adds no new examples to those accumulated in the handbooks for more than a hundred years. He follows the tradition in mixing his examples from oratory, epistles, fables, and epic.

Yet if we set Milton's chapter beside the corresponding passages in his two chief sources, the *Dialectica* of Ramus and George Downame's *Commentarii*, we discover toward the end of his definition of similars a passage that appears in neither source (in Milton's *Art of Logic* it is marked with an asterisk):

* Monendum autem est similia sive contractae formae sive explicatae urgenda non esse ultra eam qualitatem quam in utrisque eandem esse propositum assimilanti erat ostendere: sic magistratus assimilatur cani, sola nimirum fidelitate custodiae: unde illa in scholis, *nullum simile est idem, simile non currit quatuor pedibus, omne simile claudicat.*[19]

The asterisk marks Milton's most important original departure from his Ramist sources in the chapter. He puts the burden of emphasis on "the man making the comparison" (*assimilanti*)—on the poet's "intention," one might say, as declared in the specific terms for the comparison. By introducing the logical inventor (or poet?), Milton shifts somewhat abruptly from the intrinsic rationality assumed to inhere in all Ramist arguments. Moreover, in citing the school formula *omne simile claudicat*—"every likeness hobbles"—Milton diverts the general thrust of Ramist theory, which in this context begins with the proposition that "proportion not merely mathematical but also logical is common to all things" and moves (inevitably enough, perhaps, given the premise) toward the critical practice of inverting and alternating terms and elements. Significantly, Milton's caveat, apparently so skeptical on an important Ramist assumption, replaces extensive passages in the sources, where Downame and the traditional Ramist writers expand rather boldly the province of similitude. Illustrating the process with mathematical examples, Downame's passage concludes: Solent quidem hae voces a quibusdam ad quantitatum collationes

[18] *Aeneid*, I, 589: *Os humerosque deo similis* ("In countenance and shoulders like a god"); *Works*, XI, 194–195.

[19] Allan H. Gilbert's translation: "Warning, however, should be given that likes whether of short or full form are not to be urged beyond that quality which the man making the comparison intended to show as the same in both. Thus a magistrate is likened to a dog, yet merely in the fidelity of his guardianship, whence came the sayings of the schools: 'Nothing similar is identical; likeness does not run on four feet; every likeness hobbles'" (*Works*, XI, 194–195).

adstringi, verum generalis sunt significationis. Nam et similitudo omnis proportio est, et qualitas omnis ratio est.[20]

What exactly is it that Milton wishes to clarify in handing down the art of logic? As in his letter to Hartlib, Milton surely wishes to avoid the "anxious" and "subtle" employment of art which can actually trammel "those whose native abilities are active and strong." [21] But accompanying his and the Ramists' concern for the talented individual is a Ramistic stress on the limitation of the art itself, as well as of ordinary men's epistemological resources. It is true that logic is one of God's motions in men, as Milton points out in an arresting passage about invention in general:

I suppose no one doubts that the primal mover of every art is God, the author of all wisdom. . . .
The assisting causes were the men divinely taught and eminent for ability who in the past discovered the individual arts. The method of discovering these was much like the method of painting; for as there are in a picture two things—the subject or archetype and the art of painting—so in the discovery of an art, nature or practice and the example of skillful men coresponds to the archetype, and logic to the art of the painter—natural logic at least, which is the very faculty of reason in the mind of man, according to that common saying: Art imitates nature.[22]

The qualification here suggests the more normal emphasis in the handbook. Milton elsewhere defines logic as "the art of reasoning well," adding the word "well," as he says, in order "to distinguish the perfection of the art from the imperfection of the natural faculty." [23] The art of logic works at one remove from the practice or experience of perception; but Milton, speaking as a pedagogue, seems impelled to measure the utility of the art itself against human knowledge in all its frailty. Hence arises the particular value of the comparatives for "making plain," as distinct from "proving":

Before comparison is begun that which the comparatives argue by their nature should be better known and clearer to him with whom

20 "These examples are ordinarily drawn together for the comparison of quantities, but they are of general significance. For every likeness is proportion, and every quality is an argument" (my translation of George Downame, Commentarii in P. Rami [London, 1601], pp. 338–339). This copy, of a book usually studied in a 1669 reprint, is in the Folger Shakespeare Library.
21 See Works, XI, 3, 7.
22 Ibid., p. 11.
23 Ibid., p. 19.

we discuss a comparative than in the thing argued, for something equally obscure would make nothing plain. Hence the extraordinary usefulness of comparatives stands out, for by this it comes about that an unequal knowledge of things by force of comparison is made equal. Thus the consentanies are fittest for proving, the comparatives for making plain.[24]

Such a double attitude, emphasizing at once the perfection of the logical art and the frailty of human knowledge, clearly extends even to the raison d'être for Milton's own publication, which belongs somewhere between the traditional realms of logic and rhetoric.

Two elements in Milton's discussion are of particular interest to readers of his poetry. The more immediate is the role of clarification assigned to "similitude," whether it be simile or metaphor or some larger structure such as a fable. The second element is largely implicit: the underlying epistemological skepticism, the doubt of the power of men's minds. Because this element is largely implicit, it deserves further illustration. Milton is particularly concerned that *"the Theologians awake"* on the rubric of form, for example. Yet part of what emerges from the discussion is a sense of the difficulty of knowing form at all. Form is, of course, the *"cause through which a thing is what it is."* Or again, the "rational soul is the form of man generically; the soul of Socrates is the proper form of Socrates. . . . from form alone comes an essential distinction." [25] Milton allows all this, yet almost immediately he defines the difficulty basic to any knowing as being precisely the confusion between internal form and sensuous experience (i.e., "figure"—a distinction helpful in adjusting our vision to the "darkness visible" of Milton's hell):

[The fact that] cause . . . is the fount of all knowledge, is understood especially to apply to form. For the cause which especially constitutes the essence, if it is noted, above all brings knowledge. But to know the internal form of anything, because it is usually very remote from the senses, is especially difficult. In artificial things, however, the form, as being external and exposed to the senses, is more easily observed. . . .

But there is no true distribution of form. For the distribution of internal or external which some hold will not apply to all things but

[24] *Ibid.*, p. 153.
[25] *Ibid.*, pp. 59, 61.

merely to the corporeal; and the external is not less essential to each artificial thing than the internal to each natural thing.[26]

It would be difficult to surpass this emphasis on the problems faced in acquiring true knowledge. Yet substantially the same attitude pervades Milton's discussion of the relation between "definition" and "description." Since genus and form together make up the essence of a thing,[27] definition is a symbol or virtual equivalent of the thing defined. A perfect definition depends exclusively upon "the causes constituting the essence of the thing defined" [28] and is thus a "universal symbol" of those causes. But because definition requires the knowledge of such elusive entities as form, what normally takes its place is an imperfect definition or description, of which Milton writes:

Because of the obscurity of causes and especially of forms, perfect definitions are difficult to come upon. *Description* has been devised to supply their scarcity. *Description* is an imperfect *definition, defining a thing through other arguments*, that is, explaining the thing in some way from whatever is available.

So where form cannot be had (for the genera are commonly better known) a property must be accepted in place of form or distinguishing difference, as when it is said *An angel is an incorporeal substance;* or *A horse is an animal that whinnies*, etc.[29]

Although Milton does not specify the source of all this confusion—the Fall of Man—it is assumed throughout, and the art of logic exists precisely to remedy the terrible defect. Like *Of Education*, then, the *Art of Logic* helps us "repair the ruins of our first parents," and it is to that end that it points. Again, a critical problem in both treatises concerns the relation between the provinces of logic and language. Early in the book Milton explains the division of the arts in a traditional way, linking speech and reason:

The general material of the artisan is all that which really is or is feigned to be; the general material of art is what the single arts effect upon it all. Reason or speech embraces all this. Hence the general matter of the general arts is either reason or speech. They are employed either in perfecting reason for the sake of proper thinking, as is logic,

[26] *Ibid.*, pp. 61, 63; for a reminder of this kind of difficulty, see p. 253. The observation is in Downame, but not in Ramus.
[27] *Ibid.*, p. 239.
[28] *Ibid.*, p. 263. I have deleted italics.
[29] *Ibid.*, p. 267; again, in Downame, but not in Ramus.

or in perfecting speech, and that either for the sake of the correct use of words, as is grammar, or the effective use of words, as is rhetoric. Of all the arts the first and most general is logic, then grammar, then last of all rhetoric, since there can be much use of reason without speech, but no use of speech without reason.[30]

As Milton has previously indicated, the result is that logic becomes an art of reasoning well; but, more particularly, Milton wishes to dissociate logic from both words and things, to discuss simply an *affectio ad arguendum*, a "fitness for argument" technically called *ratio:*

Logic, therefore, treats neither words nor things. Although it is possible to reason without words, yet from the very necessity for speaking, logic seems with perfect right to demand that whenever it is necessary words should be employed that are distinct and certainly not ambiguous and not inappropriate. Logic leaves things themselves to their appropriate arts; it considers merely what effect or ratio for arguing they have among themselves.[31]

Words, moreover, have historically become dissociated from things, or at least from arguments, as Milton suggests most clearly in his treatment of "notation" or etymology. More is involved here than technicalities. The difficulty of discovering the nominal "symbol of some primitive argument" is simply a manifestation of the general linguistic predicament: ". . . languages, both that first one which Adam spoke in Eden, and those varied ones also possibly derived from the first, which the builders of the tower of Babel suddenly received, are without doubt divinely given; hence it is not strange if the reason [*ratio*] of primitive words is unknown." [32]

Milton enters serious reservations about the human capacity to know truly and about the possibility of recovering in language the "symbol of some primitive argument," even though languages "are without doubt divinely given." By bearing in mind these central assumptions we can best evaluate Milton's own cautionary contributions to the art of likening in logical (and thus poetic) argument. And we should notice that while the discussions are epistemologically skeptical they are also traditionally Ramist. Whatever the relevance of the *Art of Logic* to his rhetorical and poetic theory during the time Milton wrote *Paradise Lost*, the

[30] *Ibid.*, p. 17.
[31] *Ibid.*, pp. 25, 27; throughout this passage *vox* is translated as "word."
[32] See *ibid.*, pp. 219, 221.

treatment of "human names" in the poem, the "alter'd style" of Adam and Eve after the Fall (itself presented partly as an epistemological crisis), Michael's attempt to provide Adam with a new vision—all suggest that the poet's early concern with language was more than pedagogical. Although we must pick our way carefully, the *Art of Logic* is one guidepost for Milton's poems.

The *Art of Logic* itself, we may recall, is what earlier generations would have called a "rhetoric." It may be (as A. J. Smith maintains) that in using examples from literary classics Milton cannot be said to have continued the Ramist tendency to merge logic and poetry. But surely it is not too much to suggest that a logic conceived in the Ramist way, as a general art distinct from both words and things, is at least serviceable for a poetry of wisdom.[33] Within the text, moreover, Milton makes a distinction between definition and description in such a way as to suggest one province for poetry. The distinction arises in the course of a dense argument from the obscurity of causes (an important word in the opening invocation of *Paradise Lost*) to the virtual necessity of description as a mode of argument in logic and poetry.

It is dangerous, if tempting, to speak of the relation between Milton's handbook and the poems in terms more specific than these. All Ramists insist that "likes" (and all comparative arguments) are more fit for making plain than for proving, more descriptive than definitive. All agree on the importance of similars in logical strategy. And as we have seen, a common assumption in Ramist logic is the existence of a logical and mathematical proportion not quite extramental but "common to all things," an assumption likely to be indicated, perhaps, in neat, detailed correspondences between formal image and immediate context. Milton's own practice reveals a familiarity with this tradition, as James Whaler's discussion of Miltonic "homologation" amply demonstrates.[34] On the other hand, although Milton's omission of Downame's illustrative material, taken together with his caveat, obviously implies reservations about certain Ramist views, the practical implications are less clear. Certainly the claim that "every likeness hobbles" was not new when Milton wrote it; indeed, in using this school tag where

[33] See Smith, "Examination of Some Claims," p. 351; Hamilton, *Two Harmonies*, p. 116.

[34] See James Whaler, "Compounding and Distribution of Similes in *Paradise Lost*," *Modern Philology*, XXVIII (1930-31), 313-327; "Grammatical *Nexus* of the Miltonic Simile," *Journal of English and Germanic Philology*, XXX (1931), 327-334; "The Miltonic Simile," *Publications of the Modern Language Association of America*, XLVI (1931), 1034-1074.

he does, Milton confirms the impression, available elsewhere, not only that there are several Ramisms but also that each—Milton's included—accommodates elements both traditional and heterodox. Still, we must admit that Milton is not very helpful to readers of his own similes in putting the burden of the reader's attention on the intention of the poet or arguer, even if by "intention" he means an initial point of comparison. As many readers have noticed, the occasion of likeness in the similes of *Paradise Lost* accounts for only part of their total effect, schematically tight though most of them are. Milton replaced, then, Downame's emphasis on the proportion "common to all things" with a passage invoking what the "assimilating" poet or arguer proposes to show. In doing so he has implicitly refused to encourage examination of the argumentative poem itself, apart from that perplexing cause of its being, the "person" of its poet.

Even if the evidence for Milton's departure from Ramism bulked much more largely than it does in the *Art of Logic,* it would be difficult to assess fairly the question or degree of Milton's Ramism. I wish to imply no such innovation.[35] For readers of literature at any rate, the question itself seems to be asked misleadingly, too ideologically, at least if the answers are an indication. Ramism is variously held to be a cause, more or less immediate, of the Metaphysical style, the plain style, and *Paradise Lost.* One conclusion seems inevitable: either we are dealing with several discrete Ramisms or we have done little more than replace Eliot's "dissociation of sensibility" with another single-cause explanation. In any event, since Walter J. Ong's *Ramus, Method, and the Decay of Dialogue* (1958) it seems much more difficult to insist that one kind of literary strategy or style resulted from what Rosemond Tuve called "the basic realism of the Ramists, their willingness to identify thing with *ratio,* idea with thing-as-it-is." [36] We still need to know how scrupulous Milton's Ramism was. The preoccupation with whether or not Milton was a Ramist has preceded a properly detailed examination of the *Art of Logic* itself. More important, perhaps, we need to discriminate among Ramisms. There is still little agreement on what bearing such scruples as Milton's,

[35] For the most interesting and radical acceptance of Milton's Ramism, see Jackson I. Cope, *The Metaphoric Structure of "Paradise Lost"* (Baltimore, 1962), pp. 27–49; his review of the controversy over Ramistic influence is helpful, along with that of K. G. Hamilton, noted above.
[36] Rosemond Tuve, *Elizabethan and Metaphysical Imagery* (Chicago, 1947), p. 350 n. 21.

or as those of Ramism itself, might have had on the writing or reading of poetic imagery.

About the poem's (as distinct from the poet's) epistemology we can be somewhat more specific. In writing the words about the poet's "heart and intellect" with which we began, Coleridge had in mind a specific kind of poetry, as M. H. Abrams makes clear: the conventional natural description presented as the transparent vehicle for human analogues or morals, exemplified particularly in the sonnets of William Bowles.[37] Characteristically, however, in raising to the level of theory what is in part a particular stylistic objection, Coleridge obliquely helps sharpen our focus on the perceptual crisis in the narrative of *Paradise Lost:* Adam's loss of the "Presence Divine" in the universe of things and the survival only of a "track Divine," or signs of the Presence. This aspect of *Paradise Lost* was clearly central for Coleridge and contemporary readers in Europe. As presented to the reader, however, the poem's metaphysics is for the most part veiled behind what Raphael calls "process of speech."[38] Within the narrative of *Paradise Lost,* the oneness of the Almighty may be accessible to the angels and (at the moment of Raphael's lecture) to Adam. We may recall a distinction conveniently ignored by Coleridge: even before Adam and Eve sin, they do not possess the intuition of the angels. As Raphael says in the same speech, "Discourse / Is oftest yours." It does seem at times that Milton's poetic vision becomes rapt, even to the point of reaching the inexpressible mysteries of the divine wisdom. But the reader seemingly implied by *Paradise Lost* is most clearly placed by the argument of its similitudes, both formal and dissolved. More than the readers of other epics, he needs the relative clarity provided by the easier, but secondary, art of description. To Coleridge and his contemporaries, such a reader might well have seemed strangely amenable to discourse. He would have been a likely target for Blake's marginalia, if only Blake had noticed.

[37] Abrams, *Mirror and the Lamp,* p. 294.
[38] *Paradise Lost,* VII, 178.

VII
CONTRA HARTMAN:
POSSIBLE AND IMPOSSIBLE
STRUCTURES OF MILTONIC IMAGERY

Robert M. Adams

The best way to catch Geoffrey Hartman's recent article, "Adam on the Grass with Balsamum," [1] is by the tail. The last two paragraphs do a great deal to clarify an enterprise that, until then, had seemed to advance so allusively and so elliptically, in so many different and only schematically connected directions, as to be very difficult indeed of access. But the last two paragraphs make all clear, and two crucial sentences deserve quotation at the very head of the argument: "Narrative conduct [in *Paradise Lost*] is subordinated to hermeneutic structure"; and "Narration becomes, in fact, a kind of concordance."

Professor Hartman's article—to approach it now in more explanatory fashion—is an essay in hermeneutics, dealing centrally with the lines in Book VIII of *Paradise Lost* (ll. 253 ff.) in which Adam is describing to the archangel Raphael the moment of his own creation as he recalls it. The crucial phrase is that italicized below:

> Soft on the flow'ry herb I found me laid
> *In Balmy Sweat*, which with his Beams the Sun
> Soon dri'd, and on the reeking moisture fed.

---

[1] Geoffrey Hartman, "Adam on the Grass with Balsamum," *ELH*, XXXVI (1969), 168–192. For quotations from *Paradise Lost*, see Merritt Y. Hughes, ed., *John Milton: Complete Poems and Major Prose* (New York, 1957).

Through a multitude of parallel passages, analogues, sources, alliterative connections, and emblematic implications, Hartman seeks to make clear the fullness of what Milton meant by the phrase "Balmy Sweat" and why he used it here. As anyone who knows Hartman's previous work could have anticipated, the article is remarkably dextrous, informed, subtle, and perceptive; one need not here canvass all the good things that could be said about it, since they are implicit in the compliment one pays it of sustained and detailed analysis. But if stimulus often expresses itself as abrasion, and if light as well as heat sometimes results from friction, there may be some point in bringing all one's doubts and reservations into the open under the aspect of a frank polemic.

To begin with the sentences quoted from the conclusion of the article, it is a simple matter of logic that no work of explication, however excellently carried out, can yield categorical methodological conclusions of the sort laid down in Hartman's summary. Those conclusions are particularly suspect because they reaffirm the presuppositions with which the author says he started. His intention was to write a hermeneutic study; he concludes that reading Milton hermeneutically is the best of all possible ways. That is just not for him to say. If I put on pink glasses to inspect a painting, and then conclude that pink glasses are absolutely necessary to see the painting because it is essentially pink, my conclusion may or may not be right, but my logic is wrong. Concede that completely colorless glass does not exist, and that the painting cannot be seen at all without glasses of some sort; still, I ought to be suspicious of the conclusion that a painting is essentially pink because it looks pink when seen through pink glasses. There may be glasses of other colors with which to test my conclusion, which is, thus, not really a conclusion at all, but a premise. And there is all the more reason to be suspicious of Hartman's two sentences because the assumptions they convey do not answer at all well to the way in which men of other ages and cultural climates have found it desirable to read *Paradise Lost*. Andrew Marvell, who was about the best contemporary reader of Milton's epic one could have hoped for, certainly one of those most likely to have been alert to hermeneutic subtleties and overtones, did not think Milton had subordinated narrative conduct to anything else, including hermeneutic structure. When he wrote his commendatory poem for the second edition (it is too well known to quote), the narrative conduct, the argument, was precisely what he selected for the highest praise. It represented the greatest danger, and its successful management—the poem's sustained flight—represented the poet's greatest triumph. Perhaps narrative conduct was just the aspect of the poem which Marvell found easiest to discuss in public. Undoubtedly he did recognize and appreciate the sort of "hermeneutic structure" in which Hartman is interested, but that narrative conduct was subordinate to hermeneutic structure he neither said nor implied, nor did any other seventeenth-century reader with whose reactions to the poem I am acquainted.

The point (to be quite explicit) is not that it is in any way wrong to examine Milton's poem for its hermeneutic structure, but only that the decision to examine it in these terms is the critic's. The decision is not dictated by the essential character of the poem, since that essential character is still in question, or at any rate was when last heard from. Any student who takes the poem on some particular basis (as a concordance rather than a narrative, or in any other way that appeals to him) aims to persuade us that his chosen approach yields special rewards, which can then be substituted for, or combined with, the rewards yielded by other approaches, as seems most satisfying to the mind. Nobody gets privileged access to the poem in advance by virtue of his methodology.

In fact, there is every reason to think that a great deal can be made of *Paradise Lost* by studying its images in their depth and complexity, by reading the poem, essentially, as a concordance. Milton has been recognized for some time now as a poet whose diction is extraordinarily rich in echoes and overtones, not only those drawn from classical and Renaissance authors as well as the Bible, but those set up by resonances and repetitions within the body of Miltonic writing itself. Recurring in different contexts and with different coloration, certain themes form, by their mingled repetition and variation, patterns which critical scholarship has long been concerned to define. Traditionally it was supposed that these patterns were secondary implications and nuances, related to the central narrative structure but not themselves an alternative and superior structure. It was supposed that the poem was written, like many other books and all previous epics, to be read from beginning to end because a certain art controlled the disposition and ordering of its units. Not that anybody ever proposed to read *Paradise Lost* simply as a story. Far from precluding a concordance reading, a narrative reading of the poem was usually considered to provide a framework for, and a way of selecting among, the necessarily various and uneven products of concordance reading. It is no slight matter, therefore, to reverse or invert the subordination of one of these two readings to the other; a careful comparison of both reasons and consequences would seem to be in order.

To define a little more closely the method Hartman proposes: he uses the word "concordance," but I think only metaphorically; in practice, he is interested in all sorts of relations between themes and images and words and etymologies and cognates, things to which a concordance, properly speaking, gives little access and which it sometimes shuts off entirely. A concordance not only fails to help one see discords and contrasts and thematic oppositions; it deliberately segregates elements that, in the poetry itself, may be intimately united. Adam speaking to Eve after their Fall says:

                                          our Eyes
              Op'n'd we find indeed, and find we know
              Both Good and Evil, Good lost, and Evil got.
                                                    (IX, 1070 ff.)

Obviously, from a mere concordance it would be difficult if not impossible to see a set of intricate relations among the units of this speech, which reading it in the normal order makes inevitable. The concordance method implies—if it is to be truly a method and not just a convenience—not only a many-directional and many-leveled concordance, but also a discordance. This perhaps pedantic addition is particularly desirable in discussing Milton's poetry because, in my opinion, he frequently employs analogues and parallels to convey undertones that point in directions quite contrary to those in which his surface syntax seems to be moving. The concordance-discordance method of reading a poet takes relatively little notice of the order in which themes are mentioned, and not much more of the context in which they occur. Biblical hermeneutics took for granted that there was one vast divine message woven into the two Testaments, and thus that any given part of the text could best be read in the light of other parts. Samson, Joshua, and Noah were all types of Christ; the New Testament completed in rigorous detail the promises of the Old; and the Old was written to prepare men's minds for acceptance of the New. The prophecies of Isaiah prove that Christ is the Messiah, and knowing that Christ is the Messiah enables us to interpret properly the prophecies of Isaiah. Through correspondent types and shadows, through analogies and prophetic parallels, interpreters of the Scriptures attempted to extract from the sacred text the pure ore of sacred doctrinal truth.[2] What the reader is to get from Milton may be less portentous than sacred truth: it may very well be material furnishing unexampled insights into the texture of the poet's mind.

The texture of a poet's mind, however, is likely to be quite distinct from the structure of the poem he writes; you cannot really tell what sort of house a man lives in if he shows you one of the bricks out of which it is made. What is meant, then, by literary "structure"? Not simply "story," surely; not a bare sequence of events in chronological order, but those events as artistically shaped, colored, and directed to produce a controlled and ordered progression of responses in the reader. We may even distinguish two stages in the production of these responses: the reader follows the poem's action from line to line and page to page; then he looks back from the vantage point of the last line to form the book (within his own mind) into a kind of retrospective rearrangement. The two stages are different modes of perception, to be sure—the first more immediate, the second richer in the variety of possible interrelations—but both demand a kind of composition, a putting of details into patterns of relatedness which presupposes a choice between the significant and the insignificant.[3] In other words, a pattern of relationship put forward as the structure of a major poem must have a certain large and inclusive

[2] We note in passing that the Christian view of history is surpassingly chronological: between the moment of creation and the coming of the Messiah or the Last Judgment all human history is laid out on a time scale which the Bible itself follows, though inconsistently and with many interruptions. It may be worth remembering that alongside the hermeneutists, who read the Bible one way, Milton's immediate background contained highly respected chronologists, like the younger Scaliger and the famous Archbishop Ussher, who read it quite another way, as a historical record to be reconciled, whenever possible, with other historical records. For an elegant, eloquent discussion of the hermeneutic and historical approaches in their application to sacred as well as literary texts, see Helen Gardner, *The Business of Criticism* (New York, 1959).

[3] Professor Hartman tends to describe this choice, which I think pertains to the critic or the reader, as having already been made categorically by the poet. "Milton's mind," he writes, "inhabits the region *between* logos and mythos: perhaps the region of language itself, that smithy of sense. It is a region of shadowy meanings, fleeting images, but also of surprising interchanges between sound and sense" (p. 189). That is beautifully put. But it might seem more in proportion to say that Milton's mind inhabited this interesting area *some of the time*, or that it inhabited this area *among others;* and that Hartman's mind, which finds this area particularly congenial, takes pleasure and can find reward in following Milton there.

character; it must apply to the poem from beginning to end. And there is a variety of other qualifications which common sense requires, and which are so obvious that one is rather embarrassed to specify them. A structure cannot be several structures, indistinctly related; it has to be one. It has to have perceivable limits, so that we feel at the beginning of the poem that we are starting something, and at the end that we have finished something. The structure cannot depend on a selection of evidence which the exigencies of its own creation have too patently controlled. Here, not without some embarrassment, we are bound to adduce the concept of the disinterested or uncommitted reader. Without theories as to what a text is about, we see nothing in it at all; with theories, we are in danger of seeing only what they show us. Between this Scylla and that Charybdis stands at least the ideal of a mediating, critical, and uncommitted reader who tries to distinguish between a structure that satisfies the demands of a poem (making a coherent whole of it without stifling the particulars) and one that leaves it in chaos, or prevents our seeing its real qualities.

But abstractions are oily things; let us return to the particular case at hand.

The first part of Professor Hartman's article, taking off from the passage in which the sun feeds on Adam's sweat, argues that this curious passage serves to define Adam's relation to the cosmos in a specially sympathetic way. The sun, as it were, licks up the afterbirth; thus it is a very serviceable and sympathetic sun, as contrasted with the sun that Satan addresses in his first great soliloquy atop Niphates, which serves mainly to remind him of the glory he has lost (IV, 32 ff.). In thus attending to his animal needs by feeding on his reeking moisture, the sun sets Adam an example; he must feed on the universe with his mind, since eating is frequently equated with knowledge throughout the poem. The sun further exemplifies to the reader, and perhaps to Adam himself, a relationship between created things which is not a "wounding," not one creature thriving at the expense of another, but natural, sympathetic, almost symbiotic association. That is the kind of knowledge represented in the great creation scenes of Book VII; it includes the admission that one is oneself a creature. The kind of knowledge that Satan represents and Eve reaches after is bad knowledge; it includes the pretense that one is self-created and thus independent of God's creation. The sun that feeds on Adam's sweat is a creaturely sun.

Maybe it is, but one wonders how, amid so generous a compendium of reflections on the sun, Hartman manages not to quote Milton's own explicit explanation of the sun's behavior in licking up Adam's sweat. It occurs in the course of Raphael's introductory remarks on the nature of the universe; and the explanation has nothing to do with humble duties or creaturely sympathy. It is a law that applies to All—to the world, to the cosmos; it is an explanation of the observed phenomenon of evaporation:

> The Sun that light imparts to all, receives
> From all his alimental recompense
> In humid exhalations. (V, 423 ff.)

A concordance way of reading the poem discourages, if it does not prevent, our noting that this explanation of the sun's activities comes three books before Adam's description of his birth, but let us make bold to notice the fact anyhow. We may see then that the passage that Hartman's article tries chiefly to expound has been prepared for, in the poem itself, and to an effect rather different from his explanation. What the sun does for Adam, it does for universal nature; it gives light. What it takes from Adam, in humid exhalations, is recompense; that recompense it also takes from universal nature. In no way does this explanation lead us to connect the sun's eating Adam's sweat with Adam's desire for knowledge, or exemplify the condescension of a superior heavenly body to a humble earthy task. It is a process of almost mechanical interchange and circulation which Milton describes, rather like the process of interchange and circulation by which Eden is watered (IV, 223 ff.). If Milton meant us to see a good deal of what Hartman discovers in VIII, 253, he clearly prepared us for it (in V, 423) by pointing our minds in an altogether different direction.

Adam of course needs to know his cosmos in order to exercise his full range of human resources within it. We are aware, from other areas of the poem (not to mention generations of commentary), that his first paradisal state, though happily harmonious and "natural," did not require of him a strenuous participation; thus his fault, while it fractures a limited perfection (ignorant bliss), is a happy fault. That these observations are related more than peripherally (at the outermost edge of a very wide periphery indeed) to the sun's behavior in licking off Adam's sweat is, however, not clear at all. Adam is born to a world of bliss, on flowers and in the midst of a fine day; nature, a harmoniously functioning system of exchanges and balances, receives him. Any connection between the sun's appetite for liquids and Adam's appetite for knowledge is entirely the work of the critic. Natural instinct urges Adam to know, but it urges him to do all sorts of other things too—eat, drink, breathe, sleep, excrete, and copulate. The sun, by behaving as it does, teaches Adam to do those things in precisely the same measure as it teaches him to use his mind.[4]

As for the notion that the sun, by laying on itself lowly duties involving sweat, teaches Adam something about true nobility, Milton's indifference to it here is suggested by the extraordinary attentions he bestows upon it elsewhere. Our first father is insatiably curious about why the large and distinguished heavenly bodies were created for the use of inferior beings like men. In response to her questions, he lectures Eve on the point, not without a certain masculine assurance (IV, 660 ff.); then later, in her absence, he requests of Raphael, and gets, an authoritative lecture on the matter (VIII, 15 ff.). Why all this iterative curiosity about something he had been taught, in the first instant of his life, by the sun itself? To say the least, it makes him look like a very feeble hermeneutist.[5]

Here, now, a reader may well pause in proper indignation and say, "Surely this Adams is a very hard fellow to please. First he complained that Raphael gave a different explanation of the sun's behavior from that put forward in Hartman's exegesis of VIII, 253; now he complains because Milton explicitly makes the same point with regard to the functions of heavenly bodies. Won't anything satisfy him?" But it is not a matter of being captious; it is a matter of reading the passage in its narrative context, in its relation to the before and after. If Hartman's reading jars on Raphael's explanation, the argument is not that one of the two passages must be "wrong,"

---

[4] As a matter of fact, exercising his mind is not, for Adam in paradise, an un-qualified good; if the sun teaches Adam that it is his nature to know and that he should pursue knowledge indiscriminately as the sun absorbs moisture, it is con-spiring at that weakness in Adam's position which Satan shows himself so ready to exploit (IV, 512 ff.).

[5] A further question is: What do we mean, at a moment of iterative coincidence, by saying "narrative conduct is subordinated to hermeneutic structure"? When they contrast, one can choose to follow either in preference to the other. But when they coincide, is one bound to forget (suppress?) (discard?) (omit?) the literal statement as redundant, in order to follow out the richer and subtler allu-sive passage?

but that it makes relations between the two texts difficult, therefore distracting, therefore inartistic. If Adam recurs frequently to a point that has been acted out to the reader's full conviction by the sun itself, then Milton may be a great artist in VIII, 253, but he is an abominable sloven elsewhere. The natural tendency in all concordance reading is to focus all the resources of the entire poem on a single word or phrase; very frequently this process results in robbing Peter to pay Paul. One attributes so much to the image under explication that other images, passages, and even whole sections of the poem become discordant or redundant. To prevent this from happening, it was long traditional to check the results of one's concordancing against such larger structures as the pattern of developing narrative and the reader's gradually ripening attitude toward the events of that narrative. But how the checking can be done if we "subordinate" narrative conduct to hermeneutic structure is by no means clear.

A good many of the ingredients entering into Hartman's reading of Milton are familiar, even traditional, elements; only their connection with the text being explicated is questionable. For example, it is a view of long standing that Adam and Eve in paradise are underemployed and oversupplied. Their work is make-work; their comforts come so easily that their full energies are never exercised. And it is novel, as well as true, that running down the implications of the two words, "Balmy Sweat," brings us before long to connotations involving grace and labor. Balm comes from Arabia the Blest like the phoenix to which Raphael is compared when he descends from Heaven as a messenger of grace, and sweat from the curse to be pronounced on Adam as a result of the Fall. Virgil describes, in the *Georgics*, trees sweating balm as a result of special labor taken in their cultivation. Therefore the phrase gives rise to some sort of meditation on the relation of grace to labor, a meditation about which Hartman is not very precise, perhaps because the path from "balm" to "grace" is so circuitous. In any event, supposing we are to meditate on labor and grace, why should we be asked to do so just here? Adam is just born; though of middle years, he is not laboring, nor is he called on to labor. The Lord has labored, indeed, but for Him labor is synonymous with grace, so our meditations come to a quick end. To be sure, labor and grace are concepts intricately related in Milton's thought, and passages could be listed in plenty which give us to think about them; but VIII, 253, seems like a very precarious one. And by "precarious" I mean that, if one takes the two words

"Balmy Sweat" and free-associates out from them, it is really rather a special moment when the associative process leads to the conjunction of labor and grace. In making the labor-grace antithesis an operative component of the "Balmy Sweat" phrase, one is choosing (arbitrarily, it seems to me) from among dozens of potential conjunctions, such as nature-magic, activity-passivity, rank-sweet, the wearing away of life–the prolongation of life, medication-health, the wicked wealth of the Orient–a modest living tilling one's own field, death (embalming)-life, and so forth and so on. Thus, though it is certainly a general condition of Milton's universe that the real energy lurks behind or alongside the instruments and agents that ostensibly express or contain it (and Hartman has seen this with admirable insight), yet the notion that these ideas find an expression in VIII, 253, which will persuade an uncommitted reader of their operative presence seems as yet unproved.[6]

A last instance of the labor-grace theme occurs in connection with Milton's simile of the careful plowman in IV, 977 ff., where Hartman says Milton introduced the simile because he wanted us "to become, like the Plowman himself, pensive about the relation of labor to grace." When we look at the passage in context, however, the labor-grace theme seems as obliquely related to the plowman as it was to Adam's sweat. Satan is confronting an angelic *posse comitatus:*

> While thus he spake, th' Angelic Squadron bright
> Turn'd fiery red, sharp'ning in mooned horns
> Thir Phalanx, and began to hem him round
> With ported Spears, as thick as when a field
> Of *Ceres* ripe for harvest waving bends
> Her bearded Grove of ears, which way the wind
> Sways them; the careful Plowman doubting stands
> Lest on the threshing floor his hopeful sheaves
> Prove chaff.

[6] What Milton has to say about labor and grace when he openly discusses them generally amounts, it seems to me, to no more than the usual puzzled sense of their frequent disparity. Without apparent means, God often brings about results that seemingly sufficient means have been unable to accomplish (the War in Heaven). When Samson is inspired to do God's work, arms are "ridiculous"; the jawbone of an ass will serve. But God's favor comes and goes unpredictably, unaccountably. "They also serve who only stand and wait" identifies work with faith at the expense of the former; it is like throwing up one's hands before the problem.

To me the interesting thing about the metaphor is the way the patrol of guardian angels are at first sickles to cut Satan down ("sharp'ning in mooned horns" is cut off by the ending of the line from "Thir Phalanx," so that for an instant we see the angels sharpening scimitars or similar moon-shaped instruments; then abruptly we see the phalanx itself as a curved instrument stretching out its original oblong block into two sharpened and menacing points), but then become sheaves of grain to be cut down by him. Under the circumstances it seems burdensome to recall the confident motto of an emblem book, *Agricolas spes alit*, when it is precisely doubt that perplexes the angels as well as the plowman. (Perhaps it is like the ancient etymology of the Latin word for grove: *lucus a non lucendo*.) The doubt is insinuated by the movement of the metaphor itself, that starting out to be sickles, the angels may very well wind up as grain. To be sure, there is no absolute, black-and-white contrast between fighting and working; one can look upon a fight as an investment of labor in a particularly hazardous enterprise, and one can also look on labor as a battle to impose one's will on intractable materials. Because Hartman wants to use the plowman of IV, 977, to gloss the sweat of VIII, 253, he converts fighting to labor; but if his central text had been IV, 977, and he had wanted to get a comment on it out of VIII, 253, he would have found it just as easy to convert sweat into struggle into warfare and balm into victory. Thus our reading of every passage in Milton's poem is made to depend on some other passage, and we are at the mercy of our original decision to explicate this passage rather than that. Inevitably, what we create on these principles will be more like a mare's nest than a structure.

The coin has another side: a limitless choice of associative centers and directions makes any option actually taken look arbitrary. For instance, a passage toward the end of section ii in Hartman's essay challenges us to say why the sun is "presiding at Adam's birth," and answers bluntly, "It is commemorating Genesis." But is it really impossible to think of other reasons? Scripture tells us that God worked during the six days of creation; a complicated creature like man would be hard to make in the dark, even for God; since Adam was just thirty-five when created, the sun for emblematic reasons should have stood at high noon; as the noblest of heavenly bodies, the sun should have been present at the creation of the noblest of animals. There are literally dozens of reasons (simple, esoteric, artistic, practical) for the sun's "presiding" at Adam's creation, if to be in the heavens is to preside. The sun's shining on Adam's creation commemorates Genesis in the same way and to about the same degree as do the flowers on which he found himself laid. But it serves Hartman's argument, as they do not; so it is mentioned, and they are overlooked. To make the connection work in the other direction, Satan's sin is said to be that he denied the day of his birth. Once again, many alternative formulations (some much more strongly represented in the text than this one) are dropped silently out of the account because they do not serve the critic's need, which is to set one attitude toward *day* against another. It would be idle here to enumerate the names and qualities that have been assigned to Satan's sin; there are many of them. But the principle governing both these selections among alternative formulations is evidently to make a sun-Satan antithesis vis-à-vis the word "day"; and this antithesis is the critic's own, for there is no sign that Milton ever considered the matter, even to reject it.

If we start with the sun, we had better end with the phoenix. Following the eighteenth-century editors, Hartman wants to know why Raphael first appears, on his way to enlighten Adam and Eve in paradise, under the aspect of a phoenix. It is an interesting, an important, question, and Hartman's answer is a suggestive one. "The phoenix," he says, "is portrayed as an object of adoration, associated with pagan sun-worship, and engaged in a mysterious cycle of self-immolation and rebirth. The Angel's proper shape, however, emphasizes shade rather than sun, and outgoing, serviceable energy rather than self-enshrinement. Greatness is at first a phoenix, self-begot, self-centered, and self-renewed; then like Maia's son, delegated, partitive, and evangelical." He is absolutely right in considering the phoenix image here in its immediate context, as a first appearance of the angel, to be modified immediately by, or to accord with, what can only be described as the narrative conduct of the poem.

Perhaps one can define Milton's narrative problem here a little more largely and explicitly than Hartman has felt impelled to do. For the first time in his narration, Milton is faced with the necessity of making angels impinge directly on human consciousness. Up to this point in the epic, the angelic world, with all its vast dimensions and energies, has been essentially self-contained. Devils and angels have known a good deal about each other, and something about man; but man has known nothing whatever about them. Milton must do something here to accommodate divine actors and action to the human perspective: he must look at his spiritual creatures afresh.[7] And the fact is, they are like nothing we have ever known. Some sense of their extraordinary strangeness and miraculous beauty must be conveyed before their representative settles down to talk with Adam and Eve cheek by jowl, familiarly. In flight, then, and only momentarily (for it would never do to have Adam and Eve warned by a talking bird when they are about to be seduced by a talking snake!), Raphael must be something gorgeous and rare before he is reduced to the friendly, eloquent companion. I feel there is no major advantage to be gained from considering Raphael-as-phoenix an emblem of self-regarding greatness. We have seen Raphael before in the poem; as captain of the guard, as "limitary Cherub," he is the very reverse of proud, and it would be conceding too much to Satan's epithet (IV, 971) to have him even a momentary emblem of self-sufficiency. Turning him this way and then that, for the space of a few lines only, also risks reducing him to a mere allegorical convenience, a manipulated object.[8]

It should further be noted that the moral for which Raphael's very being is to be thus attenuated ("Greatness seems self-sufficient at first, but reveals its true grandeur in humility") is one of those unctuous formulas into which Milton, indeed, occasionally slipped (see, for example, IV, 201 ff.), but which are more likely to be considered the blemishes of a great poem than its rewards. Still, though accommodation need not be summarized in a moral apothegm, accommodation is definitely involved in the two appearances of Raphael, by means of which the mediating angelic orders are made brilliantly to impinge on the human mind without

[7] The poem has made do, in fact, with remarkably little description of the persons of its spirit protagonists. Satan is like a classical warrior, but he has wings (not being told how many, we are likely to suppose two) and can somehow fly in his armor; he can also dilate or diminish his stature at will. Of God, the Son, and virtuous angels we have had a few inklings, mostly indirect; Satan briefly assumed the guise of a stripling cherub, and Ithuriel and Zephon are good soldiers. There is, however, no real, full-length picture of an angelic figure comparable to the detailed, point-by-point portrait of Adam and Eve. For example, Raphael's six wings come as a surprise when they are described (V, 277 ff.), for we had not realized before that Miltonic angels have so many.

[8] That the phoenix was associated with pagan sun worship is of course true; but excellent authorities, cited by Professor Hartman, had long ago Christianized it. If Milton gave it the pagan overtones of sun worship attributed to it here, it is hard to understand why he assigned it so prominent a position toward the end of *Samson Agonistes*. That story already had vigorous overtones of pagan sun worship; yet the chorus in which the phoenix appears is precisely a celebration of the revival of "our living Dread," the God of Silo, within Samson, at the moment when he had been given up for lost.

sacrificing either their essential strangeness or their essential con-
geniality. In this context we can admire the skill with which Milton
has taken advantage of his images, with their rich history, and of
the moral overtones of descriptive details, such as blazing light and
folded wings, in order to modulate his narrative structure into a
rich and harmonious vision. It is not merely that the two views of
Raphael reflect meaning on each other; they serve to transform
the narrative perspective from that of the omniscient, surpassingly
mobile author, with whom we began, to that of the innocent, inter-
ested, earthbound listener who is to be the vehicle of Books V–VIII.
In effect, the very virtues of Hartman's account of the phoenix
are set off more brilliantly when his analysis is placed in a narrative
context, integrated with a narrative transition.

It is often useful in approaching Milton's verse to note how the
forward motion of the narrative is impeded, and enriched, by the
transverse action of the metaphors. These moments of intersection,
with their double pressures on the mind, their sense of gathering
poise and pause, are not infrequently the most rewarding of the
poem. We see this quality perhaps more clearly in the poetry of
Spenser, where the relatively desultory narrative and more static
(or at least stop-and-go) stanza form should offer an even more
fertile field for hermeneutic endeavors than Milton's epic. Yet it
is precisely in dealing with Spenser's poem that recent criticism
has been most successful in invoking the concept of meditation and
narration at fruitful cross-purposes. In dealing with Milton, too,
dialectic seems a more fruitful premise for defining the relation
between narrative movement and imagistic structure than subordi-
nation in either direction. The dialectic need not be tight; it can
be conceived as loose, intermittent, and various. One norm is that
the implications and substructures of images reinforce a statement
being made by the syntax or narration; another is that they qualify,
complicate, or undercut it. A single crucial word like "ribs" in
I, 690, has a set of reverberations that cover immense distances in
the poem and relate, in interesting premonitory ways, to all sorts
of later developments. The more variously we can conceive of the
imagery as operating with, against, and around the strain of
narrative that ties the poem togther, the better for us. On the other
hand, we can easily push our desire for image relationships so far
that they impede, not necessarily the narrative per se, but our
feelings about the narrative, the current of our managed sentiments.
Suppose Milton wants to compare Raphael, standing before Adam
and Eve, to "*Maia's* son" (V, 285). It is a fine comparison because

Raphael is winged like Mercury (and his wings are being dwelt on at the moment), because he is swift and eloquent like Mercury, and because, like Mercury, he is the messenger of the gods. He can be referred to as "*Maia's* son" because the comparison brings welcome connotations of youth, gaiety, and the freshness of May, while avoiding the disagreeable reflection that Mercury himself is currently with the rest of the Ionian gods, in hell. But how is Milton to prevent us from unraveling the full content of the image and concluding that Raphael, like Mercury, is also the patron of thieves and liars? The answer is, of course, that he can do nothing at all; he cannot disclaim the overtone without ruining the original image, or cauterize it of its unwelcome implications in any way known to man. He has to trust the reader's tact and discrimination to use the context he has been given, to accept the useful overtones and discard the unwelcome ones. It is that sort of tact and discrimation which must always adjudicate the quarrel between image and narration, between implication and assertion. When we aspire to nail the matter down so tightly that tact and discrimination are no longer required, we are perhaps inhaling more critical hubris than is good for us.

What insights of Professor Hartman's essay cannot be accommodated within the conceptual framework of a counterplay between narrative and imagery? It cannot be pretended that there are none; but a great many of his readings, like those associated with the phoenix, slip very gracefully into a narrative context that does them no harm and in fact does them some good. As for some of the others, well, it can be argued that their loss is not pure loss for Milton's poem. The consequences of enriching VIII, 253, out of proportion to its modest place in the narrative conduct of the poem is a notable impoverishment—even a kind of disintegration— of the text elsewhere. Applying the same method to half a dozen other passages threatens disastrous confusion for the poem as a whole. To come back to our architectural metaphor: the bricks of which my house is made are no doubt beautiful bricks, but four of their six sides must be subordinate to common mortar if the structure is to acquire style, rise in its dignity, and stand firm through the centuries.

VIII

MARVELL AND THE
ARS MORIENDI

Stanley Stewart

Criticism of Marvell's "To his Coy Mistress" seems destined to corroborate T. S. Eliot's view that the poem, though wittily logical in structure, is essentially like "O Mistress Mine" and "To the Virgins, to make much of Time." [1] Presumably, in theme and tone, all three poems derive from Catullus' Carmen V (*Vivamus, mea Lesbia*). In recent decades this view has gathered the acritical prestige of a commonplace. And like so many commonplaces it errs not so much in what it states openly as in what it leaves unsaid. No one doubts that "To his Coy Mistress" is a seduction poem, and so in this way generally similar to many carpe diem poems. But stress on similarities, however striking they may be, obscures the imposing differences between Marvell's poem and the legion of contemporary variations on a theme of Carmen V.

In smoothing over differences, proponents of the Catullian hypothesis must lay distorting emphasis on similarities in imagery and tone between Marvell's poem and its supposed Catullian analogues. We may read, for instance, that Marvell's treatment of

---

[1] According to T. S. Eliot, "The theme [of "To his Coy Mistress"] is the theme of *O Mistress mine*, of *Gather ye rosebuds*, of *Go, lovely rose. . . .*" Eliot identifies the mode of "Coy Mistress" by linking the poem to Carmen V (Nobis, cum semel occidit brevis lux, / Nox est perpetua una dormienda) and in general to "the intense levity" of Catullus. See Eliot, "Andrew Marvell," in *Andrew Marvell, 1621–1678: Tercentenary Tributes*, ed. W. H. Bagguley (London, 1922), pp. 66–68. For the view that "Coy Mistress" is a typical carpe diem poem, see Pierre Legouis, *Andrew Marvell: Poet, Puritan, Patriot* (Oxford, 1965), pp. 33–34. A draft of my essay was read at the 1967 meeting of the Modern Language Association in New York.

death is a "brief" and not at all unusual expression of the carpe diem tradition.[2] But is this statement true? Is the imagery of death in "To his Coy Mistress" actually like that in Carmen V? In both poems there is reference to the sun's passage. Even so, as in "To the Virgins, to make much of Time," in Catullus the speaker mentions the setting of the sun abstractly; and death is never particularized in any visual human terms. In Catullus, the mistress is told to multiply her kisses in order to hide their true number from a jealous onlooker. As Crashaw's paraphrase should make abundantly clear, seventeenth-century poets construed the tone of Carmen V to be light, even frivolous:

> Thus at last when we have numbred
> Many a Thousand, many a Hundred;
> Wee'l confound the reckoning quite,
> And lose our selves in wild delight:
> While our joyes so multiply,
> As shall mocke the envious eye.[3]   (ll. 15–20)

Similarly, in Herrick's poem, although the speaker's opening move is an almost obligatory reminder that the flower dies just as surely as the sun completes his round, the speaker's emphasis quickly turns to the effects of age on beauty and to the displeasure of prolonged maidenhood. The speaker's levity is clear in the mildness of his threat (and even in the singsong, feminine ending of the line) that, should the mistress choose to tarry now, she "may for ever tarry." [4]

The temporal imagery of "To his Coy Mistress" is closer to that

[2] Wayne Shumaker, "A Modest Proposal for Critics," *Contemporary Literature*, IX (1968), 332–348. H. M. Richmond (*The School of Love: The Evolution of the Stuart Love Lyric* [Princeton, 1964], pp. 59, 61–63) is also in general agreement with Eliot: "To the Virgins" is modeled after "pagan arguments for indulgence" made by Ausonius, Ronsard, Ovid, and Catullus. Richmond, however, allows for a more complex interpretation: he sees in "To his Coy Mistress" a dependence upon Christian "argument about, and analysis of, feeling" (p. 296). With Eliot, he sees the primary difference between "Coy Mistress" and Carmen V in the former's "sustained logic": "The texture of the two poems is very similar" (p. 14).

[3] "*Out of* Catullus," in *The Poems, English, Latin, and Greek, of Richard Crashaw*, ed. L. C. Martin (2d ed.; Oxford, 1957), p. 194; cf. *The Carmina of Caius Valerius Catullus*, trans. Sir Richard Burton (London, 1894), pp. 8–10; Alexander Brome, "Courtship," in *The Works of the English Poets, from Chaucer to Cowper*, ed. Alexander Chalmers (21 vols.; London, 1810), VI, 649–650.

[4] *The Poetical Works of Robert Herrick*, ed. L. C. Martin (Oxford, 1956), p. 84. Herrick, of course, echoes Carmen V in "*To* Anthea" (p. 24), in "Corinna's *going a Maying*" (p. 67), and in "*To* Phillis *to love, and live with him*" (p. 192). Doubtless the reader can provide numerous other examples.

of Samuel Daniel's "A Pastoral" than to that of any of the poems mentioned by Eliot. Daniel's poem, a paraphrase of the Chorus's closing speech in Act I of *Aminta*, begins with an Arcadian sketch: "O Happy, golden age! / Not for that rivers ran / With streams of milk, and honey dropp'd from trees." As in Marvell's scene, the vision of this Arcadian landscape is directly opposed by the maiden's reluctance. Were it not for her pudency, myth would break forth as reality:

> But only for that name,
> That idle name of wind;
> That idol of deceit, that empty sound
> Call'd Honour . . .   (ll. 14–17)

The poem is, in part, a process of defining paradise as an endless duration of ecstasy where man follows the constant law of instinct. But man has been undone by disobedience to this natural law, and so the lover, who has become both philosopher and casuist, presses his petition:

> Let's love—this life of ours
> Can make no truce with Time that all devours.
> Let's love—the Sun doth set, and rise again;
> But when as our short light
> Comes once to set, it makes eternal night.[5]   (ll. 64–68)

In its martial qualities, in its suggestion of mortal combat, this passage briefly displays something of the verve of "To his Coy Mistress." Time does not merely pass, it overwhelms and devours man; all that lovers can hope for is momentary satisfaction in armed resistance.

Like Marvell, Daniel presents his speaker as a rebellious if helpless victim of Time, the destroyer. Again Marvell's imagery is much more demanding and stark. The plain fact is that the imagery

---

[5] Chalmers, *English Poets*, III, 549; Daniel's paraphrase gains intensity over Tasso's "Chorus," which follows Carmen V rather closely. The imagery of warfare does not appear in the 1628 translation of *Aminta* (*Torquato Tassos Aminta Englisht* [London, 1628], sig. D2v):

> Live we in love, for our lives houres
> Hast on to death, that all at length devoures.
> Live we while we may; the wayne
> Of Heav'n can set, and rise againe;
> But we (when once we looze this light)
> Must yeeld us to a never ending Night.

Cf., however, the entire speech of the Chorus.

of the second verse paragraph of "To his Coy Mistress" stands quite apart from other poems with which it has been compared:

> But at my back I alwaies hear
> Times winged Charriot hurrying near:
> And yonder all before us lye
> Desarts of vast Eternity.
> Thy Beauty shall no more be found;
> Nor, in thy marble Vault, shall sound
> My ecchoing Song: then Worms shall try
> That long preserv'd Virginity:
> And your quaint Honour turn to dust;
> And into ashes all my lust.[6]   (ll. 21–30)

It is one thing to refer abstractly to death, to the sun's progress, to the onset of night, to the fading of the rose; it is quite another to dwell on the sensuous awareness of Time's haste, which in Marvell's poem is filled with anxiety. The speaker apprehends the sound of beating wings, and he hears them pressing from behind, as if he is running to avoid being overtaken. Further, he hears a flurry of wings approach him, and their sound is impossible to escape. The effect is one of much greater intensity than we find in Carmen V, or, for that matter, in any of the perpetually cited Catullian analogues.[7] Marvell's speaker conveys, with whatever else, a sense of terror from which he and his audience are powerless to escape. The sense is further heightened by the fact that this omnipresent threat of time concerns only the horror pursuing the lover and his mistress from behind. One of the most striking features of Marvell's poem is its pictorial treatment of the physicality of death; before the entreater and his mistress lies the even more terrible prospect of infinite time and space: "Desarts of vast Eternity."

Probably Leishman is correct in asserting that this passage and the poem generally show a lively awareness of Cowley's "My Diet": "An hundred years on one *kind word* I'll feast: / A thousand more will added be, / If you an *Inclination* have for me; /

---

[6] *The Poems & Letters of Andrew Marvell*, ed. H. M. Margoliouth (2d ed.; 2 vols.; Oxford, 1952), I, 26–27.

[7] It is well to remember that Catullus scholars have denied an explicit connection between Marvell and Catullus (see John Bernard Emperor, *The Catullian Influence in English Lyric Poetry, Circa 1600–1650* [Columbia, Mo., 1928], p. 114; James A. S. McPeek, *Catullus in Strange and Distant Britain* [Cambridge, Mass., 1939], pp. 124–126; and Eleanor Shipley Duckett, *Catullus in English Poetry* [Northampton, Mass., 1925], pp. 30, 38).

And all beyond is vast *Eternity*." [8] Leishman might further have pointed out that in borrowing from Cowley Marvell also kept in mind a striking image from the preceding poem in *The Mistress* ("The Wish"). Marvell fuses the figure of "vast *Eternity*" with the image of "desarts Solitude," and the fusion results in a startling landscape whose emptiness and loneliness confront the lovers. Of course, similarities between "My Diet" and "To his Coy Mistress" vanish when we look closely at the imagery and the rhetoric of the two poems. In "My Diet" the speaker promises to feast on "one *kind word*" from an ostensibly disinterested mistress. The luxuriousness of his fantasy is reminiscent of courtly love hyperbole, with its insistence on the detached and cool madonna-like lady (*La Vita Nuova*).

In sharp contrast, where Cowley's speaker "will," Marvell's poet "would" dally in the courtly fashion if he had time, which he does not. The prospect he presents is full of desolation, a landscape unbroken except by the monuments to his beloved's memory. (In his fantasy, the poet has already exacted the ultimate penalty on the mistress for any lack of cooperation.) The effect is amplified by the haunting figure of the poet's echoing song: no one to hear, no one to see, no one to love. The language of this passage is full of the trappings of the *ars moriendi* tradition, down to the feast of worms. Indeed, the choice presented to the mistress specifically precludes any issue of honor or virginity; in any event, the mistress must relinquish her virginity. The only question is when and how: in the palpable here and now, with at least minimal satisfaction, or later, humiliatingly, to the unresponsive worms? The speaker turns from the norms of carpe diem to the rhetoric of the "art of dying well." He presents the mistress with a choice—not between pleasure and pain, youth and age, death and life (for if she chooses correctly, she must only hasten death)—a choice of the time, place, and manner of her death. Anthony Farnham must not be reading the same poem I am reading when he suggests that Marvell's speaker tries to convince his mistress to put time "out of mind for as long as possible." [9] On the contrary, the poet insists that she seriously contemplate the ravages of time and ponder the stark images of death. Unlike the often flippant lover of carpe diem

[8] Cowley, "My Diet," ll. 18–21; J. B. Leishman, *The Art of Marvell's Poetry* (London, 1966), pp. 70–79. Leishman, of course, subscribes to the Catullian hypothesis.

[9] Anthony E. Farnham, "Saint Teresa and the Coy Mistress," *Boston University Studies in English*, II (1956), 226–239; see also Harold E. Toliver, *Marvell's Ironic Vision* (New Haven, 1965), pp. 158–159.

lyrics, Marvell's poet does not cajole or tease; he tries rather to instill awe. He hears, he sees, he feels, he knows with all his senses that death is near, and his rhetoric turns on prompting the same awareness in his undecided mistress.

Marvell's image of the decaying corpse (I know of no other such example in the so-called carpe diem poetry of the seventeenth century) is intended to be horrible, so horrible as to agitate the mistress and thus to prompt her compliance with the speaker's demands. He insists that she relinquish not only her coyness, but indeed the passivity that is, if not exactly the cause, then surely a necessary precondition of that coyness. The poet-speaker emphatically avoids any petition for passive submission on the part of his mistress; nor is that attitude even an alternative in the poem (though as Eliot and others have shown, it is definitely a conventional alternative open to Marvell in writing this kind of poem). Marvell's speaker demands an open, assertive, violent, and almost suprasexual commitment to aggressiveness in the act of love:

> Now therefore, while the youthful hew
> Sits on thy skin like morning dew,
> And while thy willing Soul transpires
> At every pore with instant Fires,
> Now let us sport us while we may;
> And now, like am'rous birds of prey,
> Rather at once our Time devour,
> Than languish in his slow-chapt pow'r.
> Let us roll all our Strength, and all
> Our sweetness, up into one Ball:
> And tear our Pleasures with rough strife,
> Thorough the Iron gates of Life.
> Thus, though we cannot make our Sun
> Stand still, yet we will make him run.   (ll. 33–46)

The language here is rife with violence. The mistress is no dove, no rose, no lily of the field. Nor is she, as in "The Canonization," to rise from the flames of passion, somehow purified, and resurrected like the phoenix. Instead she is, like her male partner, a hawk or an eagle, tearing and devouring pleasure like pieces of flesh.[10]

Critics have often been misled in their interpretations of this passage. Coming as the third, conclusive part of the lover's argu-

---

[10] In Donne's poem the imagery of annihilation is meant to suggest transfiguration, and so it operates in exactly the opposite way from Marvell's.

ment. It has been construed, for example, as a logical development of the "vegetable Love" in the first verse paragraph. Thus the culminating injunction of the lover is based on the idea of "rational love." [11] But what is rational about the subject of this third verse paragraph? The speaker confronts the mistress with two alternatives: to die quickly, or to be ground between Time's slow jaws. What does this choice mean? The possibilities opened by the pun on the word "die" need not be emphasized, but neither ought the importance of that conceit to be ignored. For the speaker's argument concerns one thing and one thing only: the speed with which the lovers are to die.

This is notably not the theme of carpe diem. In "To his Coy Mistress" the best a lover can hope for is to be devoured quickly; the pain of existence may be diminished, but it is pain nonetheless. Unlike its Catullian progenitors, Marvell's poem emphasizes the pain of life, the pain, if you will, of perfect (ergo, sexual) satisfaction. With its clearly ironic landscape, the first verse paragraph repudiates the sentimental version of courtly love, and the biblical allusiveness serves to intensify the ironic comment. As Marvell's audience knew, the practice of love "ten years before the Flood" was corrupt indeed, so corrupt, in fact, that it resembled love soon after the Flood; despite Abraham's intercession, the deluge was followed very shortly by fire and brimstone. By looking into the future to "The Conversion of the *Jews*," the speaker makes his wry commentary complete: he has encompassed the fullest temporal and spatial range of corrupt love (and this in a fantasy of prolonged dalliance which cannot lack some gentle hint of fetish).

More sardonically than ironically, the speaker moves from his Arcadian fantasy to the second stage of his appeal: he presents a contrast between a corpse, totally powerless to choose, ravished by worms, and the unattractive (but nonetheless more attractive) figures of perspiring bodies and swooping birds of prey. The latter figure suggests annihilation of sexual differences, whose sentimental exaggeration is a staple of carpe diem poetry. Abstractly, the contrast is between the corruption of passivity (a kind of death in life) and the somewhat unpleasant liveliness of actual physical passion and contact. As many critics have remarked, though the lovers may reduce Time's power to inflict a full measure of pain, in so doing they must hasten his ultimate triumph. Of course, the final couplet alludes to God's show of power at Jericho, when he gave

[11] Rufus Putney, "'Our Vegetable Love': Marvell and Burton," in *Studies in Honor of T. W. Baldwin*, ed. D. C. Allen (Urbana, Ill., 1958), pp. 220–228.

the victory over the Amorites to Joshua; hence the lovers, unlike God, cannot stop the sun.[12] But there are further implications: Joshua led the Israelites into Canaan, which represents a polar contrast to the cities of the plain. The full dimension of allusiveness here must include restatement and resolution of thematic material in the opening verse paragraph. Canaan is a type of New Canaan which will be entered by God's people only after "The Conversion of the *Jews*"; emblematically, Marvell juxtaposes the distant past and distant future. In another sense the contrast between past and future suggests the interdependence in Christian thought of time and eternity; Marvell's timeless region flowing with milk and honey, where the lover might spend eternity admiring the bodily parts of his mistress, provides a parody of the pastoral life pursued by Abraham and the destruction of Sodom and Gomorrah, where sexuality was dominant. Theologically, the contrast is between flesh and spirit.

Such biblical allusion suggests that the lovers, although they are not gods (nor are they divinely assisted, like Joshua), may still learn to exercise a degree of control over Time. As Ruth Wallerstein observed, Marvell's method derives from an inversion—indeed, a parody—of "religious echoes." [13] In particular, the obsession with time and death owes more to the *ars moriendi* tradition than to the norms of carpe diem. It was in the literature and iconography of that context that the man of the seventeenth century learned to contemplate the images of corpses and to construe their relevance to human conduct, to meditate upon the relation of life's brevity to bodily pleasures. Marvell's contemporaries were well schooled in this tradition; during the closing decades of the sixteenth and the first half of the seventeenth century, dozens of tracts on the art of dying well were published and were often reprinted, both in England and on the Continent.[14]

Not only does Marvell's poem share with the *ars moriendi* tradition a wholly argumentative purpose, but also that purpose is guided by a particular emphasis on images of temporality and death. Marvell shares with writers in this tradition—with Ninian

[12] See Walter A. Sedelow, Jr., "Marvell's *To His Coy Mistress*," *Modern Language Notes*, LXXI (1956), 6–8.

[13] Ruth Wallerstein, *Studies in Seventeenth-Century Poetic* (Madison, Wis., 1950), p. 337.

[14] For a thorough survey of the proliferation of such works, see Sister Mary Catharine O'Connor's fine bibliographic study, *The Art of Dying Well: The Development of the Ars moriendi* (New York, 1942), which, of course, I have found most useful; see esp. Part 4.

Campbell, for example—a rhetorical purpose in depicting Death as a leveler:

There is no difference betwixt dead corps, but that rich mens corps stink worse then others. . . . Let us go to the sepulchres; shew thy father, shew thy wife; where is he who was cloathed in purple? I see nothing but rotten bones, and wormes; no difference can I perceive. . . . O rottennesse thou art my father, O worme thou art my mother, and my sister.[15]

Marvell's speaker adds (to his mistress) "your lovers," for in death the Coy Mistress (like Campbell's "worme") has become promiscuous. In Campbell, as in Marvell, the aim is to shock the audience by vivid figures of death—"Beleeve me saith *Augustine*, in opened sepulchres have been found in dead mens sculs, earth-toades; in their nerves, serpents; in their bowels, worms" (sigs. E1–E1v)—and thereby to instill a sense of apprehension in the reader. By this means he is prepared for the "admonition," which usually comes in a series of phrases *de contemptu mundi:*

Use of admonition: Is death inevitable, and the stroak thereof irreparable? then let us in time thinke upon it. This is the day. . . . In the mean time, this our naturall life is but a broken reed, a cob-web to lean unto, which because of the inconstancie, uncertainty, shortnesse, naughtinesse of it, is justly compared by profane and divine writers, . . . to a . . . race, to a post, to a chariot, to a whirlegig, to a warfare . . . to grasse, to hay, to a fading flower, to a leaf, to a thought, to a dream, to a shadow, to the dream of a shadow . . . to nothing, to lesse then nothing.   (sigs. D4–D4v)

The second verse paragraph is calculated to instill the dual purpose of the *ars moriendi:* to remind the Coy Mistress of the certainty of death, while at the same time insinuating the uncertainties surrounding death, those of time, place, and manner:

The third direction is upon the manner. This is a saying repeated by many, *ad vitam unus est exitus, ad mortem paene infiniti:* There is one passage to life, *viz.* our mothers bellie, but to death, are almost infinite. *Raman* hanged *Jobs* sons, smothered the mothers of *Jerusalem,* with their younglings starved to death; *Herod* worm-eaten, those of *Sodom* burnt with fire and brimstone, those of the old world drowned with an uncomparable deluge of waters. Diverse are the kinds of the Saints

---

[15] Ninian Campbell, *A Treatise Upon Death* (Edinburgh, [1635]), sig. E1 (hereafter cited in the text).

death; *Esay* was cut through the middle with a saw; *Peter, James, Paul and John* beheaded; . . . *Bartholomew* his skin pulled off . . . him.
(sig. G4)

Similarly, the second and third sections of "To his Coy Mistress" dwell on the range of possible times and ways of dying: slowly, swiftly; painfully, less painfully.

In his famous essay on Marvell, T. S. Eliot describes the structure of the poem as syllogistic,[16] which is, of course (if, but, therefore), partly accurate. There are syllogisms and syllogisms (some of which, like the one in this poem, have undistributed middles), but what the Catullian hypothesis generated by Eliot does not account for is the drift of this particular argument toward an intense concern with the immediacy of death. Frequently, tracts on the art of dying well were divided into tripartite sequences; this division was considered an appropriate counterpart of the triad of time, place, and manner. In turn, this triad corresponded with the overriding theme of *ars moriendi*, time itself, which consisted of three parts: "The preterit time is gone, the present is a moment; and the future is uncertaine" (sig. E2v). Marvell's poem treats of this triad, though not in the usual order. As we have seen, the first verse paragraph, with its peaceful and unhurried landscape, by juxtaposing associations of the distant future and the distant past depicts a timeless region, which might well remind the Christian reader of New Canaan, a land to be glimpsed, from the human standpoint, only after time had fully run its course. The imagery conjures, therefore, a sense of the distant future. In contrast, the next verse paragraph cynically represents the future as it is known from experience rather than from faith. The reader is forced to consider the present situation from the viewpoint of the natural as distinct from the regenerate man. Finally, the exhortation of the third verse paragraph redefines the future as depicted in the first, seeing it now as the product of a simple choice between differing degrees of pain in dying. For after death all that awaits (beyond physical corruption of the body) is an eternity of loneliness.

During the course of his argument Marvell's speaker follows the *ars moriendi* tracts in many details. First and foremost, along with Ninian Campbell, he tries to focus attention on the immediacy of death:

---

[16] Eliot writes that "the three strophes of Marvell's poem have something like a syllogistic relation to each other" (*Marvell, Tercentenary Tributes*, p. 68). See also J. V. Cunningham, *Tradition and Poetic Structure* (Denver, 1960), pp. 40–58.

We die daylie, we are changed daily, yet we think our selves eternall. In the mean time, in our most lively life we may perceive the verie print and footstep of death. For we do see continually, and hear the cryes of mothers for their children; of spouses, for their husbands; of servants, for their masters; visitation of sick, mediciners, preachers, in our houses, at our bedheads, all warning us, that we are besieged by death.   (sig. G1)

In short, the reader should remember that he is presented every day with tokens of the immediate presence of death ("But at my back I alwaies hear / Times winged Charriot hurrying near"). Such an awareness necessarily prompts consideration of the maxim that man ought to live as if he were dying that very moment. Similarly, Marvell's urgent speaker, by his emphasis on the immediate aware-ness of death, intends to heighten the importance of the present choice ("Now therefore"). It is here—in the speaker's "exhorta-tion"—that one finds the crux of the argument in the *ars moriendi*.

The treatises on dying well were full of the "Use of exhortation" (sig. E2). In fact, Marvell's "Now therefore" and "Let us roll all our Strength, and all / Our sweetness, up into one Ball," and the general tone of the last two verse paragraphs, are strongly remi-niscent of *ars moriendi* rhetoric.

Yea, let us gather our selves together before the supreme decree of death passe out against us at unawares, that so wee may meet it with as much readinesse of minde, as it is willing with greedines to receive us, who should not be drifters off of repentance, like *Salomons* sluggard; or any more supersede, flatter or foster ourselves with vaine and deceitful conceits of the immortalitie of this melting mortalitie, or admire this dying carcasse, which the wormes must feed upon ere it be long, or be ravished with the astonishing fabrick of our bodies which are but clay tabernacles, and death at our flitting will dissolve the pinnes thereof.   (sigs. E2–E2v)

Recurrently in the *ars moriendi* tracts we hear the monotonous in-vocation to recalcitrant but lovely maidens: "O thou comely *Rachel*, beautifull *Bethsheba*, alluring *Dalilah*, thy pampered and wel covered skinne, in the grave shall be like that of a drudge, or vile kitchin-maid ere it be long!" (sig. E3). Indeed, both maiden and gallant shall disintegrate, and always, "ere it be long!" (sig. E3v).

Ordinarily, these exhortations were directed against "the lust of the flesh, and the lust of the eyes, and the pride of life" (1 John

2: 16), or against the five temptations most likely to assail the dying man.[17] In the former instance, since the three temptations were subsumed under the general heading "concupiscence," more often than not the *ars moriendi* author ended his exhortation by an indictment of lechery. Practitioners of the art believed that one important value of the meditation on death was its effectiveness in assuaging sexual desire. For example, the translator of Peter de Luca's *A Dialogue of Dying Wel* (1603) intends the awareness (memory) of death to diminish lust: "The third fruit of the remembrance of death is, that all desire of carnal lust is theirby easely extinguished. S. Gregorie witnesseth this, where hee saith: Nothing avayleth so much to tame the desires of the flesh, then the memorie of death, and to think what this poor flesh shal become, when the soule hath left it."[18] As a corollary to his equation of death and sexual timidity, the writer argues that the most emaciated saints had the easiest task of overcoming "fleshlie motions." Even contrary instances become grist for the writer's mill: one unfortunate hermit, though fasting to the point of starvation, could not dislodge the image or memory of a woman, now dead, whom he had desired. In order to free himself from lust he went to extreme efforts, digging "her dead body stincking and ful of wormes out of her grave, and casting himself upon this carcas licked it with his tongue, and smelling the filthy savour said to his flesh, go to now cruel and untamed beast, take now thy fil of that which thow hast affected with an unmeasurable and dissolute love."[19] It is important to note that, whatever the author's pious intent, the passage is in all respects vividly physical, even erotic, for the primary emphasis is on the passionate concentration of the hermit's mind on the need

[17] In *The Book of the Craft of Dying, and Other Early English Tracts Concerning Death*, ed. Frances Comper (London, 1917), pp. 10–12, the five temptations of the dying man are given as doubt, despair, impatience, complacence, and overconcern for the world of family and business; see also *The Craft to Know Well to Die*, pp. 58–65 (in the same volume). In *Ars moriendi* (1465) the temptations, four in number, are of faith (doubt), despair, impatience, and vainglory. A Spanish version (*Art de ben morir* [1493] [fac. ed.; Barcelona, 1951], pp. 88–104) also lists four temptations of the dying man: despair, impatience, vainglory, and avarice ("La última tentación con que el diablo mortifica en el trance de la muerte . . ."). Similarly, Robert Cardinal Bellarmine (*The Art of Dying Well*, trans. C. E. [Saint-Omer, 1622], pp. 256–276) gives the four as heresy, despair, hatred of God, and overconcern with the world.

[18] Peter de Luca, *A Dialogue of Dying Wel*, trans. R. N. (Antwerp, 1603), fol. 8*v*. Campbell writes, "O leacherous man, who sowest where thou darest not reap, deflowering virgines, defiling the honourable bed of marriage; the fierie heat of thy concupiscence shall be quenched in the flouds of oblivion ere it be long!" (*Treatise Upon Death*, sig. E2*v*).

[19] De Luca, *Dialogue of Dying Wel*, p. 9.

for an intense, close relationship with the object of his affections.

According to Cardinal Bellarmine, one of the most widely read authorities on the subject of dying well, the sole remedy for lust lay in the absolute insulation of all five senses from attractive stimuli. In "To his Coy Mistress" asceticism and coyness are treated as one and the same phenomenon; Marvell's speaker appeals to all five of his lady's senses. He encourages a fantasy of visual and tactile sensations in the first verse paragraph; in the second and third he appeals (if only in order to awe) to the senses of taste and smell. Finally—and here was the most dangerous stimulus of all—his own song appeals to her ears. Hauntingly, he presents the poet's love song to the lady's imagination, almost as if it were heard now from the vast stillness of a future grave; but the theme of that song is annihilation. Perhaps the speaker has saved his most persuasive argument for last. Had not Bellarmine insisted that, of all the senses, hearing was the most susceptible to temptation? For Bellarmine, above all, lovers were attracted by

ill wordes, that belong unto carnality, and consisteth in amorous speeches, and lascivious or wanton songes, then which by the lovers of this world no thing is heard with more delight, when as nothing is more hurtefull or dangerous: these wanton songes of Mermaydes recounted by Poets, which for no other end delighted the passengers, then that they might therby cast them into the sea & devuour them.[20]

Here Marvell and Bellarmine part ways. Bellarmine would have his reader meditate "on the four last thinges, death, judgement, heaven, and hel" (p. 177). Above all, "to overcome all the tentations of the flesh and sinnes of leachery, the only and most effectuall remedy is to avoyd idlenes, for none is so much subject unto filthy thoughts as he who hath nothing to do" but dally and talk "with his friends" (p. 178). Implicitly, the first part of Marvell's poem depicts a scene of lascivious idleness; the mistress, Bellarmine would argue, should not be listening to the poet in the first place.

Obviously, Marvell's speaker argues in exactly the opposite direction: What is the purpose of losing one's chastity at a time when all pleasure in the physical act has been foreclosed? Indeed, a good part of his rhetoric derives from an inversion of the Christian, otherworldly argument. Bellarmine's translator wrote that death actually possesses an element of bittersweet, a pain "intermingled with delight" (sig. *7v). Accordingly, proper discipline, gained

[20] Bellarmine, *Art of Dying Well*, p. 169 (hereafter cited in the text).

through years of meditation on death, reduces the fear of physical death. In effect, by a stoical relinquishing of psychic involvement with "the world," man removes death's sting. Marvell's speaker wholly rejects this view while retaining its method. He presumes, by calling to mind the images of physical death, to horrify his mistress with the vivid picture of her own annihilation. This description, however, is only the prelude to his "exhortation." Although death is inevitable, it may be more or less terrible; as the saints have written, dying to the world in the here and now not only proffers an immediate delight but also reduces the pain of the body's death. At the center of this poem is a prolonged conceit, a play with the imagery of dying, and a parody of the *de contemptu mundi* motifs of the *ars moriendi*.

It seems to me that the conceit works on at least two levels. Most obviously it functions on the bawdy level, where the idea of a swift dying (the theme of self-immolation) simply means that it is delightful to consummate the act of love swiftly. But on another level the speaker expresses the anagogic truth of this dictum for human experience: by an immediate grasping of the feel and pulse of life and love, somehow, man loses his passivity, becoming no longer the victim pursued through life by Time the destroyer,[21] whose jaws slowly and painfully devour him.[22] In terms of the contrasts working in the poem, Marvell identifies the fear of time (the more man runs from it the more slowly he is eaten, and the greater his fear) with the fear of love: coyness = fear = pain. Ironically, by overcoming this fear the lovers hurry their own end—commit suicide (for every act of love one relinquishes a day of life)[23]—but in so

[21] Marvell may be alluding to the iconographic tradition of Time as the devourer of man (see Erwin Panofsky, *Studies in Iconology* [New York, 1939], pp. 69-93, figs. 45, 46, 47, 56, 57, 60, 63, 67, 68; Samuel Chew, *The Pilgrimage of Life* [New Haven, 1962], pp. 12-17, figs. 17-23; Raimond van Marle, *Iconographie de l'art profane au moyen-âge et à la Renaissance* [The Hague, 1932], II, 112, fig. 129; 119, fig. 136, in which Time, riding in his chariot, ingests a child). This iconographic tradition owes much, of course, to the teachings of Pythagoras as presented in Ovid's *Metamorphoses*:

> tempus edax rerum, tuque, invidiosa vetustas,
> omnia destruitis, vitiataque dentibus aevi
> paulatim lenta consumitis omnia morte!   (XV, 234-236)

Like Ovid, Marvell stresses Time's capacity to gnaw at life slowly, but in "To his Coy Mistress" the lovers have a chance to hasten the process.

[22] Marvell may also have in mind another set of terrible jaws: in *Ars moriendi* (fol. 9), beneath tempted man stretch the jaws of hell, through which tormented sinners can be seen. Various contemporary versions of the same scene appeared during the late Renaissance (see, for example, *Ars moriendi* [16th cent.], fols. 1, 9, with engravings by Matthaeus Zink, or Zagel).

[23] Pseudo-Aristotle, *The Problems of Aristotle* (Edinburgh, 1595), sig. D8v.

doing they exercise a newfound power over Time. The speaker's aim has been to move his mistress's "willing Soul" to "will" this momentary limitation on Time's seemingly absolute power. If he is successful (and the final couplet seems to suggest that he is), that single, "willing Soul" joins with his own being to "will" that Time move faster: like eternity, the loneliness of indecision is painful simply because it seems endless.

As we have seen, both in *ars moriendi* and in Marvell's poem the central argument turns upon a single paradox: to live well is to die well, which is to die in the here and now of (not necessarily in) the world. Compared with poems like "The Bait" and "To the Virgins, to make much of Time," "To his Coy Mistress" presents an intense and unusual (if macabre and salacious) perspective in which the lover's invitation is urged. Bellarmine had written: "Therefore my brethren I say unto you, [since] the tyme is short," men and women should abstain from the pleasures of love, even when married (p. 10). Marvell's speaker answers that—marriage aside—since time is short, "Therefore" the lovers, in practicing the art of dying well, should most distinctly and intensely not abstain. But the speakers in both contexts would agree that this momentary dying to the world should be done in remembrance of physical death. In Marvell's poem, *ars moriendi* and *ars amatoria* are one.

If this assessment of Marvell's irony is correct, the wit in "To his Coy Mistress" is a function of the tension between the poles of asceticism and blasphemy represented in the poem. Marvell thrusts the pastoral myth into hard contrast with the world of the senses, allowing his speaker to fantasize an intense tearing of pleasures "Thorough the Iron gates of Life." Emblematically, iron suggests the contrast between iron gates and golden gates, between the mythical, Edenic world of the distant past or the distant future and the harsh reality of the actual world in which the lovers find themselves. By practicing the art of loving / dying, the couple "tear" their "Pleasures with rough strife, / Thorough the Iron gates of Life." Marvell may be suggesting an inversion of the soul's progress from time to eternity, from earth to Heaven, in the notion of an intense, cruel, painful movement by which the body makes its progress through the iron world. If so, the inversion expresses the speaker's ultimate affirmation of this world, for it is just as hard to live by the hedonistic rules laid down by Venus as to follow those enunciated by the anonymous author of the craft of dying and by the many writers during the seventeenth century who made him their literary model. Here the note of pathos is hard to miss: in this transformed Christian context, the twain of iron flesh and golden spirit can never meet. There must remain a Pyrrhic quality in man's triumph over Time.[24] As Thomas Forde wrote, something remained beyond man's power to make the contrast between gold and iron complete:

> When wee have run out the length of the threed of our life, (which by striving to *lengthen*, wee many times *shorten*; and by endeavouring to stretch longer wee crack in sunder) we *retire* into the *grave*, and go down into those *chambers of darkness*, where wee must *exuere vestes, put off* all those borrowed *clothes*, we acted in here. For as when one told *Anaxagoras*, the *Athenians* have condemn'd thee to *die*; hee answered, . . . By the decree of Nature wee were all *dead* before we began to *live. It is appointed for all men once to die:* then they must shift the *Scaene*, and begin anew. . . . For all that have gone before us have trodden the same path, . . . though their *head* have been of *gold*, their *body* of *Iron*, their *arms* of *brass*, yet their *feet* (like *Nebuchadnezzars* Image,) have been of *clay*, and they have gon into the dust.[25]

For the saint as for the sinner, the limits of the flesh are absolute.

The love pictured in Marvell's poem is no courtly or Arcadian dalliance in a summer shade; no green gowns will be donned. This consummation is a matter of animal motions, of beak and claw, both terrible and splendid. Marvell ignores the whiteness, the softness, the innocence of woman, whom he sees as hungry for the pleasures of the human animal, willing to tear her satisfactions from the resisting medium of the passing world. As in the Mower poems, she is the real woman who enters man's life as a destroyer, as if his ideal, pastoral projection of perfect love cannot survive the presence of her total physicality. She comes, like Juliana, bringing death and disintegration to the pastoral world, tearing pleasures through the "Iron gates of Life." The use of "Thorough" may suggest "along through," as if Marvell would remind his reader that, no matter what, humankind remains, even in momentary victory, Time's unseeing victim. As the lovers tear (rather than pull or push) their pleasures through life, challenging the tyranny of Time by the intensity of their lovemaking, as they tear and sweat and

---

[24] Joan Hartwig places stronger emphasis on the lovers as "momentary masters" of time ("The Principle of Measure in 'To His Coy Mistress,'" *College English*, XXV [1963–64], 572–575).

[25] Thomas Forde, *Lusus Fortunae* (London, 1649), pp. 95–96.

roll their "sweetness, up into one Ball," they propel Time to fly even faster; they hurry together to the threshold of the solitude that only moments earlier the speaker has depicted in desolate terms. Thus, man has but two choices: to go slowly, gently, but abjectly into that eternal, lonely good-night, or to hurry with his lover in a state of excitement to an end that is only the beginning of loneliness. The one alternative is passive and excruciating; the other is active, and it asserts the dignity of the human will, yet it is finally more self-destructive.

If this analysis is correct, "To his Coy Mistress" must be construed against a background, not only of pagan love poetry, but also of the *ars moriendi* tradition. When seen in both contexts the poem is just as witty as it has always been adjudged; in fact, it is even more so, for now it may be seen in its true uniqueness. More than an exercise in the mode of carpe diem, "To his Coy Mistress" is also a most intense exercise in the casuistry of love.[26] Parodying the sophistry of otherworldly moralists and theologians, Marvell's speaker, in a frame of mind to reject the claims of the soul, makes out a very good case for the primacy of the body. For to withdraw from the temptations of the flesh while one is so young and so beautiful and so soon to die is a form of blasphemy against life, a kind of loneliness that more properly belongs in the grave. There, man's capacity to choose, and by implication the meaningfulness of his existence, have been removed. "To his Coy Mistress" presents an ironic play on certain assumptions about the interdependence of life and death, about the meaning of death and the ways to die. But the wit here is not all the spark and cinder of specious logic (or, if it is, then so the argument on the other side must be for the claims of the soul): "To live well is to die well."

Blasphemer and Bellarmine would both argue that in order to learn the art of dying one must make a proper choice in the here and now. The depth of intensity in "To his Coy Mistress" rests partly on the completeness with which the speaker has accepted the major premise of this presumably Christian argument, only to reverse the conclusion by a clever act of equivocation. There are many ways of dying, many ways the text (the Word) may be con-

[26] Patrick G. Hogan, Jr. ("Marvell's 'Vegetable Love,'" *Studies in Philology*, LX [1963], 1–11), considers "To his Coy Mistress" a "devastating satire on the *carpe diem* tradition," a view with which I am in agreement as far as it goes. See also Anthony Low and Paul J. Pival, "Rhetorical Pattern in Marvell's 'To his Coy Mistress,'" *Journal of English and Germanic Philology*, LXVIII (1969), 414–421, which also emphasizes the shocking effects of Marvell's poem. The differences in emphasis between the present argument and both essays should be clear.

strued: had not the exegetes, ancient and modern, superstitious and reformed, agreed on this fundamental principle? For Marvell's speaker, the argument to his mistress is no light invitation to a roll in the hay, although it is partly that. Instead, that invitation is only one aspect of a theodicy, of an explanation of the meaning of human life, which is gained only by the speaker's construing of "love." That construction, of course, depends upon the openness of language, which allows the poet to present an argument that, while neither Catullian nor Christian, is an expression of both contexts, an argument turned in such a way as to become an ironic parody of both.

IX

DRYDEN'S *EIKON BASILIKE:*
TO SIR GODFREY KNELLER

Earl Miner

Those images that yet
Fresh images beget.
—W. B. YEATS

Most of Dryden's best poems of complimentary address have been revalued in recent years, but for some reason—perhaps its difficulty —*To Sir Godfrey Kneller* has received only incidental attention. It may therefore not be amiss to begin with a brief résumé of my analysis. The formal characteristics of the genre of the poem require that a kinship be established between poet and addressee and that a subject of common concern be developed. The kinship here is that of brother artists, each the most prominent in his medium in his time. The subject concerns the sister arts of poetry and painting. The three major movements of the poem develop a temporal, historical sequence: past, present, and future. The imagery of the poem both derives from these temporal divisions and unifies them. The past is treated in images of a sequence of nations in the progress of art; the present is a time unfavorable for creation of artistic images; in the future, Time as restoring artist will mellow the imperfections of present-day art. The sister arts become metaphors for each other, and the brother artists work in a "stupid military state" in which the rightful king (James II; the artist) is deprived of his proper subjects. The poem is pessimistic about the present but optimistic about the future, when Time will restore art to its proper position and the artist-king to his just place.

Throughout the eighteenth century and in most of the nineteenth, Dryden's editors placed *To Sir Godfrey Kneller* last among a group of "Epistles," including such poems as those to Dr. Charleton, Congreve, John Driden of Chesterton, and the Duchess of Ormond.[1] The undoubted utility of the classification is considerably diminished by the fact that neither classical nor Renaissance critics have much to say about the verse letter. They do distinguish between the amorous or elegiac epistle and the didactic or satiric form, which is to say that they identify one form following Ovid's *Heroides* and another deriving from Horace's *Epistulae*.[2] Richard Hurd is among the eighteenth-century commentators to distinguish these kinds of verse epistle in his rather miscellaneous introduction to Horace's letters.[3] No one's imagination will be strained to conceive that Dryden could distinguish a poem on love from a poem on another subject, but we are picking our way over uncertain country. Bishop Hurd also distinguished three rules: the subject must possess unity; the "method" must have "connexion"; and the "connexion" must be "easy."[4] John Warton was less prescriptive in describing *To My Honour'd Kinsman* as "one of the most truly Horatian epistles in our language, comprehending a variety of topics and useful reflections, and sliding from subject to subject with ease and propriety."[5] Such properties as variety, didacticism, associational or accretive progression, ease, and decorum bring us another step closer to Dryden, and even closer to Horace and Pope. But Dryden's variety ranges more accurately from the satiric to the historical.[6] An earlier scholar, J. C. Scaliger, wrote that the verse epistle might properly be considered with the epicede and the epitaph as belonging to the larger form of the elegy.[7] Scaliger's

[1] W. D. Christie was the first of Dryden's editors to come near to accurate dating of these poems. The second part of his rubric, "Epistles and Complimentary Addresses," better describes than does the word "epistle" most such English poems of the seventeenth century.

[2] Jay Arnold Levine ("The Status of the Verse Epistle before Pope," *Studies in Philology*, LIX [1962], 658–684, esp. 659–661) voices the irritation felt by anyone who seeks guidance from humanist or vernacular sources on the verse epistle as a form. I do not duplicate his very useful references but refer to critics whom he has bypassed. On the prose letter, see Jean Robertson, *The Art of Letter Writing* [ca. 1500–1700] (London, 1942).

[3] Richard Hurd, *Q. Horatii Flacci Epistolae ad Pisones et Augustum* (5th ed.; 3 vols.; Cambridge, 1776), I, v: the verse epistle is "but of *two* kinds; *one* of which may be called the DIDACTIC; the *other*, the ELEGIAC epistle." It is as simple as that. Hurd's introduction has much of an incidental nature to commend it.

[4] *Ibid.*, I, xiii.

[5] *The Poetical Works of John Dryden, Esq.*, ed. Joseph Warton et al. (4 vols.; London, 1811), II, 236.

[6] Warton's description does not account for Dryden's integrative powers. See the examinations of the unity of *To My Honour'd Kinsman* by Jay Arnold Levine, "John Dryden's Epistle to John Driden," *Journal of English and Germanic Philology*, LXIII (1964), 450–474; and by A. H. Roper, *Dryden's Poetic Kingdoms* (London, 1965), pp. 124–135.

comment is useful for suggesting a belief that there was one kind, or a group of related kinds, of poetry in which the poet or some fictional character addressed someone else, real or fictional, dead or alive, with feeling and by drawing upon the commonplaces (loci, topoi) of praise, entreaty, or blame.

Although such considerations seem meager criteria for getting at a difficult poem, they do raise important issues. The question as to whether or not the person addressed is real (i.e., historical or contemporary) entails complex considerations, not because the distinction is one separating art from reality,[8] but because certain artistic requirements and possible bounds of fiction are involved. Individual epistles among the *Heroides*, for example *Dido to Aeneas*,[9] afford freer fictions than do Horace's epistles to Maecenas or Dryden's poem to Kneller. In epistles based on real men or women, historical actuality necessarily controls more closely the degree of freedom and the kinds of imagery than it does in a poem like Pope's *Eloisa to Abelard*. And it presents other approaches and images. We can observe Dryden's handling of actuality in his reference to Kneller's portrait of Shakespeare, or his use of the common "place" of superior education in lines 139–144 and of the formula of the wise (brave, talented, etc.) man at home in all countries (ll. 128, 137). The use of traditional rhetorical elements is one technique employed by poets from Horace to Pope in their efforts to make poetry out of the natural elements of a letter.[10]

Consideration of "the natural elements of a letter" possesses an importance not at once apparent. Some valuable recent writing on the vernacular verse epistle has emphasized the way in which it establishes a kinship or common interest between the writer and the

[7] J. C. Scaliger, *Ivlii Caesaris Scaligeri . . . Poetices Libri Septem* (5th ed.; 1617), p. 389: Epicedia quoque, & Epitaphia, & Epistolae hoc genere [the elegy] recte conficiuntur (III, cxxxiv).

[8] E. P. Morris, who has useful things to say in "The Form of the Epistle in Horace," *Yale Classical Studies*, II (1931), 79–114, argues (as do other classicists) that the addressees in some of Horace's epistles are fictional. In his excellent *Horace* (Oxford, 1957), Eduard Fraenkel takes pains to assert the historicity of the addressees. The virtues of art claimed by Morris (see p. 101) or of reality claimed by Fraenkel (p. 310) are real virtues, but the issues they raise lack historical proof and are too simplified. It does make a difference to us, because it inevitably makes a difference to the poet, if the addressee is real. Yet the art of different poets on different occasions renders the "real" Augustus Caesar in Horace and the "real" Augustus in Ovid into different literary creations.

[9] See Dryden's translation in *The Poems of John Dryden*, ed. James Kinsley (4 vols.; Oxford, 1958), I, 197–203.

[10] The point is emphasized in Hermann Peter's useful study, *Der Brief in der römischen Zeit* (Leipzig, 1901), pp. 5, 6, 184, etc. See also Levine, "Status of the Verse Epistle," pp. 665–669.

addressee.[11] Classicists have thought this relationship important.[12] As we try to relate an unfamiliar poem like *To Sir Godfrey Kneller* to more familiar works, we see that the stress on common, shared interests marks the funeral elegy (*Lycidas;* "To the Memory of Mr. Oldham"), the love elegy (Donne, "The Perfume"; Ovid, *Amores,* I, ii, translated by Dryden), some epigrams (Jonson's on his son and daughter), the ode (Horace, *Ad Augustum;* Dryden's Anne Killigrew ode), and other forms.[13] As Scaliger suggested, the epistle is indeed related to other poetic genres. *To Sir Godfrey Kneller* resembles other poems addressed by Dryden to the dead or the living, and it is true that most of his poems formerly classified as epistles are types of complimentary address.[14] That is, they have a lineage going back to Horace and Ovid; they employ a variety of traditional resources, especially panegyric; they develop a kinship between the writer (the poet in various guises) and the addressee; they concern some topic of common interest with a Dr. Charleton, a Congreve, or a Kneller. The imagery of such poems functions to create the relationship and to develop the topic. It is typical of Dryden that he thought Horace employed rather too loose a form.[15] His aim as always was a closer unity, established by imagery, of poet and addressee in both topic and movement. It is therefore to be expected that the important images in *To Sir Godfrey Kneller* should comprehend poetry and painting, making them as it were a single art comprising the poet and the painter; that the topic should be this art of the artists; and that the movement of a poem about historical artists should itself entail history.

The imagery uniting poet and artist-addressee, and the accompanying imagery from, and of, the two sister arts, emerge very

[11] In *Pope's Epistle to Bathurst* (Baltimore, 1960) Earl R. Wasserman discusses with great thoroughness the rhetoric employed by Pope in developing the relation between poet and addressee.

[12] On Ovid, for example, see Peter, *Der Brief,* pp. 187–188. Morris ("Form of the Epistle," p. 94) speaks succinctly of Cicero, *Ad Familiares,* XIII: "Cicero's letters of introduction usually include a reminder of his relation to his correspondent, to justify the letter, some statement of his connection with the man to be introduced, and some description of his motive in seeking the introduction."

[13] Morris ("Form of the Epistle," p. 107) says that about a fourth of Horace's odes written before the *Epistulae* (i.e., *Carmina,* I–III) "are addressed to personal friends."

[14] A possible exception is the rattling verse letter to Etherege, written as if by Secretary of State Charles Middleton while Etherege was posted in Ratisbon (Dryden, *Poems,* ed. Kinsley, II, 578–580).

[15] *Poems,* ed. Kinsley, III, 1009. This fact has been observed by Levine ("Status of the Verse Epistle," p. 662).

quickly in the poem. The less obvious imagery employed to develop the sense of movement may require further consideration. There are in the poem two parallel movements followed by a brief coda, or conclusion, whose function is not at once clear. The twenty-one lines that begin the first movement present a suppressed simile of a beautiful but mute woman recalled by the poet.[16] Her beauty leads him to praise the lifelikeness of Kneller's portraits. The rest of the movement (ll. 22–72) is given over to a progress piece on painting, from its primitive beginnings to Kneller's triumph. The progress piece is an unusual one for Dryden, however, because in terms of the quality of art it shows a decided break in mid-career. Classical Rome, especially with its fall, is not one step in a ceaseless progression or *translatio studii*, but a very nadir of art. There are really two progress pieces: from the origins to Rome, and from the sack of Rome to the great rise including Raphael and Kneller. The interruption that separates them implies what Dryden's other progress pieces conceal: that if one is optimistic, as he is, that human effort is able to bring about steady improvement or refinement, then the absence or the frustration of that effort will lead to regression. Once again a certain dark shading clouds Dryden's habitual optimism. For all that, the progress piece tacitly insists on the ebullient classical and baroque commonplace, *ut pictura poesis*, the sister arts. [17] The mute woman of the initial suppressed simile is symbolic of the dumb sister art, *muta pictura*, and at the same time is praised for being a child of Nature. It does not take long acquaintance with humanist ideas to realize that something complex is occurring iconographically and historically in the opening movement of the poem.

Yet, at first, the second movement is rather harder to describe. It is a parallel movement, beginning with another artistic image, the portrait of Shakespeare, a gift to Dryden from Kneller and the occasion of the poem.[18] Before, Nature had produced the fairest

[16] For a similar, but rather less suppressed, initial simile see the first stanza of "An Ode, on the Death of Mr. Henry Purcell" (*Poems*, ed. Kinsley, II, 863–864), a poem written within two or three years of *To Sir Godfrey Kneller*.

[17] See, most obviously, l. 57, but the concept underlies the whole poem. For the background and the application to Dryden see the admirable study by Jean H. Hagstrum, *The Sister Arts: The Tradition of Literary Pictorialism from Dryden to Gray* (Chicago, 1958). The best gloss of the poem is provided in *A Parallel betwixt Painting and Poetry*, written by Dryden as an introduction to Charles du Fresnoy's *De Arte Graphica* (1695).

[18] See ll. 73 ff. For a photograph of Kneller's version of the "Chandos" portrait, now in the Fitzwilliam collection, see *O Sweet Mr. Shakespeare I'll have his picture* ([London], 1964), p. 15. Kneller's rather austere version measures 29 x 24 inches, a picture of a size that Dryden might well "place before my sight."

symbol of art; now, Kneller has produced a portrait of him whom the century regarded as England's poet of Nature. Here it is the painting, not its subject, which is mute. The unnamed woman of the first movement had led to numerous proper names falling into a historical progression. The naming of Shakespeare does not exactly take us out of history, but the emphasis is more wholly on one age than on historical progress through the ages. The problem with history had been the Goths and the Vandals. The problem with consideration of an age is the times, which are "Inferiour" (l. 118) for poetry and painting alike (see esp. ll. 117–123, 145–173). The sister arts motif symbolized by Shakespeare's portrait (as by the picture of the fair woman at the beginning of the poem) has manifold import. It accounts for the parallel history of both arts, and it explains why Dryden and Kneller alike are denied the satisfaction of working on more important schemes than they do. As the first movement provides compliment verging on panegyric, the second is so critical that it approaches satire, the obverse of praise. Dryden's satiric infusions (see l. 94, but its context must be considered) appear in many of his poems that are not properly satiric at all, and for verse addresses to be satiric in cast is a feature common in Horace and characteristic of Pope's verse epistles.[19] It is also true that Dryden is more often the panegyrist than the satirist, and that in this poem as elsewhere he reveals his "obsessive concern" with the heroic.[20]

It might well seem that some such dialectic as the Hegelian thesis and antithesis is the only explanation for two contrasting movements like these; the brief third movement (ll. 174–181) does provide a culmination of the attitudes developed in the first two movements. Praise and blame, panegyric and satire, are, however, rather means of evaluation from a common ground of "Nature" or ideal reality than they are antitheses. Each is a heightening for rhetorical effect and for moral judgment. If, therefore, a reader objects that Anne Killigrew is not a translunary poet who could bring back the music of the spheres, or that Kneller does not mark a step forward beyond Raphael, Dryden's shade would have another cause for perplexity. Anybody knows that. Judgments, however, must be made by enduring standards; men or women can be ideally lifted into realms beyond their mortal limitations; and men and

[19] Fraenkel remarks (*Horace*, p. 310) that Horace's "*Epistles* are an organic continuation of his *Satires*." No evidence is needed for Pope.

[20] No full-scale study exists of Dryden as panegyrist. On Dryden's lifelong epic preoccupations, see H. T. Swedenberg, Jr., "Dryden's Obsessive Concern with the Heroic," *Studies in Philology*, extra ser., no. 4 (1967), pp. 12–26.

women may be used to represent through their limited embodiments the perfect class to which they belong. Dryden praises no one unworthy of praise of the kind chosen. Contrariwise, his satire plays a role in showing limitations and in judging faults, again by heightening (*amplificatio*), and in satire no more than in panegyric is an author on oath as to detail. Much of the imagery in *To Sir Godfrey Kneller* is therefore necessarily directive, given to praise or blame, to amplification.

The brief third movement requires understanding in such terms; the last line says that Time will "give more Beauties, than he takes away" from Kneller's painting. The balance of hope and fear belongs to the poem as a whole. Although both the last line and other lines in the third movement are capable of being read for darker overtones, the emphasis of the conclusion is on hope. Time will mellow for later generations the "Colours" (l. 178) of Kneller's art. Given the strength of the sister arts motif and of the identification of poet and painter, there is no doubt also a suggestion that Time will mellow the rhetorical "Colours" of the panegyric and satire in Dryden's poem. The continuing connection between the two arts is only implicit in the conclusion. In it Dryden mentions neither himself nor poetry, nor is there any reference to himself by so much as a pronoun. No topical allusions are to be found, and there are no proper names. It almost seems as though the last movement is detachable from the poem, applicable to any other painter of importance. It is this quality that makes the passage difficult: the preceding 173 lines obviously require some treatment, if only implied, of subjects dealt with earlier. But in what ways is the requirement satisfied?

The poem's inner relationships, or its complex ordering of many parts (ll. 172–173), seems to me best studied where least evident. The first half of the last movement serves the purpose admirably:

> More cannot be by Mortal Art exprest;
> But venerable Age shall add the rest.
> For Time shall with his ready Pencil stand;
> Retouch your Figures, with his ripening hand.
>
> (ll. 174–177)

The personification is obvious: Time the retoucher or restorer is the final artist. And time in various forms is one unifying motif of the poem. *Pictura*, the fair woman created by Nature at the beginning of the poem, and Kneller's portrait of Shakespeare lie in one sense outside time. (By introducing a painting of so great a poet, Dryden ensures that the sister arts motif will operate without his calling attention to himself.) They are immortal, the latter a product of a "Godlike Art" (l. 35) and the former a symbol for it. But by the end of the poem the scope of the artist has lessened. His is now a "Mortal Art." Earlier, when the capacity of art seemed greatest, the results were apt to be more discouraging than when the scope of art is reduced and the artist is aided by Time. The various guises of time, as well as of art, help shape Dryden's careful formulation. We first observe time in the progress piece (*translatio studii*) of painting (ll. 28–72). Time is conceived of as historical improvement, halted though it was by "the *Goths* and *Vandals*" (l. 47). The progress piece also divides into prehistoric times for which "Perhaps" (l. 30) is the careful word, and then into ages expressed in terms of nations: Greece (ll. 35–44), Rome (ll. 45–56), Italy (ll. 61–64), and England (ll. 65–72). Ostensibly each unit of time, each *aevum*, each nation, improves on its predecessor. Ostensibly the present era of Kneller in England is the culminating triumph. But the long second movement of the poem alters both the conception of time and the sense of progress. Now the emphasis is not on history, on the successive ages of man, or on time, but on "this Age" (ll. 117, 146). It is here not time, but the times, that deprive poetry and painting of the chance to be what historically they might be, as the culmination of their centuries-old tradition. The optimistic possibility afforded by time and open to human effort is not lost. It is rather frustrated by the way in which "this Age" deprives the artist of his scope in treating great subjects.

What has gone wrong? Dryden seems to have been suffering from a degree of literary pessimism, having on his mind Ovid's four ages, culminating in the Iron Age.[21] But this is only to say that Dryden used certain literary recollections to express his disenchantment with the early 1690's. The satiric coloring of his criticism of the age in the second movement of the poem is, after all, but a relatively faint version of the remarkable outburst near the end of *Eleonora*:

> Let this suffice: Nor thou, great Saint, refuse
> This humble Tribute of no vulgar Muse:
> Who, not by Cares, or Wants, or Age deprest,

[21] See l. 57. In *Examen Poeticum* (1693; *Kneller* was perhaps written that year or the next) Dryden included his translation of Book I of the *Metamorphoses*. His recollection of Ovid's story about Prometheus' creating man (his translation, ll. 98–112) is evident in *Kneller*, ll. 22–25.

> Stems a wild Deluge with a dauntless brest:
> And dares to sing thy Praises, in a Clime
> Where Vice triumphs, and Vertue is a Crime:
> Where ev'n to draw the Picture of thy Mind,
> Is Satyr on the most of Humane Kind:
> Take it, while yet 'tis Praise; before my rage,
> Unsafely just, break loose on this bad Age:
> So bad, that thou thy self had'st no defence,
> From Vice, but barely by departing hence.[22]

The common moral and rhetorical grounds of praise and satire are evident, and the tone is far stronger than that of the poem to Kneller. But in both poems the satiric denial provides a darker shading for the brighter panegyric. When Dryden said to Kneller (l. 94) that satire entered wherever he wrote, his remark must be understood in its local context and in the context of his career. His references to himself as a satirist are confined to a brief period, to those few years when his translations of Juvenal and Persius were in his mind.[23] Of his career as a whole it is more accurate to say that where panegyric, history, and epic usually prevail, satire may enter at any time.

With Juvenal and Persius lingering in his mind, then, Dryden turned in displeasure on his age, that is, on William III, one of the most admired and least loved of English kings. To Dryden he was neither English nor a king, but a usurper, a man not only of the wrong blood but a man of blood. In the dedication of *Examen Poeticum*, Dryden clearly speaks of "this *Iron Age*,"[24] and for once he criticizes even Homer, who

stirs up the irascible appetite, as our Philosophers call it, he provokes to Murther, and the destruction of God's Images; he forms and equips those ungodly Man-killers, whom we Poets, when we flatter them, call Heroes; a race of Men who can never enjoy quiet in themselves, 'till they have taken it from all the World.[25]

[22] Ll. 359–370. The image of the artist ("Muse," l. 360) defying the immoral oppression of the age "with a dauntless brest" is echoed in *Kneller*, l. 79. The image appears to be formulaic. See also the last paragraph of the epistle dedicatory of *Eleonora*.

[23] It is also true that many of Dryden's poems and translations in *Examen Poeticum* are nonsatiric; that Dryden was next setting to work on Virgil; and that the poem on Purcell (1696) is wholly optimistic. The political concerns I discuss next may be overstressed; they must not be taken out of the context of Dryden's other interests at the time.

[24] *Poems*, ed. Kinsley, II, 797.

[25] *Ibid.*, pp. 798–799.

So much for King William and his wars. It would not do to say simply that Dryden no longer esteems (or had never esteemed) the bravery he had praised in *Annus Mirabilis*, in Barzillai's son (that is, Ossory; *Absalom and Achitophel*, ll. 829–861), or in the heroic plays. It may well be argued, and I think it profoundly true, that Dryden's deepest hopes lay in what man might achieve in peace. That attitude, nevertheless, did not preclude admiration for bravery; in another context of portraits Dryden had praised Anne Killigrew's portrait of James II for revealing the king's "Warlike Mind" (l. 131). But James was a king by law and by divine right, not a de facto usurper or conquerer; like "the *Goths* and *Vandals*" William III was of "a rude *Northern* Race" (Kneller, l. 47):

> Thus in a stupid Military State,
> The Pen and Pencil find an equal Fate.
> . . . the rude delight
> Of Brutal Nations, only born to Fight.
>
> (ll. 51–52, 55–56)

Later in the second movement (ll. 155–156) the Jacobite poet complains, with most of his contemporaries, of the levies exacted for King William's wars. In brief, Dryden's historical view, though optimistic in general, is momentarily very pessimistic over the situation of the artist "in a stupid Military State." The image of the military times rudely challenges the vision of time as history of human progress. The cry is very much "O tempora! O mores!"

The brief third movement, with its image of kindly, restoring Time, brings therefore an accommodation of the frustrating times to the basic progressivist historical view of *translatio studii*. It is significant that there are three optimistic versions of time in the last eight lines. How optimistic they are can be judged by the passage from Ovid which had reechoed in Christendom for centuries: *tempus edax rerum tuque invidiosa vetustas* (*Metamorphoses*, XV, 234), or, in Dryden's version, "Thy Teeth, devouring Time, thine, envious Age, / On Things below still exercise your Rage." In the coda of the poem to Kneller, on the other hand, the Ovidian *invidiosa vetustas* is softened altogether to "venerable Age," a kindlier way of adding the last touches needed in painting (and in poetry). Time is no longer the devourer of things but the retoucher, "with his ripening hand." Finally, Dryden looks ahead to "future ages" with hope that more will be gained than lost.[26] The

[26] To Dryden, "age" is the English for both *saeculum* and *aevum*. Although the Latin words are also ambiguous, Dryden's usage includes "century" (*saeculum*

images of time in the poem are, then: first, a succession of ages in the progressivist historical *translatio studii;* then the sorry William- ite times; and finally three personifications, "Age," "Time," and "Ages." The poem ends with personification, as it had begun with a prosopopoeia of painting, *Pictura,* the mute "fairest of her Kind." It also ends with "Ages," as the progress piece had begun with them unpersonified. Moreover, since the temporal personifications are treated as artists in time, they play a special role as images in a poem about artists and represent something of a bond between Dryden and Kneller, poet and painter, two image makers. Thus the reader is led to think back to the first artist in the poem, another personification, "Nature" (*natura naturans*). The two mortal but somehow "Godlike" artists dwell with their counterparts of all ages between the natural demiurge, "the vicaire of the almyghty Lord" (as Chaucer terms Nature), at the outset of the poem, and at the end Time in various personified guises. Man is set in a great historic panorama beginning with the central principle of creation and extending to future times. Indeed, the poem works out the movement, characteristic of Dryden's poems, from the essential principle and the past to the present and on to the future.[27] This movement affords consolation for the unhappy state of the times, provides a historical scheme inclusive of Dryden and Kneller, and creates a bond between the two artists which is appropriate in a poem of address.

The three passages thus far considered create images that are at once connected with paintings, form the relation between painter and poet, and establish three orders of time. These images—of the fair woman, of the portrait of Shakespeare, and of Time-Age as retoucher—reveal a tendency for a poem written to a painter about painting to take on painterly characteristics. Like the Anne Killi- grew ode, Dryden's poetry and the cast of his imagery in this poem tend to encroach on the province of painting. In other poems Dryden's protean art may take on the harmonies of music when music is the subject (*A Song for St. Cecilia's Day,* the Purcell ode, *Alexander's Feast*); it may turn historical in poems about history (*Annus Mirabilis, Absalom and Achitophel*); and it may turn into a dramatic skit when the poem is about drama (*Mac Flecknoe*).

rather than *aevum*), as in *The Secular Masque,* and "age" or "era." Often, as in the Kneller poem, it is difficult to determine his precise meaning. Dryden's theme of Time's kindly mellowing develops a commonplace, *Tempore cuncta mitiora* (see Geffrey Whiting, *A Choice of Emblemes* [Leyden, 1586], no. 206).

27 I have treated this movement in *Dryden's Poetry* (Bloomington and London, 1967), pp. 195–196, 200–204, 274–276.

As in *The Medall,* so in the poem to Kneller Dryden is casting images, asking his poetry to assume the role of her sister art:

> Thou hadst thy *Charles* a while, and so had I;
> But pass we that unpleasing Image by.   (ll. 100–101)

Or, again:

> For Hymns were sung in *Edens* happy Earth,
> By the first Pair; while *Eve* was yet a Saint;
> Before she fell with Pride, and learn'd to paint. (ll. 90–92)

The latter passage is very much in the seventeenth-century line of wit. Like Donne's it is serious levity; like Marvell's it puts in question what it affirms. Dryden's emphasis is, however, more upon an emerging and interrelated whole than upon detail. Since wit resides in detail, the shock of Dryden's wit is lessened until we force ourselves from his (and our) envisioned whole to some remarkable parts. As the arts are sisters, so imagery from another biblical source makes the artists brothers:

> Our Arts are Sisters; though not Twins in Birth . . . (l. 89)

> For oh, the Painter Muse; though last in place,
> Has seiz'd the Blessing first, like *Jacob*'s Race.   (ll. 95–96)

Certain essential tendencies of Dryden's imagery emerge in such passages. Imagistic structures tend to rise into large patterns from details that at first seem to have no relation to one another. Dryden's conceits (e.g., "thy Pictures look a Voice") tend to yoke elements together with little apparent violence, because the yoking is after all so appropriate. And there is a constant tendency to derive poetic imagery from a seemingly alien subject, here rendering details associated with Kneller's art into figurative language.

Dryden's praise of Kneller's eloquent, his (so to speak) poetic, painting begins with the initial image of the beautiful woman and the suppressed simile for Kneller's art:

> True she was dumb; for Nature gaz'd so long,
> Pleas'd with her work, that she forgot her Tongue:
> But smiling, said, She still shall gain the Prize;
> I only have transferr'd it to her eyes.   (ll. 3–6)

The conception of a tongue transferred to the eyes, though sufficiently baroque, is merely incidental to the wit. More funda-

mental is the idea, at least as old as Simonides, which is para-
phrased by Thomas Flatman:

> For pictures are dumb Poems; they that write
> Best Poems, do but paint in Black and white.[28]

The idea that speechlessness is a defect in a woman is a nice play
on what the Duchess of Malfi confessed to be her last woman's
fault. Paradoxically, the woman is after all eloquent, but with her
eyes, and to male understanding this kind of eloquence is appropri-
ate. Within five lines Dryden applies the paradox to Kneller in
another conceit: "At least thy Pictures look a Voice" (l. 11). In
the local context as well as in the development of the poem, one
idea-image begets another of a similar kind.[29] In a later passage
Dryden envies painters their international freedom from the need
for translation: "The Pencil speaks the Tongue of ev'ry Land"
(l. 127). The mute sister is multilingual, even omnilingual—with
her looks.

A central feature of the poem is the principle of likeness: the
likeness drawn by a painter or by a poet, and the likeness of the
painter and the poet as well as of the painting and the poem. As
Dryden says of Kneller's painting,

> Likeness is ever there; but still the best,
> Like proper Thoughts in lofty Language drest.
> When Light to Shades descending, plays, not strives;
> Dyes by degrees, and by degrees revives.
> Of various parts a perfect whole is wrought:
> Thy Pictures think, and we Divine their thought.[30]

The principle of likeness is creative, not static; it is esemplastic,
working through resemblances to make "Of various parts a per-

---

[28] Thomas Flatman, *Life and Uncollected Poems*, ed. Frederic Anthony Child
(Philadelphia, 1921), p. 26 (cited by Hagstrum, *Sister Arts*, p. 112).

[29] Dryden's use of "Idea" for the image of the woman in l. 2 seems to carry the
original Greek senses of ιδέα or εἶδος with something of the Platonic meaning (see
Hagstrum, *Sister Arts*, p. 5).

[30] Ll. 67–72. The imagery subdued in wordplay is very nice: consider "drest"
and "Dyes." Again, the last line leads to Kneller's portrait of Shakespeare. Cf. also
the very subtle wit, in the context I have drawn, of ll. 158–159. L. 68, "Like
proper Thoughts in lofty Language drest," closely resembles the definition of wit
Dryden took pride in until he decided that Aristotle had anticipated him. See *John
Dryden: Of Dramatic Poesy and Other Critical Essays*, ed. George Watson (2
vols.; London and New York, 1962), I, 207; II, 210–211, 304–305 (Watson's
glossary).

fect whole." The same principle is alive as well in the more nega-
tive second movement of the poem, as when Dryden speaks of the
ways in which the lofty aims he shares with Kneller are compro-
mised by the unfavorable times. In themselves, most of the lines in
the passage seem to speak of literature as much as of painting:

> Else shou'd we see, your Noble Pencil trace
> Our Unities of Action, Time, and Place.
> A whole compos'd of parts; and those the best;
> With ev'ry various Character exprest.
> Heroes at large; and at a nearer view;
> Less, and at a distance, an Ignobler Crew.
> Where all the Figures in one Action joyn,
> As tending to Compleat the main Design.   (ll. 166–173)

The echo of the passage quoted just before (almost a hundred
lines earlier in the poem) is evident enough. So is the fact that the
first two lines here speak of the painting as if it were a play. The
second couplet is neutral, or rather inclusive of both arts. The
third moves in reverse direction, using descriptive poetry to paint
a scene. The concluding couplet, like the second, is applicable to
both arts; and, as the preceding four lines had concluded with a
multivalent verb, *exprest,* so the second quatrain concludes with a
multivalent noun, *Design.* Dryden's imagistic art in this poem, in-
deed in most of his best poetry, is shown by the principal words—
three verbs and three nouns—in the concluding couplet of the
passage, an imagistic art "Where all the Figures in one Action
joyn, / As tending to Compleat the main Design."
    Earlier, in distinguishing three "movements" in *To Sir Godfrey
Kneller,* I used a term suggestive of Dryden's "Action" so as to
stress the temporal directions of the poem. Although the imagery
possesses a reciprocal "Action" in which poetry becomes painting,
and painting poetry, the principle of temporal movement in the
imagery is expressed in a metaphorical process. The process leads
to "a perfect whole," to "the main Design"; in other words, the
"Godlike" arts produce immortal works lying outside the ravages
of time.[31] In a fairly simple example, this complex conception of
creative reciprocal processes leads to perfected design toward the
conclusion of the progress piece on painting:

---

[31] On Dryden's concept of the immortal as an order of time lying between the
mortal and the eternal, see my *Dryden's Poetry,* pp. 200–204.

Thence rose the *Roman*, and the *Lombard* line:
One colour'd best, and one did best design.
Raphael's like *Homer*'s, was the Nobler part;
But *Titian*'s Painting, look'd like *Virgil*'s Art.   (ll. 61–64)

The detail of resonant words is best left to the reader's consideration, but I should like to stress the place of the two couplets in their larger context. The four lines present time in its historical aspect; Dryden is setting forth the last development of painting before Kneller's culminating skill. The second couplet of the passage harks back to two earlier stages in the history of art, to Greece (cf. ll. 37 ff.) and to Rome (cf. ll. 45 ff.), by moving forward to modern painters; or rather, it is moving forward to modern painters by harking back to classical poets. Dryden's imagistic art is revealed in the very rhetoric (perhaps one should simply say syntax): "*Raphael*'s [part] like . . . *Virgil*'s art," even while "*Homer*'s . . . *Titian*'s" provides, as it were, the rhyme or imagery of ideas with the other phrases. Or, in a couplet from the second movement on the unpropitious times, "But we who Life bestow, our selves must live; / Kings cannot reign, unless their Subjects give" (ll. 154–155), the syntax and context force the metaphor upon us: artists are kings (as in *Mac Flecknoe*, in the Anne Killigrew ode, and in the poem to Congreve), and "Subjects" (political or artistic) must pay for the rule of the monarchs. The point is that the subjects of the usurping King William pay so much in taxes in the "stupid Military State" of the times that they are no longer fit subjects for great art. Better times may be hoped for, however, and the concluding movement of the poem appropriately makes Time or Age do what "Mortal Art" in such an age could not achieve, so completing a design in which history and art, time and the artist, poetry and painting, the poet and the painter, are at one in a temporal and imagistic movement.

A given kind of imagery in the poem, and the individual image as well, constantly beget imagery, or an image, of another kind. The poetic image appropriates the pictorial, and the pictorial, the poetic. The static art of painting is immersed in time and the times, while the progress of painting in time is completed only when Time becomes the painter. Such an imagistic process—unquestionably witty in the seventeenth-century manner—may be termed one of "fancy wit," of wit discovering likeness in things that are, according to the faculty psychology of the century, apparently different. At the same time, or in passing time, a complementary process of "judgment wit" differentiates between things that are apparently like.[32] The differentiating process is closely related to the temporal sequence, to imagery of various stages in the progress piece, and to contrasts between what ideally might have been as opposed to what so unfortunately is, in the sorry Williamite times. The fancy wit constantly seeks out likeness, as the differentiating wit of judgment discriminates between things that are otherwise brought together. The fancy wit plays especially, though not restrictedly, on artistic matters; the judgment wit, on temporal. At the end the two are made one when Time is judged and fancied to be the artist.

Dryden's enduring but vain Jacobitism is too well known to require emphasis. What has not received adequate attention is his identification of the poet or the artist with monarchy.[33] In the same sense that the Royal Society was "truly Royal" in *Annus Mirabilis* (ll. 661 ff.) for seeking knowledge to the greater glory of God, Flecknoe is a false king because he is a dull poet. In *Threnodia Augustalis* (ll. 364 ff.) the King is the miraculous phoenix, and poets are similarly extraordinary birds of paradise. In the Anne Killigrew ode (st. vii) the poet re-creates the artist re-creating the image of the King and Queen, and (in st. vi) the artist herself is likened to an imperialist king. In *Threnodia Augustalis* (ll. 356 ff.) and in the poem to Congreve (ll. 6–10) the King is himself artist, as Charles II cultivates the age. In the poem to Congreve, however, the lawful king (James II) and the laureate poet have been deposed. The same situation exists in *To Sir Godfrey Kneller*. As he looked about him in the 1690's, Dryden seems to have felt himself, the lawful monarch of wit and imagery, deposed. In fact, the allusion to Jacob and Esau (ll. 95–96) suggests that the poet, lawful prince of artists, has been passed over in the succession for his younger brother, the painter. Whether the poet actually holds primacy over the painter may be a matter open to question, but certainly the vain, temporizing Kneller was willing to paint whoever would pay. Dryden's lines, "But we who Life bestow, our selves must live; / Kings can not reign, unless their subjects give" (ll. 154–155), hold numerous meanings, one of them being that

---

[32] For the validity of "fancy wit" and "judgment wit" in describing seventeenth-century poetry, see my book *The Metaphysical Mode from Donne to Cowley* (Princeton, 1969), pp. 144–145.

[33] George R. Levine has, however, sought to explicate the king as musician in *Absalom and Achitophel* on the basis of "the Davidic *figura*" ("Dryden's 'Inarticulate Poesy,' " *Eighteenth-Century Studies*, I [1968], 291–312, esp. 298, 299–309).

Dryden's poetic subjects had been disaffected from what right and history might have made them. Not many months before, in the "Discourse" prefixed to *The Satires*, Dryden had made a bid for the support of the nobility so that he could write a national and monarchic epic. But the king and the artist-king were deposed: it is not far from the truth to say that in his poem to Kneller, Dryden wrote his own *Eikon Basilike*. For, as Davenant had recognized more than four decades earlier in *Gondibert* (II, vi, 73), the artist is a king: "By an imperial Pencil this was wrought." Ultimately, Dryden was to spend the last years of his life not so much the poet-king as the poet-regent, translating Virgil and producing that incomparably mellow collection, *Fables*. It is a happy thing that something of the warmer light of those last years shines in the concluding section of the poem to Kneller. Dryden's recollection of the picture of the dumb sister, *Pictura*, Kneller's painting of Shakespeare, and Dryden's role as poet-king will be restored by Time. To the old tag, *ut pictura poesis*, Dryden had added, "As the King, so the Poet." And, although he was witnessing the failure of many hopes during the adversities of the 1690's, he could yet add in his final image: "As the Artist, so Time."

X

THE BEAUX' STRATAGEM:
IMAGE AND ACTION[1]

Alan Roper

To complete the patterns of literary history, it sometimes seems that if Farquhar had not existed, it would be necessary to invent him. In the customary division of neoclassic comedy into forty years of wit and sex and some eighty years of sentiment and love, Farquhar is that necessary thing, a transitional writer. He began his dramatic career in 1698, at a time that was "in many profound respects a period of transition."[2] By the laws of sociological determinism it is, then, not surprising to find that his heroes are "too sincerely eloquent and passionate lovers to be the rakes of Restoration comedy, and are too joyously abandoned to dissipation to be the exculpated prodigals of sentimental comedy."[3] Farquhar, we learn, is "the connecting link between the older generation of the Restoration and the rising tide of Cibbers and Steeles"[4] (both of

---

[1] A shorter version of this essay was read at the 1966 meeting of the Modern Language Association.

[2] Dale Underwood, *Etherege and the Seventeenth-Century Comedy of Manners* (New Haven, 1957), p. 72.

[3] Ernest Bernbaum, *The Drama of Sensibility* (Boston and London, 1915), p. 84.

[4] Henry Ten Eyck Perry, *The Comic Spirit in Restoration Drama* (New Haven, 1925), p. 108. Ronald Berman ("The Comedy of Reason," *Texas Studies in Literature and Language*, VII [1965], 161–168) finds *The Beaux' Stratagem* to be "a farewell to mores. . . . In the most general sense it marks a move from the world of Hobbes to that of Shaftesbury" (pp. 167–168). In their edition of *The Beaux' Stratagem* (Great Neck, N.Y., 1963), Vincent F. Hopper and Gerald B. Lahey say "it would be heretical to approach Farquhar . . . without invoking the word *transitional*," but they find the word "too ambiguous a label to affix to the diverse ingredients that make up *The Beaux' Stratagem*" (pp. 16–17).)This edition is cited hereafter as Hopper and Lahey.)

whom, incidentally, were older than Farquhar). Therein lies his sorrow. "As the child of a transition, he was caught between two sets of antagonistic values; he necessarily formulated no harmonious values of his own." [5] Poor Farquhar! It was a cross fate that visited upon such a child of his age the combined sins of Rochester and Jeremy Collier.

These formulas of literary history depend customarily upon what may be called a principle of moral extrapolation. Values and attitudes that are, at least potentially, contributions to a total structure of words are detached from that structure, scrutinized in themselves, and allocated a position in a pattern composed of similarly detached pieces from other plays. These pieces may be scenes, statements about the nature of fool, rake, or gentleman, or something to be ranged beneath the awful banner of themes. Such an activity is not especially perverse when it confines itself to descriptive classification, but it rarely does confine itself thus. Moral values are intoxicating things to critics, and soon lead to the loud confrontation of ethical preferences. We are all familiar with the cries in this ethicocritical war: cynical, immoral, maudlin, mature, immature, responsible, frivolous, aware, myopic.

Critical reaction to one scene may serve to illustrate the possible consequences of such combat. In the fifth act of *The Beaux' Stratagem*, Archer, the unregenerate beau, gains entry into the bedchamber of Mrs. Sullen, a provoked wife of developed sensuality and enfeebled virtue. Archer woos Mrs. Sullen in a mixture of mock-heroic rant, impatient exhortation to hurry on to the right, true end of love, and a nervous reminder to Mrs. Sullen to keep her voice down. He kneels before her in randy excitement, and she, weak, womanly vessel that she is, knows the imminent capitulation of her virtue. "Rise," she explains, "rise thou prostrate Ingineer, not all thy undermining Skill shall reach my Heart." [6] Rarely has the trope of chastity's besieged fortress been put to more pointed comic use. Archer's erotic tunneling is not, after all, directed to her heart. Abandoning the soft sell of persuasion by mythological tropes, Archer lays hold of Mrs. Sullen. "Thieves, Thieves, Murther," she cries. Enter Scrub, the butler, calling "Thieves, Thieves, Murther, Popery," and bringing news that a band of robbers has broken in. With seduction interrupted,

[5] Louis Kronenberger, *The Thread of Laughter* (New York, 1952), p. 183.
[6] Quotations from Farquhar follow the text of *The Complete Works of George Farquhar*, ed. Charles Stonehill (London, 1930).

Archer's attention is given to apprehending the burglars. To one critic, Archer's "violent wooing" of Mrs. Sullen "provides a very emotional scene," one of the "slight sentimental touches in the love-affair" between them. But, fortunately for comedy, this sentimental moment is "interrupted by a farcical burglary."[7] To another critic, the scene exemplifies Farquhar's consistent failure to be either artistic or realistic, because his heroes, torn between "license and honor,"

will not commit themselves to either one. Occasionally an Archer steps completely into the comic picture, but then by his side there is always an Aimwell to spout high morality or a Gibbet [the chief burglar] to interfere with the impulses of nature. Archer is the last effort of the Comedy of Manners to maintain its position in the teeth of Jeremy Collier and eighteenth-century propriety.[8]

To the first critic the wooing is sentimental and the interruption a welcome return to the business of comedy, even if at the level of farce. To the second critic the wooing is comic apparently because it exhibits "the impulses of nature," and the intrusive Gibbet is the rather startling avatar of Jeremy Collier.[9] Their disagreement partly results, I suspect, from an examination of the scene in itself and a measuring of it against some external standard of the comic. But what is important is the demonstrable fact that the scene is a necessary contribution to the total statement of the play, the sum of its doings and sayings. And the fact is important, critically important, just because it is demonstrable.

It was William Archer who pointed somewhere in the direction we should look. He drew a distinction between the dramatist as dramatist and the dramatist as social essayist. In the plays of Wycherley, Congreve, and Vanbrugh he found that the action

[7] Bernbaum, *Drama of Sensibility*, p. 102.
[8] Perry, *Comic Spirit*, pp. 127–128.
[9] Eric Rothstein, in his sensitive and informative *George Farquhar* (New York, 1967), is generally successful in keeping historical elucidation and critical evaluation separate, but he does occasionally simplify the complexity of historical elucidation. Like Hopper and Lahey, he contrasts the unconsummated seduction of Mrs. Sullen with the successful seduction of Berinthia in *The Relapse* as evidence that Farquhar was, in part, responding to a change in "the subject matter of comedy" in "the decade or so before *The Beaux' Stratagem*" (pp. 144–146). We ought to bear in mind not only *The Relapse* and Dorimant's way with Bellinda in *The Man of Mode*, but also such things as Fondlewife's fortuitous interruption of his wife and Bellmour in *The Old Bachelor* and the near misses in the third act of *Marriage A-la-Mode*.

frequently stands still "while the characters expatiate in reflection, generalisation, description, and criticism of other characters; in short, in essays or leading articles broken up into dialogue." Farquhar, by a contrast all in his favor, "confines his characters within the action, and keeps the action moving. . . . He is much less given to the elaborate portrayal of a Jonsonian 'humour' for its own sake." [10] For William Archer, *The Country Wife* and *The Way of the World* were *The Spectator* struggling to come into being. Archer certainly underestimated both the dramatic effectiveness and the significance of the conversational mode in the best Restoration comedies. But he was right to distinguish it at least from Farquhar's final dramatic mode, in which the means of social definition are a combination of saying and doing, of significant action as a source of verbal analogy.

Such a dramatic mode differs from what we find in a play like *The Old Bachelor* where, instead of action as a source of verbal analogy, we have speech, proper and improper, as the effective action. Congreve's first play exhibits various acceptable and unacceptable life styles, styles that reveal themselves in the way characters use language. These uses of language require for their proper exposition an analysis more detailed than the limits of the present essay permit. But part of the use of language is the use of metaphor, and the use of metaphor in *The Old Bachelor* is not only interesting in itself; it also provides us with some of the terms with which to define, if disjunctively, the use of metaphor in *The Beaux' Stratagem*.

With *The Old Bachelor* before us, it is tempting to say that the wit of the best Restoration comedy is radically metaphorical. Certainly, *The Old Bachelor* displays a life style that uses language, especially metaphor, with a due sense of its signification and implication. This style also reveals itself negatively by indicating the reliance of those evidencing an improper life style upon cliché and a complacent display of rhetoric for its own sake—those false or would-be wits who have caught a trick of speaking without grasping the reason for so speaking. Such propositions will surprise few readers of Restoration comedy, and they may therefore be demonstrated briefly by reference, first, to an exchange between Belinda and Bellmour in *The Old Bachelor* (II, ii):

BELINDA. Prithee hold thy Tongue—Lard, he has so pester'd me with Flames and Stuff—I think I shan't endure the sight of a Fire this Twelvemonth.

[10] William Archer, ed., *George Farquhar* (New York, 1959), pp. 24-26.

BELLMOUR. Yet all can't melt that cruel frozen Heart.

BELINDA. O Gad I hate your hideous Fancy—You said that once be-
fore—If you must talk impertinently, for Heav'ns sake let it be with
variety; don't come always, like the Devil, wrapt in Flames—I'll not
hear a Sentence more, that begins with an, I burn—Or an, I beseech
you, Madam.[11]

Let us say, then, that proper speaking as an expression of a proper
life style requires most conspicuously, in the use of image, an
awareness of the concrete significance of vehicles and the necessity
to hold to the tenor.

One way in which such proper speaking manifests itself is
through the pursuit of a (generally cliché) metaphor or simile,
showing the required mental agility by elaborating upon the ve-
hicle in a manner consonant with the tenor. A second way is by
drawing attention to another person's foolish or desperate use of
cliché, especially the clichés of overstatement. Sometimes one
character will ridicule the clichés of another, as in the "fiery"
exchange between Belinda and Bellmour. Sometimes a character,
already established as witty, will use ranting tropes he knows or
believes acceptable to another in order to gull him:

BELLMOUR. Well, I promise.—A promise is so cold.—Give me leave
to swear—by those Eyes, those killing Eyes; by those healing lips.—
Oh! press the soft Charm close to mine,—and seal 'em up for ever.
                                                              He kisses her.

LAETITIA. Upon that Condition.

BELLMOUR. Eternity was in that Moment.—One more, upon any
Condition.

LAETITIA. Nay, now.—(*aside*) I never saw any thing so agreeably
Impudent.   (IV, ii)

And so to bed. A variation on this principle is operative in Archer's
unsuccessful use of mythological tropes to seduce Mrs. Sullen. In
exchanges of this kind the audience must respond, without explicit
direction from a character, to the deliberate "abuse" of language
in the interests of deceiving one presumed incapable of seeing the
abuse: the application of the clichés of adoration to a persuasion to
merely physical indulgence.

A similar perception by the audience is required when a Heart-
well engages in such rant as the following:

---

[11] Quotations from *The Old Bachelor* follow the text of *The Complete Plays of
William Congreve*, ed. Herbert Davis (Chicago, 1967).

Is not this *Silvia's* House, the Cave of that Enchantress and which consequently I ought to shun as I would infection? To enter here, is to put on the envenom'd Shirt, to run into the Embraces of a Fever, and in some raving fit, be led to plunge my self into that more Consuming Fire, a Womans Arms. Ha! well recollected, I will recover my reason and be gone. (III, i)

The ludicrous inappropriateness of this rant to the situation is pointed for us when we recall Antony's tragically apt exclamation on his seeming betrayal by Cleopatra: "The shirt of Nessus is upon me; teach me, / Alcides, thou mine ancestor, thy rage." An incongruity or inappropriateness located in a single word or phrase is evident in Bluffe's thrasonical huff: "I'll call a Council of War within to consider of my Revenge to come" (III, i). This has something of the wit of Terence's *hui! universum triduum!* whose elegance Dryden commended in his essay *Of Dramatick Poesie.*[12]

The practice of the proper life style, revealing itself in an intelligent awareness of language, both permits one to be a social predator, ridiculing, patronizing, and fooling others, and offers a defense against the sallies of other social predators. The aristocrat of intellect must not be outfaced by being caught in an unexamined use of language or by taking himself and others seriously, especially in matters of love. Above all, he must not be laughed at. To put oneself in a position to be laughed at by one's social peers is at least to smirch one's intellectual honor, and perhaps to lose title to the aristocracy or to be revealed as possessing a false title. It is, in fact, to make oneself the butt of a Hobbist laughter, those "grimaces" prompted by the "passion" of "sudden glory," a laughter that is provoked by the folly and misfortune of others because the spectacle of their folly or misfortune ministers to our sense of superiority to others.[13] Such laughter accompanies the application of La Rochefoucauld's maxim, used by Swift in his verses on his death, that there is always something in the misfortune of our friends which does not displease us. Dorimant anticipates the application of this maxim when, outfaced by Mrs. Loveit with Sir Fopling in the Mall, he turns in supplication to Medley: " 'Twere unreasonable to desire you not to laugh at me; but pray do not expose me to the town this day or two." [14] Heartwell also anticipates his social disgrace as a result of pursuing Silvia, that "De-

---

[12] *Essays of John Dryden,* ed. W. P. Ker (New York, 1926), I, 51.
[13] Hobbes, *Leviathan,* ed. Michael Oakeshott (Oxford, 1960), p. 36 (I, 6).
[14] Etherege, *The Man of Mode* (III, iii), ed. W. B. Carnochan (Lincoln, Neb., 1966).

licious, Damn'd, Dear, destructive Woman! S'death how the young Fellows will hoot me! I shall be the Jest of the Town" (III, i). And so it proves, after Heartwell's supposed marriage to Silvia:

BELINDA. I swear, at the Month's End, you shall hardly find a Married-man, that will do a civil thing to his Wife, or say a civil thing to any body else. *Jesus!* how he looks already. Ha, ha, ha.
BELLMOUR. Ha, ha, ha.
HEARTWELL. Death, Am I made your Laughing-stock? (V, ii)

If the poised, skeptically intelligent wit must not be caught out in seriousness or earnestness, then it is easy to see why the subject of love must be approached cautiously. The life style as fully practiced scarcely allows for the intimacy of love, in which one is, at least to some extent, at the mercy of another. Sex and adultery may be approached flippantly, but flippancy is easily if not necessarily destructive of love. Hence the difficulty of "sententious Mirabell" in being serious with Millamant until, in their proviso scene, they achieve an extension of the life style of independence into the mutuality of love, the affection and sentiment fully understood, leaving the mind and tongue free to continue the game. More often, the poised flippancy of courtship requires a conversational style radically different from that needed for serious love and serious marriage. This disjunction is phrased most clearly by Belinda in *The Old Bachelor*, retorting to a sentimental sketch of marital bliss. "Courtship," she says, is "to Marriage, as a very witty Prologue to a very dull Play" (V, i). Fortunately, the conventions of comedy permit a large emphasis upon the vicissitudes of courtship, with the prospect of a marriage of love sketched in the last scene with a few vows, prognostications, and, perhaps, a festive dance. The very economy with which the prospect is sketched disguises the actual disjunction between the style of living and speaking appropriate to courtship and the sex hunt and the style appropriate to marriage and a marriage of love, a disjunction between independence and mutuality.

Comedy, it is true, had customarily concerned itself in various ways with an abdication of responsibility, or a reluctance to enter upon responsibility, or an aberration from a pattern of behavior explicitly or implicitly endorsed within the play. The movement of such plays, and it is at least partly a narrative movement, is toward a final acceptance or reconciliation from which only the

completely incorrigible are excluded, driven from court with
Shylock or locked up as a madman and then laughed out of the
house with Malvolio. The commonest preoccupation of such
comedies is with permutations upon the motives that bring together
the sexes—appetite, prudence, sentiment—often in order to en-
dorse the wisdom of Tennyson's "Northern Farmer, New Style":
"Doänt thou marry for munny, but goä wheer munny is!" Such a
preoccupation permits a clearly marked movement through the
competition of motives to an acceptable reconciliation of them. If
this movement is most obviously ideological, it also has evident
possibilities for illustration in character and plot.

Plays like *The Old Bachelor* and *The Man of Mode*, however,
are notable less for a movement toward acceptance or reconcilia-
tion than for their display of a life style and various aberrations
from it. Elements superficially contributory to narrative, princi-
pally the details of intrigues, are present not so much to forward
a plot or to anatomize motives as to provide matter for discourse
and the consequent display of proper and improper life and con-
versational styles. Despite the evident concern with bed, or clothes,
or money, it is an intensely cerebral life.

And it demands an answering intelligence in the playwright who
ventures to record it. To employ the distinction favored by Dryden
in the preface to *Annus Mirabilis*, "wit written" will not occur
unless the author is capable of "wit writing." [15] The major fallacy
of explanations of literary disparity in terms of historical shifts in
taste and manners is that they unduly neglect the large contribu-
tion of the inequality of talents. Farquhar was simply less intelli-
gent than Etherege or Wycherley, Vanbrugh or Congreve. The
proposition can be illustrated by comparing the way in which a
character in *The Old Bachelor* and a character in *The Beaux'
Stratagem* ridicule the reliance of another upon the clichés of
précieuses exclamations. Here is Congreve:

VAINLOVE. Did I dream? Or do I dream? Shall I believe my Eyes, or
Ears? The Vision is here still.—Your Passion, Madam, will admit of no
farther reasoning.—But here is a silent Witness of your acquaintance.—
Takes out the Letter, and offers it: She snatches it, and throws it away.
ARAMINTA. There's poison in every thing you touch.—Blisters will
follow—
VAINLOVE. That Tongue which denies what the Hands have done.
ARAMINTA. Still mystically senceless and impudent.—I find I must
leave the place.   (IV, iii)

15 *Essays*, ed. Ker, I, 14.

Nothing, indeed, can exceed the elegance of that "mystically," superficially a mere intensifying adverb, amusing by its hyperbolic incongruity, but actually justifying itself by its pointed reference to Vainlove's "visionary" exclamations and by the weight and appropriateness it gives to "senceless." The wit writing here, as so often in Congreve, produces in what is wit written an intelligent pressure on the words. Now Farquhar:

> ARCHER. Well, but heark'ee, *Aimwell*.
> AIMWELL. *Aimwel!* call me *Oroondates, Cesario, Amadis*, all that Romance can in a Lover paint, and then I'll answer. O *Archer*, I read her thousands in her Looks, she look'd like *Ceres* in her Harvest, Corn, Wine and Oil, Milk and Honey, Gardens, Groves and Purling Streams play'd on her plenteous Face.
> ARCHER. Her Face! her Pocket, you mean; the Corn, Wine and Oil lies there. In short, she has ten thousand Pound, that's the English on't.
> (III, ii)

Archer is ridiculing less a lapse of style, a loss of poise, than what he takes to be a loss of candor, a self-deceiving cant. The jeering explicitness of "Her Face! her Pocket, you mean" and "that's the English on't" is remote from the sensibility responsible for Araminta's "still mystically senceless and impudent." It is very close to Rymer's brusque *Short View of* [and shortest way with] *Tragedy*, or Fielding's bluff English response to epic simile and heroic hyperbole in *Tom Jones*, or to Dr. Johnson, that *Jean Bull philosophe*, kicking the stone and thus refuting Berkeley. With such a passage as this between Archer and Aimwell before us, and with the memory of Araminta's snub of Vainlove, it is not hard to see how Pope, in his imitation of Horace's epistle to Augustus, came by his opinion of Farquhar's "pert low Dialogue."

If there were nothing more to say about this exchange between Archer and Aimwell, there would be no reason to see or read *The Beaux' Stratagem* with a greater expectation of pleasure than we might bring to Cibber's *The Careless Husband* or Susanna Centlivre's adaptation of *The Gamester*. But the exchange, whatever its inadequacy as humor, is also one of the many moments in *The Beaux' Stratagem* in which a concern with motive in matters of love finds expression in terms of metaphors drawn from the play's continuous movement, physical and ideological, between two places, the inn and the house. What Farquhar gives us in *The Beaux' Stratagem*, and to a lesser extent in *The Recruiting Officer*, is a play notable for a conspicuous (if at times forcibly imposed) integrity of action, character, dialogue, and setting. By making the moral world of his play commensurate with fully realized places, he is closer, for all the lesser comprehensiveness and intensity of his imagination, to Shakespeare and Jonson than he is to Congreve and Etherege.

In Congreve and Etherege, the recurrence of related metaphors —epithets of the underworld, celestial tropes, images of fashionable materialism, mirrors, clothes, china—may encourage a search for patterns of metaphorical meaning. But the contribution of such patterns is obscured by the concentration on the local use of what were, after all, the cliché commonplaces of the age: Is the local cliché wittily renewed or complacently retailed? The relevant holism, what associates these local uses with one another, is the contribution of each part, each metaphor, not to the significant total meaning of the metaphors—a materialist society, say, desperately in search of a proper theology and a proper morality— but to the significant way in which metaphor is used to reveal proper and improper life styles founded on conversation. Farquhar, less intelligent than the best of his predecessors, produced, finally, a dramatic mode in which the smaller local pressure on the use of metaphors freed them to relate, manifestly, to one another and, by deriving from the action, to underline its meaning.

It was not so at the beginning of Farquhar's career. *Love and a Bottle*, his first play, offers an intrigue plot with a complex and farcical life of its own. As a vehicle for socially satiric conversations on love, friendship, soldiers, wine, seduction, foppery, snuff, dancing, poetry, theaters, fencing, Oxford, it is distracting in its robust complications. The protagonist is no self-aware honest man, but a randy Irishman just arrived in London, ready to chase off-stage with a priapic bellow in adolescent pursuit of a passing woman (IV, iii). As the most lustful example of lusty *juventus*, he prompts not a set of analogies based upon clothes and cards, fruit and mirrors, but a series of quasi-theological references to paradise, forbidden fruit and forbidden knowledge, serpents, devils, flesh, and fall. Driven out of Ireland, that venomless paradise, by fleshly indulgence in forbidden fruit with his whore, he comes to London to enter into sin (I, i), to be a rakehelly rascal (III, i). He seeks in the back door to his mistress's house "the narrow Gate to the Lovers Paradice" (IV, iv). Reclaimed at the end by the love of a good woman, he pensions off his whore, rejecting her as a stale iniquity, and is ready to pronounce the moral: *"Paradice was lost by Woman's Fall; / But Vertuous Woman thus restores it all."*

The theology is, obviously, confused by the indiscriminate use of paradise as a source both of moral definition and double entendre. In addition, the physical activity implied by the paradise references has only a tenuous likeness to the physical activity of the intrigues. Paradise organizes a set of quasi-theological glosses upon an action to which it is only superficially analogous.

In subsequent plays Farquhar several times took up a favorite topic of some of his predecessors: the social falsity of travel in providing, not a broadening of a gentleman's understanding, but matter for his folly or iniquity to feed upon. Both *The Constant Couple* and *Sir Harry Wildair* are dominated by the past or future travels of a number of the main characters. But the kind of character definition the travels provide has, once again, little reference to the details of what these busy characters actually do. The drift of the plays is to the working out of relationships by a reclamation from folly or incontinence or by the removal of misapprehension over identity or personality. Travel certainly contributes to misapprehension and redeemable incontinence, and it is to some extent a unifying motif since so many of the characters are affected by it. But there is no necessary connection, no true analogy. Incontinence and misapprehension can originate elsewhere, as they do in *The Constant Couple* when the vallain revenges himself on the hero by persuading him that the heroine is a whore, her mother a bawd, and their house a brothel.

It was in *The Recruiting Officer* and, less clearly, in *The Twin Rivals* that Farquhar found his way to uniting the busy activity of his intrigue plots and the social definitions implied by the occurrence of related metaphors in conversation. The very title of *The Recruiting Officer* suggests those twin concerns with enlisting soldiers and getting wives which serve not only as a means to revitalize such aging literary preoccupations as love and honor and the trope of the love battle; they also provide parallel actions that are mutually revelatory because they are analogies for each other. Especially do they share a concern with financial trickery in the purchase of recruits or mistresses and the monetary disposition of daughters in marriage. The two activities are united by the heroine's disguising herself as a young man in order to be "enlisted" by the hero so that she might test his love and worth and prove to her father the falsity of disposing of her only to a high bidder. The enlistment intrigues are both a source of metaphor for the love intrigues and the means by which the complications of the love plot are resolved. The chief weakness of *The*

Recruiting Officer is that the important subplot of the civilian second lovers expresses its analogy with the main plot wholly in terms of the conventional tropes of the love battle, in contrast with the metaphorical density of the main plot itself—with its paralleling, often identification, of wenching and enlisting, fighting for money and marrying for money, false honor on the battlefield and false love at home. Consequently, the revitalized analogy emerges as true of a recruiting officer's situation, but lacking full relevance for more general social concerns as they affect sex relations and marriage. The Petrarchan tropes of the subplot insist upon an analogy with the main plot which exists only tenuously. If *The Recruiting Officer* is not completely satisfactory, however, it does point clearly to the grounds of success in Farquhar's last and best play, *The Beaux' Stratagem.*

The Beaux' Stratagem chiefly establishes its meanings by a fruitful juxtaposition of its two, alternating scenes of action, the inn of Boniface and the house of Lady Bountiful, and by an interrelation of hospitality and sexual emotion—love or appetite. In each place and activity it is chiefly the attitude toward money which distinguishes the right from the wrong way.[16] Such a movement and such attitudes are reminiscent of *The Merchant of Venice,* with its alternation between Venetian streets and the walks of Belmont.

Boniface's hospitality is, as his name promises, only superficially good. He bustles about, providing food and drink to distract from his chief concern with tricking guests out of their money. He overcharges the French prisoners of war, and when he thinks Aimwell and Archer are highwaymen, he plans to betray them and thus gain the £200 they deposit with him (I, i). To prove his suspicions and gain the means for betrayal he is willing that his daughter Cherry be debauched by Archer, who is disguised as Aimwell's servant. He will harbor no rogues but his own Gibbet, Hounslow, and Bagshot, highwaymen and housebreakers based at his inn. But when they are caught he absconds with all

[16] If the scene changes whenever the stage is cleared of characters for a moment, then there are seventeen scenes, only eleven of which are marked in the text (II, ii, and V, i, comprise two scenes each, and Act IV, marked as one scene, contains five). There are two inn sets—the entrance hall and the beaux' chamber —and three or four house sets, principally the gallery and Mrs. Sullen's bedchamber. The first act is set entirely in the inn, and the ethos thus established is recalled by brief inn scenes in each of the remaining acts, which are principally set in various apartments of the house. For a reconstruction of the probable method by which these sets were changed see George L. Hersey's note on staging in Hopper and Lahey's edition of the play (pp. 45–60).

the money he can lay hands on, leaving the highwaymen to swing (V, iv). This false, financially motivated hospitality contrasts with the true hospitality of Lady Bountiful, who lays out half of her income "in charitable Uses for the Good of her Neighbours" (I, i). Lady Bountiful's care for the poor is given dramatic, if negative, realization in the scene between Mrs. Sullen and the country-woman with a sick husband (IV, i). Mrs. Sullen's reaction to the countrywoman, her issuing of maliciously false advice, is so delib-erately overstated as to effect a comic neutralization of any outrage at her careless cruelty. Her advice, reminiscent of Medea's instruc-tions to the daughters of Pelias for the "rejuvenation" of their father, has something of the inventive hyperbole of Lady Wish-fort's ritual commination of Foible in *The Way of the World*. Mrs. Sullen's response is, of course, that of the townee bored with the simple pieties of the country.

These contrasting attitudes to hospitality parallel in the main intrigue of courtship and marriage the distinction between those who approach marriage for love and those who approach it for money. Charity is the social counterpart of the private virtue of love. At the beginning of the play both Aimwell and Archer are fortune hunters, and marriage to them would be more tolerable than marriage to Squire Sullen, Lady Bountiful's son, with his similar financial motivation, only because they are more witty and agreeable. Sullen assures his wife's brother when he comes to take her away from an unhappy marriage that he has no quarrel with his wife's fortune, he only hates his wife (V, i). In the final scene of separation by mutual consent, Sullen readily parts with his wife, but has to be forced to part with her portion by Archer's handing over the husband's papers to Mrs. Sullen's brother.[17]

[17] Just why Archer's act should force the restitution of the portion constitutes a minor crux, as is noted by Hopper and Lahey (p. 36). The solution is probably to be found in Gellert Spencer Alleman's *Matrimonial Law and the Materials of Restoration Comedy* (Wallingford, Pa., 1942), although Alleman's own explicit solution is unsatisfactory: he simply notes that by possessing Sullen's "writings" Archer or Freeman would have Sullen at his mercy (p. 112). A fuller solution is implied by the data Alleman supplies on pages 107–108. Dorinda and Mrs. Sullen agree that there are no grounds for a "Case of Separation" in the ecclesiastical courts (II, i). The only possibility, then, is separation by mutual consent, the form the Sullens go through in the final scene. The law of the time provided for alimony for the wife in all cases of separation or divorce, even if she was an adulteress. The alimony consisted of her refunded portion and an allowance de-termined by her husband's income. Alleman describes a case in which a couple who separated by mutual consent disagreed, apparently over the terms of the settlement. Their case was heard by a civil court, which ordered the refund of the wife's portion and a small allowance. Since Sullen had gone through a separa-

Aimwell is intent upon marrying the fortune of Dorinda, Lady Bountiful's daughter, although his final reclamation to selfless love is prepared for in the opening scene by Archer's characterization of him as "an amorous Puppy . . . [who] can't counterfeit the Passion without feeling it." Archer can, and he demonstrates his sexual virtuosity by busying himself with minor speculations in sex and money with Cherry at the inn and an amour with the susceptible Mrs. Sullen at the house as incidental relief from intriguing on Aimwell's behalf. His appetite for Cherry is sharpened when she tells him she has £2,000, but he rejects her suggestion of marriage: "what need you make me Master of your self and Money, when you may have the same Pleasure out of me, and still keep your Fortune in your Hands" (II, ii).

In one of the early conflations of women and property, Archer remarks, "I love a fine House, but let another keep it; and just so I love a fine Woman" (I, i). Like the beaux, Mrs. Sullen, understandably embittered, thinks in terms of money. Her thoughts run on her dowry, and she observes shortly afterward that "Women are like Pictures of no Value in the Hands of a Fool, till he hears Men of Sense bid high for the Purchase" (II, i). Immediately, Mrs. Sullen is concerned with the property approach to women, but her simile prepares for the wooing of herself and Dorinda by the beaux in terms of the pictures in the house. When the women compare notes afterward, it emerges that Archer "thought" Mrs. Sullen the original of a Venus, while Aimwell took Dorinda "for *Venus* her self" (IV, i). The mythological eroticism of the paintings recurs in the trope Archer indulges in when he first enters Mrs. Sullen's bedchamber (V, ii), thus completing the circle of pictures, property, mythology, and eroticism.

Even the innocent Dorinda has to lose her social and financial taint, her wish to marry a title. "Why," she says to Mrs. Sullen, "my Ten thousand Pounds may lie brooding here this seven Years, and hatch nothing at last but some ill natur'd Clown like yours:— Whereas, If I marry my Lord *Aimwell*, there will be Title, Place and Precedence, the Park, the Play, and the drawing-Room,

tion by mutual consent before witnesses, he apparently hoped to keep his wife's portion by denying, if the dispute came to court, that she had brought him one. His "writings," which included the articles of marriage, would prove the contrary. Moreover, if the case came to court, Sullen would also have to make his wife an allowance proportionate to his income. His "writings" further contained the evidence on which that allowance would be based. He therefore compounds and refunds the portion. Farquhar's handling is certainly careless; one sentence from Archer or Freeman would have been sufficient to resolve the crux.

Splendor, Equipage, Noise and Flambeaux" (IV, i). When Aim-well's love for Dorinda has brought him to "prefer the Interest of my Mistress to my own" and to confess that he has pretended to the title of his brother to trick her, she, in return, finds herself prouder that he is without title and fortune than she was when he apparently possessed them: "Now I can shew my Love was justly levell'd, and had no Aim but Love" (V, iv). Shortly afterward, Sir Charles Freeman, who has come to take away his sister Mrs. Sullen, gives the news of Lord Aimwell's death. Although Freeman and his news are usually and with some justice taken as a facile deus ex machina allowing virtue to live happily ever after,[18] Lord Aimwell's death accomplishes two things, one quasi-symbolic, the other morally realistic. When Aimwell's conscience works on him and makes him declare to Dorinda "I'm all Counterfeit except my Passion" (V, iv), he not only echoes Archer's early marking of his inability to counterfeit a passion without feeling it and the later discussion of imperfect imitation in paintings, he has also, morally speaking, ceased to be counterfeit at all. He is accordingly rewarded by becoming the veritable Lord Aimwell. Dorinda and Aimwell do not need his title and wealth, for they would still have £5,000, half her portion, the other half going, in accordance with the beaux' agreement, to Archer. They "earn" the title and fortune as soon as they renounce them. Aimwell's access of wealth also enables him to propose a Solomonic test of motivation by offering Archer not half of Dorinda's portion, but a choice between Dorinda and her whole fortune. Archer takes the £10,000.

Love and hospitality are, then, paralleled in a manner richly productive of incidental metaphor. The principal form of these metaphors is to compare love with a dwelling or property, as in Aimwell's rapture over Dorinda's cornucopian beauty and Archer's jeering response to it. When Mrs. Sullen asks Archer how he got into her bedchamber, he replies, "I flew in at the Window, Madam, your Cozen Cupid lent me his Wings, and your Sister *Venus* open'd the Casement" (V, ii). The visitation of Cupid is also implied in Archer's catechism of Cherry: "Where does Love enter?" (II, ii), and it recurs in Mrs. Sullen's exclamation to Dorinda, "I own my self a Woman, full of my Sex, a gentle, generous Soul,—easie and yielding to soft Desires; a spacious Heart, where Love and all his Train might lodge. And must the fair Apartment of my Breast be

18 Berman, "Comedy of Reason," p. 164; Hopper and Lahey, p. 21. Rothstein (*Farquhar*, pp. 156–157) discusses Freeman as "a narrative and thematic agent who precipitates a resolution that he has never effected."

made a Stable for a Brute to lie in?" (IV, i). When, earlier, Dorinda endeavors to console Mrs. Sullen with the recollection that her husband makes her an allowance, she retorts, "A Maintenance! do you take me, Madam, for an hospital Child, that I must sit down, and bless my Benefactors for Meat, Drink and Clothes?" And with such a low view of charity, she naturally goes on to express contempt for Lady Bountiful's benevolence: "spreading of Plaisters, brewing of Diet-drinks, and stilling Rosemary-Water with the good old Gentlewoman, my Mother-in-Law" (II, i).

In addition to producing incidental metaphors, the paralleling of love and hospitality is accompanied by a conventional discrimination of their values into selfishness and selflessness which is fully implicated into character, action, and setting. The schemes of the beaux involve Aimwell's pretending a fit calculated to play upon Lady Bountiful's hospitality and so bring them within the house. Because such an entry is devious and is designed to gain money, or sexual gratification, or both, it may properly be associated with the sexual and financial atmosphere of the inn. The beaux are intent upon carrying the values of the inn to the house. The infiltration, in fact, has already begun. Mrs. Sullen is involved in a liaison with Count Bellair, a captured French officer who lodges at the inn, by which she hopes to put a jealous edge on Sullen's dull appetite for her. But Sullen himself is also occupied in carrying the values of the inn to the house, for he spends long hours at the inn, returning to the house with an aching head to call for food and drink as if he were still at the inn, or, as Mrs. Sullen puts it, returning late at night to come "flounce into Bed, dead as a Salmon into a Fishmonger's Basket; his Feet cold as Ice, his Breath hot as a Furnace, and his Hands and his Face as greasy as his Flanel Night-cap.—Oh Matrimony!" (II, i). The nature of matrimony at the inn is further revealed in the exchange between Boniface and Sir Charles Freeman. Boniface asks, "Are not Man and Wife one Flesh?" and Freeman replies, "You and your Wife, Mr. Guts, may be one Flesh, because ye are nothing else—but rational Creatures have minds that must be united" (V, i). The inn's values are flesh and money.

Lest there be any doubt about the nature of the values and social distinctions involved in character, action, and verbal analogy, there is in the activities of the highwaymen a superficially inconsequential subplot which is, in fact, integral with the total meaning and action of the play. The highwaymen, principally Gibbet, their leader and spokesman, are the most conspicuously predatory representatives of the inn at which they are based. Their attempted robbery of the house at the instigation of Boniface parallels the beaux' attempt to gain money from the house by pretended love. Just as the analogies in *The Recruiting Officer* depend in part upon the trope of the love battle, so the importance of Gibbet and his gang depends in part upon the convention that highwaymen are "gentlemen of the road," a convention, of course, which Gay later put to good use in *The Beggar's Opera*. The parallel between the beaux' stratagem and Gibbet's housebreaking is present in his insistence that "there's a great deal of Address and good Manners in robbing a Lady, I am the most a Gentleman that way that ever travell'd the Road" (IV, i). We should not forget that Aimwell and Archer are also gentlemen who travel the roads of England in search of a lady's fortune. When they first put up at Boniface's inn, he mistakes them for highwaymen because, like Gibbet, they have a box of money and keep their horses saddled. Gibbet laments that he is "only a younger Brother" (V, ii), a condition of notorious financial consequences which he shares with Archer (II, ii) and also with Aimwell, of course. The analogy between Archer's sexual housebreaking and Gibbet's monetary housebreaking is further prepared for by Bellair's remark that if Sullen "but knew the Value of the Jewel he is Master of, he wou'd always wear it next his Heart, and sleep with it in his Arms" (III, iii). When Mrs. Sullen, her husband's neglected jewel, rallies her virtue to cry "Thieves, Thieves, Murther" at Archer's offered familiarity, the echo of Scrub's "Thieves, Thieves, Murther, Popery," inspired not by her plight but by the presence of robbers, serves to identify the activities of Archer and Gibbet. Lest the point should still prove elusive, Scrub proceeds to mistake Archer for one of the housebreakers, and Archer cheerfully admits that he too has come to rob Mrs. Sullen, but of a different jewel.

In addition to making even clearer the moral status of the beaux' stratagem, the highwaymen's adventure contributes largely to the comic resolution of the play. In the last act the inn and its values make a bodily assault upon the house and its values. Gibbet's housebreaking not only interrupts Archer at a crucial moment, it moves Cherry to rouse Aimwell to the rescue because Lady Bountiful is her godmother and she loves Dorinda. With the collapse of the burglary, Boniface absconds, robbing his own inn. It is, moreover, during the burglary that Sullen's papers are confiscated by Archer and handed over to Mrs. Sullen's brother to force the restitution of her portion. At the end of the play the forces of the inn are scattered, although none will be too severely punished, for even Gibbet has £200 in reserve to buy his life at the sessions. Gibbet and his gang may appear to operate, inconsequentially, within a buffo subplot, may be permitted a few rough jests from time to time, and may be ready, at authorial fiat, to dissolve sentiment into comedy or, perhaps, comedy into sentiment. But the presence of Gibbet, what he says and does, confirms the propriety of reading *The Beaux' Stratagem* as a play in which image and action are mutually enriching: what one character does provides others and himself with metaphors for conversation. I confess to a great fondness for Gibbet, and am reluctant to sacrifice him to those who would find him Jeremy Collier in disguise or the Comic Spirit made flesh. I think him an ineluctable highwayman, a gentleman of the road, and not the less interesting for that.

XI

SOME REMARKS ON
SEVENTEENTH-CENTURY IMAGERY:
DEFINITIONS AND CAVEATS

Pierre Legouis

Having been asked, at rather short notice for one so slow as I, to write on seventeenth-century imagery, I beg leave to do it somewhat erratically and in a rather unscholarly way: I shall trust to a (tired) memory without reading, or rereading through, what has been written on the subject for the past forty-odd years. In 1920, indeed (old men are allowed to be reminiscent), I chose for the subject of my *thèse complémentaire* a study of Donne's imagery; I even corresponded with Grierson on that project and he wisely warned me that "metaphors out of context are rather dead things." Undeterred, I set some of my brighter students to write *mémoires de diplôme* (intermediate between M.A. and Ph.D. theses) on subjects cognate with my own. But by the time I had completed my *thèse principale* a new idea had dawned upon me, less dangerous and more limited. I do not regret having adopted it, since *Donne the Craftsman* at least made a stir (mostly protests). Yet I missed an opportunity of doing what is called by the younger generation, somewhat patronizingly, "pioneer work" on imagery, before this field became popular. A lecture to the English Association branches at Oxford and Southampton in 1930 was the only outcome of my earlier project. It adumbrated some of the views that Rosemond Tuve was to set forth in a masterly way and with a wealth of erudition which holds me in awe.

By 1924 I should not, however, have come first in the field, even among my contemporaries. In that year came out an important and original book, Henry W. Wells's *Poetic Imagery Il-lustrated from Elizabethan Literature*, where "radical metaphors" are proposed as the chief characteristic of Donne's poetry. My own study of the *Songs and Sonets* was intended to correct Wells's thesis, to some extent, obliquely, but I fought shy of meeting him frontally; it seemed too soon to plod across the ground he had traversed in striking style.

And then came the flood. Even by 1951 the bibliography in Wolfgang H. Clemen's *The Development of Shakespeare's Imagery* had grown impressive, and I must confess unacquaintance with most of the books on his list, as with many more that have appeared since. What remains, then, but to carp at those research workers who have used the spade and taken risks in the analysis of their finds? The editor of this volume seems to expect from me definitions and caveats: here they are in approved schoolmasterly manner.

Imagery is so comprehensive a term that in teaching it proves dangerous, or at least tricky. I shall not try to trace its semantic history further back than the *Oxford English Dictionary*, which records no earlier instances than those in Puttenham's *Arte of English Poesie*. There imagery is only one of the three "sorts" of "resemblance," made specific by its equivalence to "Pourtrait" and to the Greek "Icon." So far so good. Later, Puttenham flounders somewhat: judging by the instances he gives from his own poetry one of the terms (the tenor in Richardsian terminology [1]) should be a person; the other (the vehicle) may be "any other naturall thing," not only an animal but a vegetable, or a mineral, or (in modern parlance) an artifact. The gratuitous limitation of the tenor (man alone deserving to be portrayed in words as well as in paint?) seems to have been Puttenham's exclusively. It need not bother us.

Let us take a long leap to Hobbes. He does not, as far as I can see, use the collective noun "imagery," but he has a paragraph on "Images" in the preface to his translation of the *Odyssey*.[2] Like Puttenham he considers "image" as the equivalent of "icon" in the critical vocabulary of the ancients, but he goes further than Puttenham in limiting its meaning: it "is always a part, or rather the ground of a Poetical comparison." Then it is only the vehicle;

---

[1] I am grateful to Professor I. A. Richards for coining two convenient terms to designate the components of the image, but that is all I have assimilated of his philosophical theories, known to me, I must confess, mostly at second hand.

[2] See J. E. Spingarn, ed., *Critical Essays of the Seventeenth Century* (3 vols.; Bloomington, Ind., 1957), II, 71.

if you add to it the tenor "you have the comparison entire." Whether we adopt Hobbes's definition or not, I consider that his method went in the right direction because it aimed at greater precision. The modern tendency has been, on the contrary, to extend the meaning of critical terms beyond recognition. More of this anon.

Dryden uses the word "imagery" twice in his poetry, both times as a term belonging to the fine arts and entirely unmetaphorical. I do not remember meeting the word in his prose. But what of his use of "imaging"? It is not free from ambiguity (a fault): in *The Authors Apology for Heroique Poetry*, for instance, he seems to give "imaging" its widest meaning when he proclaims it "in itself, the very height and life of poetry," [3] calling to his support Longinus, whose notion of "images" is no more specific. And even in the instances of the word "image" listed in the glossary of Watson's edition under the meaning "trope, a rhetorical analogy," we are none too sure that Dryden does not include "descriptions," a term several times linked by him with "images" by means of the conjunction "or," which may be translated either *aut* or *vel*. On one occasion at least Dryden passes a description for an image: Camilla flying over wheat field or sea, as painted "in the 8th of the Aeneids," if a trope at all, comes under hyperbole, not simile or metaphor (Watson, I, 202).

The embarrassing ambiguity has continued from Dryden to our day. In the second paragraph of her capital book, *Elizabethan and Metaphysical Imagery*, Rosemond Tuve noted that the "theorist of the Renaissance . . . takes far greater care . . . than do the authors of modern discussions of poetry, to preserve the important logical distinction between such imagery [viz., "mere descriptive detail"] and imagery introducing the element of metaphor and similitude." In order, presumably, to illustrate this modern lack of "care" she at once quotes five instances of Elizabethan and early seventeenth-century imagery, at least two of which—one from *Hero and Leander* and one from *The Faerie Queene*—are mere description. As she herself points out, the five instances have in common that they are "deliberately and richly sensuous"—but that is all. And yet her book is really concerned with the image as (part of) a metaphor or similitude.

The more extensive sense of "imagery" indeed proves convenient for such studies as Caroline Spurgeon's, aiming primarily at discov-

[3] See George Watson, ed., *John Dryden: Of Dramatic Poesy and Other Critical Essays* (2 vols.; London and New York, 1962), I, 203 (hereafter cited as Watson).

ering the man and his tastes behind the poet. Rosemond Tuve's objections (pp. 422–423) do not seem to me decisive enough to dismiss altogether this approach (derisively called "Spurgeonism" by a recent critic [4]), even if we grant that it has its limitations and its deceptions, and that it remains superficial so far as poetry is concerned. Of course the hunting grounds for images are largely commonplaces, *loci communes*. Take, for instance, warfare: Marvell, who apparently never saw a battlefield, draws largely upon it. But when Sidney in his *Arcadia* borrows many images from the fine arts—I could provide a list—it shows the connoisseur.

No less insistently than Caroline Spurgeon, but more openly, Wolfgang Clemen rejects any limitation of the term "imagery" and allows it to include descriptions that entail no comparison. One instance is common to the two critics: in Othello's speech beginning "Farewell the plumed troop . . . ," down to "circumstance of glorious war," all is graphic but nothing is metaphorical; the passage calls up the facts of military life, as Othello has experienced them.[5] I am not censuring Clemen any more than Caroline Spurgeon. I only regret the absence, or nonexistence, of a term that would mean "comparison and metaphor" and nothing else. If someone should object to "comparison" itself as too broad and indefinite a word I would readily substitute "simile" as more technical, widely used by critics and rhetoricians in the seventeenth century, and still current, it seems, in schools.

Whether named "comparison" or "simile," the figure announces itself and is obvious to a fault, some moderns deem. Yet the presence of "as," "like," "such," and so on, does not automatically certify that the vehicle of a comparison follows. For instance, when near the end of Dryden's *All for Love* Charmian maintains that Cleopatra's death "is well done, and like a Queen, the last / Of her great Race," the critic [6] should not list this passage as a comparison: Cleopatra *is* a queen, and the last of the Ptolemies. Here

---

[4] Bernard N. Schilling, *Dryden and the Conservative Myth* (New Haven, 1961), p. 8.

[5] When Professor Clemen says (*The Development of Shakespeare's Imagery* [Cambridge, Mass., 1951], p. 167) that in "the whole tragedy" of *Antony and Cleopatra* "we see before us the gleaming multi-coloured image of the changeable queen, now whore, now courtesan, now royal lover," he seems to give the word "image" a newly developed (American?) meaning. In Shakespeare's time calling a woman a whore (i.e., unchaste) was no metaphor but just a bit of plain speaking.

[6] Otto Reinert, "Passion and Pity in *All for Love*," in M.-S. Røstvig et al., *The Hidden Sense and Other Essays* (Oslo, 1963), p. 192.

"like" is an adjective meaning "characteristic of; such as one might expect from" (*OED*, 6b). The first instance is from Pepys's *Diary*, in the year 1667; this use of "like" was apparently unknown to Shakespeare, who makes Charmian say: "It is well done, and fitting for a princess. . . ." By the way, that speech, borrowed from Plutarch, is to my mind the noblest one in either play.

"Metaphor" should require no comment: the term proved remarkably stable in meaning since its introduction into English (more than two centuries after its introduction into French!) until recently when a tendency has appeared to blow up (in the photographic sense) that figure, hitherto characterized by brevity and compactness. Through no fault of its own, it now risks the fate of Phaedrus' frog which, inflated, blew up in a sinister sense. For instance, the whole of *Absalom and Achitophel* has been considered as one metaphor because English history is continuously translated into Jewish history.[7] There is nothing in the etymology of the Greek word, I grant, to prevent such a use, but I question its convenience, its advisability. Why not call *Absalom and Achitopel* an allegory since this figure is "an extended or continued metaphor" according to the *Oxford English Dictionary*, which barely modernizes Puttenham's "a long and perpetuall Metaphore"? True, Fowler prefers to call allegory "an extended simile," but by his own distinction a simile is explicit, "a comparison proclaimed as such," whereas an allegory remains tacit, implicit, like a metaphor: the tenor "in a full allegorie . . . should not be discovered but left at large to the readers judgment and conjecture"; otherwise, says Puttenham, it is only a "mixt" allegory. Therefore I, for once, incline to disagree with Fowler. And "allegory" applied to *Absalom and Achitophel* certainly means no detraction if we follow Puttenham, who calls it not only a "Courtly figure" but "the chief ringleader and captaine of all other figures." Let us admit, however, that between a single word, or phrase, and a whole poem we often meet intermediate extensions for which we have no specific name. We may call them continued metaphors or brief allegories as they come nearer to the one or the other pure form.[8]

[7] Earl Miner, *Dryden's Poetry* (Bloomington and London, 1967), p. 110. I entertain similar doubts about the imagistic discussion of *Absalom and Achitophel* in Arthur W. Hoffman, *John Dryden's Imagery* (Gainesville, Fla., 1962).

[8] A remarkable instance of continued metaphor is quoted (in *The Talent of T S Eliot* [Seattle, 1929; Chicago, 1969]) by the much-regretted George Williamson (who, however, calls it a comparison) from *Prufrock*, ll. 13–22. It is peculiar in that it opens with a plain introducing of the tenor, "The yellow fog," which at once turns into a cat without the animal being mentioned—we have to intuit

When in the twenties I read the philosophical statement, "All language is metaphor," I was impressed by that arresting generalization. But on second thought it seems to mean that before a word was used to mean anything it had been used to mean something else, which looks like an Irish bull. I have just read in a French *thèse de doctorat ès lettres* (which approves) that Owen Barfield "est persuadé que la métaphore était là à l'origine" of language, which sounds somewhat like the same conception, but I must suspend judgment until I have read *Poetic Diction*.

Also in the twenties I read an article by one of Bergson's disciples proving that all the Aristotelian logic was reducible to analogy. It might be argued, and probably has been argued, that all rhetorical figures also are. But this technical term, "analogy," has already suffered from undue extension involving degradation. The definition given by Samuel Johnson, "resemblance of things with regard to some circumstances or effects," was not considered obsolete by the *Oxford English Dictionary* in 1888, but I am afraid it is now regarded by logicians only; the vaguer meaning, "agreement between things, similarity," currently replaces it. I am not sure I have not sinned myself in this respect. Yet it is a pity to reduce this word to a mere synonym of "resemblance."

I protest more strongly against the abuse of "type," at least in scholarly criticism of seventeenth-century works and, a fortiori, of works produced in earlier ages. In the mid-nineteenth century, when democratization and journalism began to play havoc with the vocabulary in all progressive countries, "type" drifted from its high position in the language of divinity to become an equivalent to "kind" or "class" and even to designate a representative of a class; hence the modern colloquial "an energetic type," almost as bad as the present vulgar French use in which *un type* by itself means a chap or a bloke. In the field of imagery I should never use "type" unless I could name the "antitype": for instance, "Heywood

---

it; all the predicates are among those currently attached to the vehicle, and few readers could have guessed that the fog was meant had they not been told from the start.

I do not agree with Geoffrey H. Hartman ("'The Nymph Complaining for the Death of Her Fawn': A Brief Allegory," *Essays in Criticism*, XVIII [1968], 113–135) that "The Nymph" is an allegory at all. Yet I must concede that Hartman speaks (pp. 130–131) of "brief allegory" as his "own coinage, on the analogy of Milton calling the Book of Job 'a brief epic.'"

H. W. Fowler is quoted from *A Dictionary of Modern English Usage* (2d ed.; Oxford, 1965), p. 559 (as in 1st ed., *s.v.* "simile and metaphor"). George Puttenham is quoted from *The Arte of English Poesie*, ed. G. D. Willcock and A. Walker (Cambridge, Eng., 1936), p. 187 (II, xviii).

and Shirley were but types of" Shadwell.[9] Accordingly, "typology" (if we have to use the word, unknown to the seventeenth century) can mean nothing else than the study of types and antitypes.

Similarly we should never use "emblem" without bearing in mind the pictorial origin of the term, when we write on an age during which collections of prints entitled *Emblems* gave its most popular support to poetry—of a sort. Normally the vehicle, as a word picture, would be the emblem of the tenor, that is, the subject in hand. At least once, however, Dryden inverted the terms when he called Phaleg "An Emblem of that buzzing Insect Just / That mounts the Wheell, and thinks she raises Dust," in fact, La Fontaine's *mouche du coche* (*Absalom and Achitophel*, Pt. II, ll. 336–337). The taunt is more insulting turned that way since the man stands for the fly instead of the fly's illustrating the man's character.

"Symbol" is often preferable because of its less restrictive seventeenth-century use. This term should, however, retain something of its corporeal origin. An abstraction can hardly be symbolic. People can and do speak nowadays of sexual symbols, but sex itself cannot be a symbol; much less can "Alexas' sexlessness" be "one of the play's major symbols" in *All for Love*.[10] Rosemond Tuve has wisely warned us not to read sixteenth- and seventeenth-century poets through the theories of the *Symbolistes*. And it will serve no useful purpose to allow "symbol" to encroach upon "allegory."

Another annexionist is "myth," of which Bernard Schilling says that it "has become so useful in literary study that it can defend or illustrate almost any position one chooses." [11] This remark, however, is far from ironical, and the critic does not deplore this extension of the term, but enumerates all the uses it can be put to in order to justify his adoption of it in the title of his own book. Granting that his "conservative myth" bears some likeness to the myth of the Golden Age, yet the latter retains the notion of a tale, a narrative, even if it blooms into a description. Personally, I should consider the vogue enjoyed of late by "myth" a reason for eschewing it. But I may also be prejudiced against it by the skeptical French use of *mythe* as the contrary of reality, almost a lie.

[9] Let us hope the phrase "a prototype of Christ," applied to Samson, is only a lapsus; it should not become a precedent. See H. T. Swedenberg, Jr., "Dryden's Obsessive Concern with the Heroic," *Studies in Philology*, extra ser., no. 4 (1967), p. 22.
[10] Reinert, "Passion and Pity," p. 190.
[11] Schilling, *Dryden and the Conservative Myth*, pp. 1–2.

I have sufficiently denounced elsewhere the craze for ambiguities not to deal with the term at length here. It came in as a more respectable substitute for the French, or quasi-French, *double-entendre*. Of course all the ambiguities discovered in seventeenth-century poets are not fictitious; but do even the genuine ones take place among images, though the old rhetoric did not include them in its classification? I see no reason to reject them provided one of the meanings is concrete enough to be visualized. The French critic of today has copied his English colleague: he duly discovers and praises *ambiguité(s)*. But the true *dixseptièmiste* prefers to use *pointe(s)* for the sort of ambiguity that is something of a metaphor. Lanson says it consists in the taking of a word successively or simultaneously in two different acceptations, "comme le propre et le figuré." But is there assimilation of the one meaning, as tenor, to the other one, as vehicle? If so it could rank among the metaphors, if not comparisons. In fact *la pointe* lends itself to opposition, to antithesis we might say, as in Racine's line (possibly his worst) instanced by Lanson: "Brûlé de plus de feux que je n'en allumai"; *feux* is at once figurative as object of *Brûlé* and concrete enough as antecedent of the relative pronoun. We might say that this play on the two meanings, bad as it is, revives the well-nigh dead metaphor in "les feux de l'amour." Thus *la pointe* does what *le calembour* cannot do. The latter plays not on cognate meanings but on mere homonymy. I own that it is not always easy to decide whether two words, pronounced alike, have a common etymology, and even less easy to guess whether Shakespeare, for instance, no great linguist, thought them to be one word, so that he may well have occasionally ignored the distinction. It remains obvious, however, most of the time. To the English critic, however, *calembour* and *pointe* alike are "puns," a term he works very hard. He seldom resorts to "paronomasia," probably for fear of being considered pedantic; yet it is a satisfactory equivalent to *calembour*, tone apart. Personally I used "quibble" until English friends warned me it was obsolete in this sense; if so I wish it could be revived and given a technical definition. A good instance would be Bacon's famous remark to his rival lawyer Coke in an age when "precedent" and "president" were pronounced alike.

"Irony" has little in common with the terms reviewed so far, except that it has been as great a sufferer as any in recent years. Of course it had already undergone a metamorphosis passing from the Greek into the Western languages; but as early as the fourteenth century Oresme gave in French the definition of it I learned in my childhood: "Yronie est quand l'en [= on] dit une chose par quoy l'en [= on] veult donner a entendre le contraire." In English the earliest instances and definitions are awkward, vague, and even misleading. Puttenham tells several anecdotes, not one of which seems relevant. Dryden rarely uses the word, says George Watson, who gives only one instance, unimpeachable but far from explicit: there is irony in Lucian. In the eighteenth and nineteenth centuries, however, the word seemed to have settled down for good; but the twentieth is witnessing an inordinate extension of its meaning. Critics discover irony everywhere. Even funeral odes contain a dose of it, and not, as might be expected, of the bitter sort, but of the playful variety. In Dryden's *To the Pious Memory of . . . Mrs Anne Killigrew* there are "ironic undertones," which the critic does "not wish to overstress" but which "must be admitted on principle." That remark applies to lines 83–87, dealing with the chaste spinster's verse on love (but not love verse), and may be understood literally, if only at the cost of charging Dryden with bad taste and humor out of place. But a few pages later we read that the "irony which had never been too far away in earlier parts of the poem, nor ever too close," is again detected in lines 168–171.[12] If so, is the meaning of the term the same as before? Since Anne's brother, a naval captain, ignorant as yet of his sister's death, is advised to "Slack all [his] sails," if there is irony at all here it should be of the very special category known as "dramatic irony," as when Oedipus is advised not to try to learn what the audience already knows (and yet persists).

Other critics do insert the epithet "dramatic" before "irony" with much zest. Are they always justified in doing so? The index to Clemen's great work lists eight references to "Irony, dramatic." I am afraid it is hardly found there, in the strict sense. Of the two conditions required—knowledge on the part of the audience, ignorance on the part of the character concerned—either the one or the other seems to me to be missing. At the first performance of that romantic comedy, *The Winter's Tale*, how many spectators knew that Polixenes would, "by his subsequent action against his son, himself deviate from the procedure" he had recommended earlier in the same scene "as an organic law" (p. 204)? And, while it is true that "the audience knows that the curve of destiny is already taking a downward trend" for Antony and Cleopatra (p. 166), Antony himself is fully aware of it when he utters the speech quoted by Clemen as containing "a fine dramatic irony" (III, xi, 73);

12 Miner, *Dryden's Poetry*, pp. 257, 263–264.

a fortiori, is the same thing true of Cleopatra's speech that he also adduces as evidence (IV, xv, 43)? But I can hardly censure those who use *irony* loosely since *ironie* fares no better in my mother tongue, where, however, the term *ironie dramatique*, as I have found experimentally, is unintelligible to any but *anglicistes*.

Speaking of Shakespeare, I must confess I cannot share the admiration of English and German critics for some of his imagery. Here is one example, called "magnificent characterization" by a scholar [13] who is both judicious and sensitive:

> His face was as the heavens; and therein stuck
> A sun and moon, which kept their course, and lighted
> The little O, the earth.   (*Antony and Cleopatra*, V, ii, 79–81)

Emile Legouis, certainly no lukewarm devotee of Shakespeare, said such a comparison made one squint. Decidedly the French, even the best of them, have a spice of Voltaire in their composition.

A hackneyed quotation from *Hudibras* might here remind us that "a rhetorician's rules / Teach nothing but to name his tools" —after all, a mere preliminary to real work. And the study of imagery might occasionally dispense with the learned, or pedantic, "tools," which at any rate would be preferable to mishandling them. Many years ago I wrote of "le déguisement biblique" used by Dryden in *Absalom and Achitophel*,[14] and I could argue now that the homely term, even if metaphorical, suits the poet's device best. He wants to deal with present English politics, not with Jewish politics of long ago; only so much of the latter will be used in the presentation of the former as is required to save appearances (after all Monmouth was held to have royal blood in his veins) and give a literary varnish to the facts. The motto from Horace— *Si propiùs stes / Te capiet magis*—invites the reader, no doubt, to relish the niceties of style and versification, but it also asks him to look for the application of the superficial meaning to the substantial lesson.[15] Therefore the equal importance attached by some critics to the means and to the end, to the vehicle and to the tenor, or the reciprocity they attribute to the two components, even to the length of asserting that the metaphorical vehicle of biblical history has swallowed up the "metaphorical tenor of Restoration

---

[13] Clemen, *Shakespeare's Imagery*, p. 162.

[14] See my edition of selected poems by Dryden, *Poèmes choisis* (Paris, 1946), p. 19.

[15] Here I agree with Hoffman (*Dryden's Imagery*, p. 72), but later he drifts from that position.

history," [16] strikes me as a witty paradox but leaves me unconvinced. As Rosemond Tuve has shown, the tenor is the master, the vehicle the servant for the men of the Renaissance; Dryden, the poet of argument, held, I think, to this principle. The biblical names and vocubulary impart dignity to the poem. Besides, Monmouth as Absalom and Shaftesbury as Achitophel stand at once convicted, the one of vain, and the other of crafty, ambition. Although the biblical disguise has been used before, it can still do service and bias the reader of 1681 against the Whig leaders; having performed this service it should become as thin as possible. The only detail that does not fit Charles while it fits David is "th' old Harp on which he thrums his Layes: / Or some dull *Hebrew* Ballad in your Praise" (ll. 439–440); ostensibly it is Achitophel's sarcasm against David, whereas in fact it is Dryden's little joke at the unsuitability of the part of the Psalmist to his witty but uninspired sovereign, a joke of the sort Charles could appreciate even if he cut a ludicrous figure in it. In an earlier passage, apparently serious (ll. 196–197), must we see only David stringing "his tuneful Harp" without any (deliberately incongruous) reference to Charles? But the preceding lines, of which we are now given the conclusion, fit Shaftesbury closely and the biblical Achitophel not at all. The "Immortal Song" (certainly not Dryden's poem but one of the Psalms of David) that would have been accompanied on the harp may be referred to Charles in the same spirit: here, if anywhere, there might be an ironical undertone. But I must stop, lest I incur the charge of overingeniousness brought forth by me against so many of the New Critics.

[16] Miner, *Dryden's Poetry*, p. 109.

INDEX

Entries include names, major topics, and titles of works by seventeenth-century English authors (under author's names). Well-known members of the nobility are indexed under their most familiar titles, disregarding prior or later enlargement of titles. Less familiar nobility are entered in fuller citation, usually under surnames. Index entries make no distinction between text and notes.